CULTURESHOCK!

A Survival Guide to Customs and Etiquette

AUSTRIA

Julie Krejci
Susan Roraff

Marshall Cavendish
Editions

This edition published in 2007 by:
Marshall Cavendish Corporation
99 White Plains Road
Tarrytown, NY 10591-9001
www.marshallcavendish.us

Other Marshall Cavendish Offices:
Marshall Cavendish International (Asia) Private Limited. 1 New Industrial
Road, Singapore 536196 ▪ Marshall Cavendish Ltd. 119 Wardour Street, London
W1F 0UW, UK ▪ Marshall Cavendish International (Thailand) Co Ltd. 253 Asoke,
12th Flr, Sukhumvit 21 Road, Klongtoey Nua, Wattana, Bangkok 10110,
Thailand ▪ Marshall Cavendish (Malaysia) Sdn Bhd, Times Subang, Lot 46,
Subang Hi-Tech Industrial Park, Batu Tiga, 40000 Shah Alam, Selangor Darul
Ehsan, Malaysia

Marshall Cavendish is a trademark of Times Publishing Limited

ISBN 10: 0-7614-5399-7
ISBN 13: 978-0-7614-5399-4

Please contact the publisher for the Library of Congress catalogue number

Printed in China by Everbest Printing Co Ltd

Photo Credits: All photos from the authors except page 11 (Carol Roraff),
pages 47 and 93 (Gary Krejci), page 43 (J. Jurkin), page 201 (Gerhard Krejci)
and pages 134–135, 184–185, 196–197 and 216–217 (Photolibrary)
▪ Cover photo: Photolibrary

All illustrations by TRIGG

ABOUT THE SERIES

Culture shock is a state of disorientation that can come over anyone who has been thrust into unknown surroundings, away from one's comfort zone. *CultureShock!* is a series of trusted and reputed guides which has, for decades, been helping expatriates and long-term visitors to cushion the impact of culture shock whenever they move to a new country.

Written by people who have lived in the country and experienced culture shock themselves, the authors share all the information necessary for anyone to cope with these feelings of disorientation more effectively. The guides are written in a style that is easy to read and covers a range of topics that will arm readers with enough advice, hints and tips to make their lives as normal as possible again.

Each book is structured in the same manner. It begins with the first impressions that visitors will have of that city or country. To understand a culture, one must first understand the people—where they came from, who they are, the values and traditions they live by, as well as their customs and etiquette. This is covered in the first half of the book.

Then on with the practical aspects—how to settle in with the greatest of ease. Authors walk readers through topics such as how to find accommodation, get the utilities and telecommunications up and running, enrol the children in school and keep in the pink of health. But that's not all. Once the essentials are out of the way, venture out and try the food, enjoy more of the culture and travel to other areas. Then be immersed in the language of the country before discovering more about the business side of things.

To round off, snippets of basic information are offered before readers are 'tested' on customs and etiquette of the country. Useful words and phrases, a comprehensive resource guide and list of books for further research are also included for easy reference.

CONTENTS

PREFACE

Austria! You've just found out that you are moving to Austria. Beautiful images pass through your mind of Baroque churches, castles and classical music, or maybe you think of heading directly to the Alps for a bit of skiing. Everyone you know is envious and you are excited at the prospect. Then it suddenly hits you that this is not a two-week vacation, but the next few years of your life! Thoughts turn to what it will be like to actually live in Austria and whether you will like it.

Relax. It will not be that difficult, and if you keep an open mind and welcome new experiences, you will find yourself crying when the time comes for you to leave. Austria is a lovely country that is full of possibilities. After you learn what is expected of you and become well versed in the local etiquette and customs, you will do just fine. The main problem with being an expatriate is that you don't always know why people do what they do, and in turn, you are uncertain as to what you should do. You don't want to appear rude or do something embarrassing, but it happens to just about every new arrival. This book will help you understand the little things as well as the major points about Austrian society so that you can start off on the right foot.

There are a few things you can do before you leave home. Probably the most important is to become familiar with basic German. Most Austrians in the major cities and quite a few in smaller towns speak very good English (besides other European languages), so knowing German isn't vital, but it will help lessen the culture shock. Being able to read some of the signs and advertisements, or understanding the weather report on the radio, will help you feel at home in Austria. If your departure is somewhat sudden, there are plenty of excellent and not too expensive places to learn German in Austria. Studying there will also provide you with an excuse to get out and about in your new home and allow you to meet people who are in similar situations.

Meeting new people is the second major weapon in the fight against culture shock. If you are heading to Austria with a job or are already enrolled in a school or university, you will have several opportunities to socialise. However, if you are giving up your job or studies and your social life back home to accompany your spouse or partner, it is essential that you make new friends and build your own life in Austria. Obviously, meeting people from your home country through clubs and organisations is the easiest path to follow, but why stop there? Although opportunities to meet and socialise with Austrians do not jump out at you every day, it is not impossible to make good friends. It can be very easy to isolate yourself from your host country and its people, but if you do, you'll find that something is missing. Seek out Austrian friends and your efforts will be well rewarded.

Finally, staying busy will help keep homesickness at bay. Austria is an outdoor lover's paradise. You don't have to be an excellent skier to enjoy the fresh air. In fact, the most popular pastime is *wandern* (hiking). If that's too much exercise for you, the cities are bursting with museums, shops, concerts, opera and theatres. Every little town is a jewel to be discovered. Learn about the rich history of this land and take advantage of all that it offers. Do as much as you can and your time in Austria will fly by. If you follow this simple advice, we believe that your stay in this wonderful country will be as pleasant as ours has been.

ACKNOWLEDGEMENTS

The authors recognise that this book could not have been written without the help of many people. Our heartfelt thanks go to Julie's husband Gary, the Schwanzer family, the Zanetti family, Adele Jibidar and Brian Roraff for contributing valuable information, answering endless questions and/or reviewing the manuscript. We would also like to thank Lisa Boucher, Peter Siavelis, Colleen Galvan, Carol and Robert Roraff, Pilar Peikoff, many teachers at the American International School in Vienna and the students of Central University of Iowa for their comments and insights. We are indebted to the many Austrians who have made us feel welcome in their country and who have shared their historically-rich culture with us. We would like to thank Jitka Dvorackova for keeping Benjamin smiling and Suzanne Kuhnard for entertaining Natascha while their mothers worked. Finally, we recognise that any errors are the responsibility of the authors.

To our beautiful children,
Natascha and Daniela,
Benjamin and Tomás,
who motivate us with their boundless energy
and inspire us with their unending curiosity.

MAP OF AUSTRIA

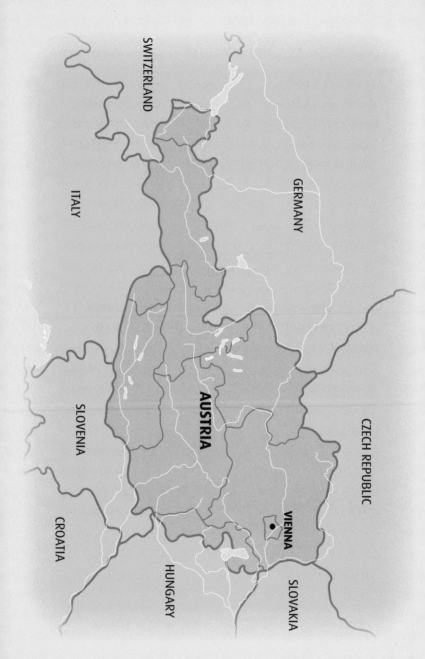

FIRST IMPRESSIONS

CHAPTER 1

'Illusions commend themselves to us because
they save us pain and allow us to enjoy pleasure instead.
We must therefore accept it without complaint when they
sometimes collide with a bit of reality against
which they are dashed to pieces.'
—Sigmund Freud, founder of psychoanalysis

MOST LIKELY YOU ALREADY HAVE an impression of Austria, even if you've never set foot in the country before. The mention of Austria conjures up images of a grand empire that has made enormous contributions to music, the arts and architecture. Surely you've heard of the Vienna Boys' Choir, Wolfgang Amadeus Mozart, *The Blue Danube* waltz by Johann Strauss Jr, and have seen Gustav Klimt's famous painting, *The Kiss*. This is, in fact, your first impression. Yet many people do not have a clear idea of what to expect from a modern-day Austria. What are the people like? What are the day-to-day realities? Once you arrive, will your first moments in this history-rich country live up to your expectations?

First, we must point out that we are all shaped by our previous experiences and personal values. This, in turn, has an impact on how we view other countries and their people. Obviously, a person moving to Austria from another European country will have a different experience from someone moving from the United States, Asia, the Middle East, Africa or Latin America. For some, the differences between Austrian society and their own may be huge, for others, less of an adjustment will be necessary. Likewise, for those who have travelled across the globe, their first impressions will be different from those of someone leaving their home for the first time. Furthermore, there are many different ways to live in Austria. Students will have a completely different experience from those who go to Austria to work. (Susan knows this first-hand as she went to Austria to study and returned 14 years later with her husband for his job. It was almost as if she experienced two different worlds.) Single people will also find their experiences differ from those who arrive with their family. (Julie is familiar with both situations, having arrived on her own and later marrying an Austrian and becoming part of an Austrian family.) Given all of these variables, we can only provide you with our impressions and highlight what we find to be worth knowing before going. In essence, this is a book of opinions and generalisations and just as people in your own country are not all exactly alike, the people of Austria do not conform to a rigid interpretation. We hope that this book will be of help to you as you begin to make Austria your home.

Don't be surprised if you tell someone that you are moving to Austria and they immediately start to talk about 'down under'. Although worlds apart, their similar names has led to some confusion among the geographically challenged. So much so that you can find T-shirts in Vienna stating that there are no kangaroos in Austria.

There are several ways to arrive in Austria and numerous stepping off points. Susan's first trip to Austria took her to Innsbruck. It was everything she had thought an Alpine city would look like. Towering snow-covered mountains, ski resorts, quaint streets lined with small shops, a palace, baroque churches and monuments, delicious restaurants and typical souvenir shops. In many ways, it resembled its postcard image.

Many others have the same experience. A friend's travels took her to Salzburg. A city rich in history, all she could see upon arrival was the fortress overlooking the city, Mirabell Palace, Getreidegasse with its picturesque shops and Mozart's image everywhere. Inspired by *The Sound of Music* (many people's idea of Austria), she took a tour. More than finally seeing where the movie was shot, she realised the rural beauty of Austria. The beautiful lakes and small towns that surround Salzburg opened her eyes to the fact that Austria is much more than its cities.

The beauty of Europe is that you can travel by train, bus or plane. Undoubtedly, travelling by plane is the least romantic. As is true of most cities, airports lie on the outskirts, often in industrial areas. For example, arriving at Schwechat airport in Vienna, the first thing you see are the towers of the huge Schwechat oil refinery. Certainly not the image one would expect. Susan was fortunate enough to have arrived in Vienna for the first time by train. Stepping out of the Westbahnhof, she immediately came face to face with the city in all its grandeur. How can you not be in awe of such a beautifully ornate city, so rich in history that you know there is a story behind everything you see? As she headed towards the city centre, her head spun around trying to catch a glimpse of the Opera House, the Kunsthistorisches Museum, the Rathaus, the Hofburg, etc. It seemed as if one magnificent landmark superseded another. All she wanted to do was to get out and walk around the city and breath it all in.

When Julie moved to Austria, her first impressions were of space, cleanliness, a beautiful countryside, wonderful wines and a sense of a well-balanced lifestyle. She was struck by the well-functioning infrastructure and incredible public transportation systems in the cities and towns. This allows newcomers to easily access information and get around without any major difficulty. Furthermore, even though she had not studied German beforehand, she found that getting around was easy because most people studied English in school and have a passable knowledge of the language. Most importantly for her, as a single woman, she felt safe and secure wherever she went.

For those of you who, upon arrival, see a country steeped in history, your second impression will be that of a very modern country. Austrians may be a traditional and conservative people, but they have enthusiastically embraced the 21st century. Life in Austria is a wonderful mix of quiet cafés and mobile phones, leisurely strolls in the woods and speeding along the Autobahn, Mozart and jazz, tuxedos and green hair, Baroque buildings and the 51-storey Millennium Tower skyscraper, small family-owned stores and the largest shopping mall in Europe with probably the shortest opening hours. It is a country that, although no longer an empire, is an active member of the European Union and the seat of several international organisations. Geographically, the country

The *Handy* (cell phone) is part of a truly modern Austria, yet the country maintains its old-world charms.

is much smaller than it was at the height of the empire, yet what remains contains some of the most breathtaking scenery, too many castles and churches to count, and one of the most vibrant, culturally-rich capitals in all of Europe. You'll be hard pressed to take in all of the attractions that the cities have to offer, visit the picturesque villages tucked away in the mountains, and take advantage of the numerous world-class sports facilities.

Upon meeting the Austrians, you will find them friendly and willing to help the newcomer, although a bit reserved. You get the idea that your visit will go much smoother if you adhere to the rules of society. If you travel to rural areas, you will find the Austrians to be very pleasant and welcoming.

Due to the fact that there are so many tourists throughout the country, your presence will cause no stir or controversy. Tourists are pretty much treated the same as Austrians, and in turn are expected to behave like the locals.

On weekends, you will see families out and about, enjoying their time together and taking full advantage of the outdoors, summer or winter. Many first-time visitors also comment on the Austrians' love of dogs. Not only do dogs of all sizes accompany their owners practically everywhere, but you will notice how they are doted on and treated with much affection.

Meeting the Austrians

A friend who had much experience travelling around southern Europe was amazed at the hushed tones of Austria. People go on their way quietly, without drawing attention to themselves, and save you from having to make idle chit-chat with complete strangers. Yet when he needed help, he found that the Austrians were incredibly polite and more than happy to provide information, which they always did with a smile. This contrasted with his preconceived ideas of a cold and grumpy people. He remarked that in Vienna, a city bursting with tourists, he was surprised to find so many locals willing to aid yet another foreigner with poor German-language skills.

REGIONAL IMPRESSIONS

Austria is a federal republic consisting of nine *Bundesländer* or autonomous provinces. Beginning in the west and moving in an eastwardly direction, the states are Vorarlberg, Tyrol, Salzburg, Carinthia, Upper Austria, Styria, Lower Austria, Vienna and Burgenland. These provinces have marked differences in topography, customs, dialects, traditional dress and personality. Geographical and cultural differences have given rise to a strong sense of regionalism. People often consider themselves Tyrolean or Viennese more so than Austrian. Thus, as you travel throughout the country, you may find yourself with many different 'first impressions'.

Vorarlberg, Austria's most westerly province, lies between the Bodensee (Lake Constance) and Arlberg Pass. For those who enter Austria here, you could feel like you've landed in Switzerland instead of Austria, as it closely resembles a Swiss canton. Before the 14-km Arlberg tunnel was opened in 1978, linking this province with Tyrol, Vorarlberg was practically cut off from the rest of Austria during the winter months. Over the centuries, it had forged close ties with neighbouring Switzerland. Thus, customs, homes and food in Vorarlberg are similar to those found in that country. The traditional dress, which is not commonly worn today, also differs from the *Trachten* worn throughout the rest of Austria. This is especially true of the hats, which include wide black straw hats, fur hats and cone-shaped hats. Also, the German they speak is much closer to Swiss German than to the German spoken in the rest of Austria.

Tyrol is a unique province known for snow-covered mountains, winter sports, folk customs and tourism. The inhabitants speak a dialect that may be difficult for other German-speakers to understand, and their customs and clothing differ greatly from the rest of the country. Even so, there are marked differences within Tyrol itself. Prior to World War II, Tyrol was a much larger area encompassing Südtirol (Southern Tyrol). Austria was forced to cede this area to Italy in 1919, yet the region remains culturally closer to Austrian Tyrol than to the rest of Italy. As a result of the change in borders, East Tyrol became geographically separated from the rest of Austrian Tyrol and it remained somewhat isolated until the Felbertauern tunnel was built in 1967. Thus, it has closer ties to the neighbouring province of Carinthia than to the rest of Tyrol. Furthermore, the Ausserfern, a small part of Tyrol, shares much more with Vorarlberg and Swabia, Germany, due to its geography.

The Salzburg region did not become part of Austria until 1816. Originally part of Bavaria, in the 14th century, it became an independent entity within the Holy Roman Empire and was ruled by prince-archbishops as absolute sovereigns. Thus, people from this province consider themselves citizens of Salzburg first and Austrians second. The region gets its name from the salt that has been mined here for centuries. The capital city of Salzburg, known the world over as the birthplace of Mozart, is a very important cultural centre, noted for its museums, musical performances, theatres and festivals.

Upper Austria borders Bavaria and Salzburg and is primarily an agricultural province. It is home to the largest section of the Salzkammergut, noted for its lakes and picturesque towns. Some of the largest and most beautiful lakes, such as Attersee, Traunsee, Mondsee and Hallstättersee, can be found here. The town of Hallstatt has been referred to as the most beautiful lakeside village in the world. Bad Ischl is said to be the centre of the Salzkammergut. Emperor Franz Josef spent his summers here and his presence led the aristocracy and other important people of the 19th century to make it their summer resort as well. The best-known artists, composers, writers, poets and actors of the day were drawn to the town.

Carinthia (Kärnten) is another of Austria's Alpine provinces. Yet, Carinthia might be more popular in summer because of its many lakes. Principal among them is the Wörthersee near the capital, Klagenfurt. The province borders Slovenia and is home to a sizeable Slovenian population, particularly in the Gail, Rosen and Jaun valleys in the southern part of the province. Although some Slovenian customs and traditional costumes remain and the Slovenian language is sometimes heard, the Carinthians are all Austrian. In fact, following the breakup of the empire in 1918, they voted to remain part of Austria instead of joining with Slovenia in Yugoslavia.

Styria (Steiermark) is lovingly called the 'green province' of Austria. Forests cover about half the province and pastures and vineyards cover almost another quarter. Styria also happens to be the country's most heavily mined province. In addition to iron ore, lignite and magnesite are two of the other economically important minerals found here.

Lower Austria (Niederösterreich) is the largest province in terms of area. More significantly, it is considered to be the cradle of Austria. This was the very place that was referred to as the Ostarrichi or Eastern Realm of Charlemagne's Frankish Empire. It is from this word that Austria's name in German, Österreich, is derived. Because of its strategic importance, Lower Austria was heavily fortified and ruins dot the landscape today. This region is also primarily agricultural

Bildstock, distinctive shrines featuring different religious scenes on each of their four sides, are common in Carinthia.

in nature and is divided into *viertel*, such as the Weinviertel (Wine district) and the Waldviertel (Woods district).

Burgenland was formed in 1921 from the German-speaking border areas of Hungary. The region was annexed by Austria in 1920, a development which resulted in sporadic fighting. A plebiscite was held the following year, and the residents of the area's main city Sopron voted to remain with Hungary. When you look at a map, you'll see that Sopron sits on a little finger of Hungary that juts into Burgenland. In terms of the landscape, this province is quite different from the rest of Austria. This is where the Hungarian Plain or Puszta begins. The gentle scenery gives a sense of peace

Burgenland may be Austria's smallest province, but it is full of castles like Burg Lockenhaus where you can stay overnight or attend a concert.

and relaxation. In fact, some Viennese complain that the pace is too slow, and joke that the clocks run slower there. The ethnic mix of Burgenland is also somewhat different from that in the rest of the country. While the majority are German-speaking Austrians, there are significant Hungarian and Croatian minorities, which is reflected most of all in the region's cuisine.

The city of Vienna is both the capital of Austria and a federal province. Its history dates backs to the Celts and the Romans, but it only flourished in the 12th century when the Babenberg dynasty made it the imperial residence. The Habsburgs assumed power in the 13th century, and remained in control until 1918. Under their rule, the empire grew and the city blossomed along with it. Palaces, churches, museums and gardens beautified the city. Austria's intelligentsia were drawn to it. Architecturally, culturally and politically, Vienna became one of the most important capitals in Europe. Most of the city's architecture, art and music were influenced by each other and by events within the empire. The Baroque period left Vienna full of ornate palaces and churches. Biedermeier focused on comfort, simplicity and function in architecture and furniture. Historicism saw the removal of the city wall and the creation of the Ringstrasse and many parks and

Schönbrunn Palace in Vienna, the summer residence of the Habsburgs, evokes images of imperial Austria.

green areas. Jugendstil left its mark on architecture and art. Add to this the architecture of Red Vienna, a period noted for its massive public housing projects, and you have a strange mixture of styles that can only be Vienna.

Today, Vienna is a curious mix of its imperial past, its ties with socialism and its modern development. It promotes an image of emperors and palaces, but that is merely one level of a highly complex city. We have heard Vienna referred to as a capital without an empire, and that is true to some extent. But it remains an elegant and proud city, an integral member of the international community. Vienna is easily accessible, enjoyable and safe. For a capital city, its crime rate is remarkably low. Visitors have commented that Vienna has all the culture and interests of Paris, but because of its smaller size, has a cozier atmosphere. It is a city that entices and enthrals without overwhelming or intimidating.

THE HISTORY OF AUSTRIA

CHAPTER 2

'Let the strong fight wars; thou, happy Austria, marry:
What Mars bestows on others, Venus gives to thee.'
—attributed to King Matthias Corvinus of Hungary, 1477,
referring to expansion of the Austro-Hungarian empire
through marriage instead of war

THROUGHOUT ITS LONG HISTORY, Austria has often been right at the centre of events in Europe, not only politically but also in the arts and sciences. Living in Austria, one is constantly reminded of its glorious past. Having a sense of this history helps in understanding the Austrians of today.

EARLY HISTORY

Present-day Austria has been inhabited since prehistoric times. The Venus of Willendorf, a remarkable 20,000-year-old figurine in the shape of a woman symbolising fertility, was unearthed in the Wachau valley. As early as 2000 BC, the area was populated by the Illyrians, early Iron Age miners who reached a high degree of civilisation between 1700 and 700 BC. The Celts were next to populate the area and remained until the first century BC. Their kingdom, known as Noricum, thrived on salt mined from the Salzkammergut and iron ore from the Styrian mountains. The Celts were the first to settle in present-day Vienna, which they called Vindobona.

Vienna became an important settlement thanks to its location. The Amber Route, which ran from the Adriatic Sea to the Baltic, crossed the Danube River here. Bronze weapons and pottery from the south and amber and whale tusks from the north were traded along the route. By the year 15 BC, the Romans had extended their realm into the region, establishing a military camp on the banks of the Danube at present-day Vienna that was to stand for 400 years. Other

Roman settlements at this time included Iuvavum, presently Salzburg, Brigantium at Bregenz, and the largest, Carnuntum, a major city with approximately 20,000 inhabitants located east of Vienna.

Eventually, the Romans were overtaken by their enemies and withdrew from the area in the 5th century AD, leaving Austria to the so-called Dark Ages. During this time, Austria was at the centre of shifting populations, which included Germanic tribes, Teutons, Huns, Slavs, Magyars and Avars.

Between 791 and 796, the Frankish ruler Charlemagne founded the Holy Roman Empire to succeed the Roman Empire. Austria became the eastern border of the empire, and was referred to as Ostmark or the Eastern March. At the end of the 9th century, this area succumbed to the Magyars. The region remained under Magyar control until their defeat by King Otto the Great. In 976, his successor, Otto II, presented the province to Margrave Leopold von Babenberg.

THE BABENBERG DYNASTY

The Babenberg family ruled the Ostmark for 270 years, gradually expanding their territory. The Babenberg holdings increased when Leopold V obtained the duchy of Styria in 1192. Vienna was granted a city charter in 1221 and cultural life at the Babenberg court flourished. Under its leadership, Austria became one of the richest duchies in the Holy Roman Empire, and Vienna the second most important city. In 1246, the dynasty ended suddenly when Duke Friedrich II, who was childless, was killed in a battle against the Magyars.

A dispute erupted as to who would rule the duchies of Austria and Styria. King Ottokar II Przemysl of Bohemia had the support of the Austrian nobility and assumed power. Rudolf of Habsburg, a minor count from Switzerland, was elected Holy Roman Emperor in 1273 by the German princes, who assumed erroneously that he could be controlled. Instead, they helped create a powerful dynasty that would rule Austria for over 600 years. Rudolf of Habsburg challenged King Ottokar's rule over Austria. King Ottokar was killed in 1278 in the Battle of Dürnkrut, and Rudolf assumed power.

THE HABSBURGS DYNASTY

The Habsburgs consolidated their rule in the early 14th century. In the mid-14th century, Rudolf IV, later known as Rudolf the Founder, took the throne. He moved to establish Vienna as one of the premier cities of Europe. During the 14th and 15th centuries, the Habsburgs gained Carinthia, Tyrol, Vorarlberg, Slovenia and Trieste. Friedrich III raised the duchy of Austria to that of an archduchy within the Holy Roman Empire, and consequently from 1438 until its dissolution in 1806, the Habsburgs were the hereditary emperors of the empire.

Marriage Diplomacy

During the 15th and 16th centuries, the Habsburgs peacefully obtained by marriage more lands than they ever could have won in battle, gaining Netherlands, Burgundy, Naples, Sicily, Sardinia and large territories in the Americas. The line split when Emperor Charles V's son, Phillip II, took possession of the Spanish and Dutch lands, while Charles's brother, Ferdinand I, became regent not only of the German-speaking lands, but through shrewd marriage policies of his own gained Bohemia and Hungary.

THE 16TH AND 17TH CENTURIES
The Turks

The Ottoman Empire was also interested in expansion. The Turks set their sights on Vienna in 1529, but thwarted by the city's strong defenses and the approaching winter, they failed in their siege. Although they did not take Vienna, they maintained control of Hungary and remained a powerful and ever-present enemy on Austria's doorstep.

The Thirty Years War waged from 1618 to 1648, pitting Catholics against Protestants, and left Austria somewhat weaker for the ordeal. The situation was compounded by the Plague, which devastated Vienna in 1679. Thus Vienna seemed easy prey to the Turks, who once again laid siege to the city in the summer of 1683. Prince Eugene of Savoy, a clever military commander, proved instrumental in the struggle against the Turks, who were finally firmly defeated. As a consequence, the Turks ceded control of Hungary (which included present-day Romania) and Croatia to Austria.

THE 18TH CENTURY
War of the Spanish Succession

In 1700, the Spanish line of the Habsburgs died out. The War of the Spanish Succession erupted as the Austrian line of the Habsburg dynasty attempted to reclaim its former territories. Ultimately, Austria lost the Spanish possessions, but was able to regain control of Italy and the Netherlands.

The Baroque Period

With the Turks no longer a threat, and with the end of a second plague in 1713, new life was breathed into Vienna. As the Habsburgs and the accompanying nobility moved into the city, it became an imperial melting pot of Czechs, Poles and Hungarians, among others. During the 18th century, the population doubled to 200,000. No longer needing the protection of walls, the city overflowed into the suburbs. Economically, the region surged forward. The arts were summarily promoted and there was a frenzy of creative activity in literature, music and architecture. Austria enthusiastically entered the Baroque period, which reached its highest point under Karl VI.

Maria Theresa (1740–80)

In 1713, Karl VI, who had no male heir, changed the law to allow daughters the right of succession, and thereby ensured

Holy Trinity columns were erected in towns all over Austria in the late 17th century to give thanks for the end of the Plague epidemic.

that his daughter Maria Theresa would take the crown after his death. However, upon Karl's death in 1740, Maria Theresa faced challenges to her rule: Austria lost Silesia in the Silesian War, also known as the War of the Austrian Succession (1740–48), and an attempt to regain it in the Seven Years War (1756–63) was unsuccessful.

In 1745, Maria Theresa's husband, Franz Stephan of Lorraine, was crowned Holy Roman Emperor, Franz I. Although her father's edict had allowed her to become ruler of Austria, gender prevented Maria Theresa from becoming the Empress of the Holy Roman Empire. When her husband died in 1765, she named her son, Josef II, co-regent, in effect retaining power. She was respected and popular because of her reforms, which included making general education compulsory and building an efficient centralised administration, albeit at the expense of local governance. Yet one of her most impressive feats was not political at all. While concerned with the affairs of the empire, she gave birth to sixteen children, one of whom, Marie Antoinette, would lose her head during the French Revolution.

Josef II (1780–90)

When Josef II came to power following his mother's death, he began to institute his own reforms. Influenced by the Enlightenment, he issued the Toleration Patent in 1781, granting freedom of religious worship. He also set out to curtail the powerful Catholic Church. In addition, Josef II abolished serfdom, made the aristocracy liable to taxation, and opened the Prater, the imperial hunting grounds, to the public. More famously, he allowed vintners to sell their own 'new wine' or *Heurige*. The government was unable to keep pace with the reforms, and following his death, many of them were repealed.

THE 19TH CENTURY
The Napoleonic Years

As was true for many European monarchies, the Habsburgs were threatened by the ideals of the French Revolution and the subsequent rise of Napoleon. Fighting erupted in 1792 when France declared war on Austria and most of Europe. In 1804, Napoleon crowned himself Emperor of France. To compensate, Franz II raised Austria from an archduchy to an empire and named himself Emperor of Austria as Franz I. In spite of his efforts, Franz was forced to renounce his crown as Holy Roman Emperor when Napoleon consolidated his own power. Vienna was occupied by French troops in 1805 and 1809. In yet another attempt at marriage diplomacy, Franz's daughter Marie Louise was married to Napoleon in 1810. This marriage produced a son, who, after Napoleon's downfall and exile, was closely guarded at Schönbrunn Palace until he died at 21 from tuberculosis. Austria eventually took up arms again as part of the coalition comprised of England, Prussia and Russia that finally defeated Napoleon in 1814.

The Congress of Vienna (1814–15)

At the Congress of Vienna, 200 delegates from across the continent met to re-establish the traditional balance of power. Borders were redrawn and Austria regained lands lost to France. The Congress was more famous, however, for its extravagance as the delegates spent more time at dinner and balls.

Vormärz

The period between the Congress of Vienna and the revolution of March 1848 is known as the Vormärz (the period before March). Prince Metternich, chancellor during the reign of Franz I, was in charge of government policy. Metternich was extremely conservative and employed harsh repression and censorship to uphold the absolute power of the monarch. As a result, many people turned inward, focusing on family life instead of venturing out under the careful gaze of the secret police. Among the upper and middle classes, culture replaced political and economic activities, ushering in the Biedermeier period. Music, literature and the other arts flourished during this time.

Revolution of 1848

The police state could not restrain the demands of a society entering the industrial age. The middle class led calls for increased freedoms, and the working class wanted better living and working conditions. On 13 March 1848, a large group of students and workers protested, precipitating Prince Metternich's flight to England. Emperor Ferdinand eventually agreed to set up a parliament, and the first deputies took office in July. By 31 October, after 2,000 people had died, the rebels were finally subdued.

The regions of Hungary and Bohemia were anxious to secure their independence and saw their opportunity in this unrest. The Bohemians were brought under control first, but the Hungarians proved a formidable enemy. Only with the help of Russian troops was the Hungarian revolt finally suppressed. On 2 December 1848, Emperor Ferdinand, who was epileptic and not in full command of his faculties, abdicated in favour of his nephew, Franz Josef.

Franz Josef (1848–1916)

Only 18 years of age when he became emperor, Franz Josef was a popular monarch, closely associated with the memories of imperial Austria. Under his rule, the second half of the 19th century came to be known as the *Gründerzeit*, or Founder era, and Vienna shone as one of the jewels of Europe. Yet Franz Josef also ruled during a time when the Austrian Empire began to break apart. Austria lost Lombardy in 1859. Following the Austro-Prussian War of 1866, Austria lost dominance among the German states and ceded Venice to Italy.

Meanwhile, the Hungarians were still demanding independence. Given their military losses, Austria agreed to negotiate. In 1867, the Austro-Hungarian dual monarchy was created. Each state would be autonomous, and a separate parliament was established in Budapest. In return, the Emperor of Austria would also be crowned King of Hungary and the two states would share the same defense, foreign and economic policies.

Civilian Government

By the end of the 19th century, three main political parties had been formed in the Austrian part of the empire: the Austrian Social Democratic Party, the Christian Social Party and the German National Party. Austria enjoyed a relatively free press. Universal male suffrage was granted in 1907, and the first general elections were held for the imperial parliament, although Franz Josef remained in firm control.

There were growing concerns within the empire: the working class was demanding better pay and working conditions; nationalistic tendencies among the many ethnic groups were on the rise, but German-speaking Austrians were reluctant to grant them more rights; and tensions were running high. The emperor was also plagued by personal problems: while Franz Josef had survived an assassination attempt in 1853 by the Hungarian Janos Libenyi, his wife, Empress Elisabeth (better known as Sissi), was killed in Geneva in 1898 by an Italian anarchist. Earlier, his son, Crown Prince Rudolph, had committed suicide after killing his lover, Baroness Maria Vetsera, in Mayerling in 1889.

THE 20TH CENTURY
World War I
On 28 June 1914, Crown Prince Franz Ferdinand and his wife were assassinated in Sarajevo, Bosnia-Herzegovina (which had come under Austro-Hungarian rule in 1878), by the young Serbian nationalist, Gavrilo Princip. About two months later, Austria declared war on Serbia. Russia came to its fellow Slavic country's defense.

Russia's allies, France and Britain, joined in and World War I was under way. Austria, aided by Germany, was unable to claim victory on the battlefield. Emperor Franz Josef died in 1916 and his successor, Kaiser Karl I, tried unsuccessfully to keep the empire intact. Austria eventually signed an armistice treaty on 3 November 1918. Eight days later, Karl I renounced participation in the government, although technically not the throne. South Tyrol was lost to Italy, Galicia went to Poland, and Yugoslavia was formed, encompassing some of the former Habsburg possessions. Hungary finally received its long-awaited independence, as did the Czechs and Slovaks. Austria was reduced to one-eighth its former size with one-ninth its former population, primarily the German-speaking areas of the former empire.

The First Republic
Delegates to parliament proclaimed the Republic of German Austria on 12 November 1918. Like many citizens,

especially those in the Alpine provinces, the three major political parties were all favourable to a union with Germany. However, this would not have been in the best interests of Austria's World War I adversaries, and thus any merger was expressly forbidden by the treaty ending the war. So the country was called merely 'Austria' and in February 1919, the Social Democrat Dr Karl Renner was elected the first state chancellor. The coalition that had brought Renner into power broke down the following year. The conservative Christian Social Party won elections in October 1920 and in essence ran the federal government until 1938. The inter-war years were marked by economic crisis, inflation, unemployment, hunger and violence.

Red Vienna

Constitutional reform in 1922 granted Vienna special status as a *Land* or semi-autonomous province. The Social Democrats governing Vienna introduced a number of important social reforms, which ushered in the period known as Red Vienna. They instituted a massive housing programme, building

Red Vienna produced a large number of public housing complexes, but the Karl-Marx-Hof in the 19th district is the most famous.

about 63,000 apartments for workers between 1923 and 1933. These complexes were quite innovative for their time in that they included amenities like indoor plumbing and community facilities such as kindergartens, cooperative food stores, medical services, meeting halls, libraries and green courtyards.

Growing Tensions

While the Socialists had a lock on Vienna, the Christian Socials ran the federal government. The two were constantly at odds. Political tensions were heightened by the existence of paramilitary organisations linked to the political parties whose ranks swelled as unemployment grew. In July 1927, a strike was called to protest the acquittal of three right-wing men accused of killing a man and a boy who had been marching in a Socialist parade. Clashes between demonstrators and the police in Vienna left 91 dead.

Civil War

The country was heading for civil war. By the late 1920s, the Nazi movement had entered Austria through the western provinces. By 1932, Austrian Nazis had begun to hold elected positions. The Christian Democrat Engelbert Dollfuss became chancellor. He took advantage of the resignation of the Speaker of the House and his two deputies following an impasse in parliament and quickly imposed an authoritarian regime. His right-wing government was hostile to both Social Democrats and the Nazis, a position that would ultimately lead to his downfall and the disappearance of Austria as a political entity. Instead of aligning with the Social Democrats against the threat of the Nazi government in Germany (Hitler had risen to power in May 1933), he faced both enemies simultaneously.

On 12 February 1934, civil war finally broke out, pitting the Social Democrats against the federal government, led by the Christian Socials and supported by the police and the army. The Social Democrats were summarily defeated and their hold on power was broken. The party was outlawed and the leaders were either exiled or imprisoned.

The Anschluss

In July 1934, the Austrian Nazis attempted a coup, and Dollfuss was assassinated. His successor, Dr. Kurt Schuschnigg, allied himself with Italy's Mussolini, as Dollfuss had done. When Hitler and Mussolini became friendly, Schuschnigg was forced to enter into the Austro-German Agreement of 1936, which recognised Austria's sovereignty on the grounds that Austrian Nazis be pardoned and included in the government. As the Austrian Nazis grew more powerful, Schuschnigg tried hard to secure true independence from Germany. This resulted in Hitler demanding the chancellor's resignation. Schuschnigg looked to the international community for help, but received none.

On 11 March 1938, Schuschnigg resigned, stating that he did not want fighting to erupt. The next day, German troops marched into Austria, which put up no military resistance. Hitler was greeted by cheers in Linz and Vienna. After a hefty dose of propaganda, he held a plebiscite on 10 April and the *Anschluss* (annexation of Austria) was approved by 99.73 per cent. Austria ceased to exist and the region became known as Ostmark, a province of the German Reich.

The Jews

Systematic persecution of the Jews began immediately. Jewish property was quickly Aryanized, or expropriated by non-Jews without any sort of payment rendered to its rightful owners. Jews were harassed and forced to wear the yellow Star of David. 10 November 1938 saw the infamous *Kristallnacht* take place. Throughout the German Reich, synagogues and Jewish stores and homes were destroyed. Only one synagogue in present-day Vienna dates from before 1938. Penniless and denied entrance visas by most countries, Jews found it very difficult to emigrate. By 1941, the government banned all Jews from leaving the country and shortly thereafter began to send them to concentration camps. Mathausen, near Linz, was the largest camp in Austria.

Anti-Semitism was not new to Austria. Persecution of Jews began with their expulsion from Vienna in 1421. About 200 who were unable to flee were burned at the stake. Jews returned to the city eventually, but periodically faced more repression, culminating in further expulsions. Empress Maria Theresa was an outspoken anti-Semite on religious grounds, but she chose to overlook the fact that many of her financiers were Jewish, as was Josef von Sonnenfels, one of her most important advisors. Dr Karl Lueger, the Christian Social Party mayor of Vienna from 1897 to 1910, was also famous for his anti-Semitic rhetoric. Because of his harsh comments and policies, he was prohibited three times from taking his post by Emperor Franz Josef. One of Lueger's admirers was Adolf Hitler, who praised him in *Mein Kampf*. While most high-ranking Nazis were German, Hitler himself was Austrian.

World War II

Austria was spared most of the fighting until near the end of World War II. The Allies carried out a massive bombing raid that culminated with major damage to the State Opera House, National Theater and Saint Stephen's Cathedral on 12 March 1945. The Battle of Vienna between the Germans and the Soviets (4–13 April) was the worst seen on Austrian

Flak towers, like this one in the Augarten, were built in Vienna by the Nazis to protect anti-aircraft artillery. They cannot be destroyed without damaging nearby buildings due to their 10-feet thick concrete walls.

soil. The Soviets finally liberated the city, and were initially welcomed by the hungry and distressed Viennese.

Post-World War II

By 1945, Austrians had come to dislike the Nazis, but soon the Red Army was hated even more. Soviet soldiers terrorised society. The country and the capital were divided into four zones (just as Germany and Berlin were), to be occupied by each of the Allied nations (France, Great Britain, the United States and Russia). The inner city was declared an international sector and kept intact. Patrols consisted of one soldier from each of the four nations, so the post-war period came to be known by the term 'four in a jeep'.

In November 1943, the Allies had stated in the Moscow Declaration that Austria was a victim of the Nazis and as such should be re-established as a free and democratic state. Thus, international borders were re-established using 1 January 1938 maps.

The Second Republic

The Second Republic was founded in 1945 by three parties from the pre-World War II era. A fourth party, the Austrian Nazi Party, was forbidden by the occupying forces to participate in politics. The Christian Social Party re-emerged as the Austrian People's Party (ÖVP). The Social Democrats became the Social Democratic Party of Austria (SPÖ). The first postwar elections were held in November 1945. The ÖVP and the SPÖ won most of the seats in parliament, with the communists (KPÖ), who had never had a strong following, winning only four seats. The provisional government was headed by Dr Karl Renner (SPÖ) as president and Leopold Figl (ÖVP) as chancellor. The two main parties formed a 'grand coalition', which would govern Austria for most of the rest of the century.

The 1920 constitution, amended in 1929, was reinstated in May 1945. The federal government holds most of the political and economic power, while the nine *Länder* (provinces) have their own local governments and maintain authority over other areas. The president is elected for a six-year term, but is primarily a figurehead. It is the chancellor who runs the federal government. Parliament consists of two houses, the *Nationalrat* and the *Bundesrat*. The *Nationalrat* is the upper house and has greater powers, including the mandate to pass legislation. Its 183 members are directly elected by the population for four-year terms. The *Bundesrat*, or lower house, is mainly concerned with safeguarding the rights of the provinces. Its 63 members are elected by the parliaments of the federal states. The number of representatives per province ranges from three to 12 and is based on the size of its population.

The Austrian Parliament is made up of two houses, the *Nationalrat* and the *Bundesrat*.

> ### The SPÖ and ÖVP
> The Socialists (SPÖ), founded in 1889 by Viktor Adler, have
> always spoken for the working class. Thus, much of their support
> has come from the cities. They were in power for most of the
> postwar years, either on their own or at the head of a coalition
> government. The conservative ÖVP is backed by businessmen,
> farmers, and, unofficially, the Roman Catholic Church. It
> promotes greater individual freedoms and less bureaucracy. From
> 1986 until 1999, the ÖVP was the junior member of a SPÖ–ÖVP
> coalition government.

Proporz

In an effort to avoid the internal conflict that led to civil war in
1934, the new Austrian government unofficially established
the *Proporz* system, whereby the two main political
parties (the SPÖ and the ÖVP) agreed to divide among
themselves jobs in the government bureaucracy, nationalised
businesses and public services. Cabinet positions all the way
down to civil service posts were divided according to political
party. Austrians began to question this practice and showed

their unhappiness in the 1999 elections with increased support for the FPÖ. Although the system still exists, it has diminished some following Austria's membership in the European Union.

Social Partnership

The First Republic had been torn apart by political infighting and civil strife. To avoid repeating earlier mistakes, the *Paritätische Kommission* (Parity Commission) was created in 1945. The Commission is part of a mechanism, referred to as 'social partnership', that brings together organised labour, businesses and government to discuss and settle labour and economic issues, especially wage and price increases. It has no legislative powers, but wields considerable influence nonetheless. Labour conflicts are often settled quietly through negotiation and compromise, although not always in the best interest of the general public. On the other hand, the level of cooperation is such that Austria does not suffer from paralysing strikes. In fact, time lost by strikes per person is counted in seconds, not hours.

Independence

In 1955, the Allies finally reached an agreement on Austria. The Cold War was well under way and the East and West had already established their zones of influence. The Soviet Union agreed to withdraw from Austria on condition it remained neutral, did not join NATO and refused foreign military bases. On 15 May 1955, the State Treaty granting Austria independence was signed. Foreign Minister Leopold Figl waved the State Treaty out of the window of the Upper Belvedere to the crowds below and yelled, "Austria is free!"

In its new form, Austria turned outward in an effort to recapture some of its previous importance in global affairs. Because of its history, geographical location and neutrality, Austria was a logical place for East-West relations to develop during the Cold War. Known to be a hotbed of spying activity, Vienna also made more honourable contributions to East-West relations. As security issues were of premier importance,

Vienna became the headquarters of the International Atomic Energy Agency (IAEA) in 1956. One year later, OPEC, the Organization of Petroleum Exporting Countries, located its permanent secretariat in the capital as well. The city also hosted two key East-West summit meetings: between President John F Kennedy and Premier Nikita Khrushchev in 1961, and between President Jimmy Carter and Premier Leonid Brezhnev in 1979.

Cold War Refugees

Austria's geographical location and neutrality also made it a transit point for many immigrants from the East. Hungarians were welcomed following the Soviet invasion in 1956, as were Czechoslovakians after the 1968 uprising. Poles made their way to Austria when the Solidarity movement was banned in 1981. Hundreds of thousands of Soviet Jews passed through Vienna on their way to Israel, the bulk coming during the 1970s. When relations between the two superpowers were good, a great many refugees flooded into Vienna. When tensions were high, few would arrive at the train station.

Bruno Kreisky

Between 1945 and 1966, the SPÖ and ÖVP jointly ran the Austrian government. In 1966, however, the Socialists were forced into opposition when the ÖVP won an absolute majority and formed a one-party government. The Socialists, under Bruno Kreisky, made a strong comeback and governed Austria alone from 1970 until 1983. During his term as federal chancellor, Austria prospered amidst political and social stability, and he became affectionately known as Emperor Bruno.

Kreisky strove hard to strengthen Austria's role in international affairs. He argued that Vienna should be home to as many international organisations as possible because this would help prevent it from ever again falling victim to aggression by a larger country, as it had to Hitler's Germany. In 1979, Austria was chosen as the site of the third major United Nations headquarters, following New York and

By hosting international organisations such as the United Nations, Vienna sought to remake its image as a world-class city.

Geneva. In addition to the IAEA and the United Nations Industrial Development Organization (UNIDO), which had been established in Vienna in 1967, the city continued to attract more agencies, among them the UN International Drug Control Program (UNDCP), the Comprehensive Nuclear-Test-Ban Treaty Organization (CTBTO), the UN Office for Outer Space Affairs (OOSA), the UN Commission on International Trade Law (UNCITRAL) and the Organization for Security and Cooperation in Europe (OSCE).

The FPÖ

In 1983, the Socialist government lost its clear majority in parliament and entered into a coalition government with the Freedom Party of Austria (FPÖ). This far right party was founded in 1955. When Jörg Haider was elected party leader in 1986, the Socialists called an end to the coalition and the following year once again joined forces with the ÖVP. They ruled together for the next 13 years.

The FPÖ is an ultranationalist and populist party that has garnered harsh criticism and rejection by virtue of its leadership. Haider has been severely criticised for his pro-Nazi and xenophobic remarks. He was elected governor of Carinthia province in 1989 but was forced to resign in 1991 after having praised Nazi employment policies. Yet he did not disappear from the political scene.

The sensitive issue of racism was brought to the fore during the 1999 elections as the rightwing FPÖ gained support and was ultimately invited to join a coalition government with the ÖVP.

The Waldheim Affair

It was also around this time that another Austrian stirred up controversy. Kurt Waldheim, who had been Secretary-General of the United Nations from 1972 until 1981, ran for the presidency of Austria in 1986. This time, however, his involvement in public life led to an international backlash as accusations of his participation in Nazi-era crimes surfaced. During the war, he had served as a lieutenant in the German army in the Balkans, at a time when the Nazis were deporting Jews from Greece, rounding up slave labourers and carrying out reprisals on Yugoslavs and Albanians. Questions arose as to just how much he knew about such atrocities, and whether or not he had been involved.

In spite of, and to some extent in defiance of, the international uproar, Austrians elected him president. The United States later declared him an undesirable alien and put him on its watch list, which prevented him from visiting US territory. The Austrian government set up an international commission to investigate Waldheim's past. It found no proof of his direct involvement in any war crime. However, it noted that he had lied about his past and that he had known about what was taking place, although his ability to prevent war crimes was limited. While there were some protests and calls for his resignation, he remained president and Austria was ostracised by the international community for the duration of his six-year term.

The End of the Cold War

Soon after the fall of communism, Austria sought closer ties with Western Europe. In 1989, it applied for membership to the EU, and negotiations were completed in 1994. A national referendum was held, and Austrians voted overwhelmingly in favour of membership. On 1 January 1995, Austria joined the EU.

The country maintains its permanent neutrality status. As such, it cannot join NATO, but in February 1995, it entered into the NATO Partnership for Peace. Militarily, this means Austria can only take part in humanitarian and peacekeeping missions, as it did with conflicts in the Balkans.

The Green Party

The Green Party was formed in 1986 as a left-wing pro-environment party. The original founders included ecological farmers, peace activists and left-wingers. Their level of support was small, but sufficient to keep them active in the political arena. In the 2006 elections, they came in third place for the very first time, with 11 per cent of the vote. They ran their campaign promoting issues such as alternative energy policies, women's issues, anti-xenophobia, non-violence and organic foods.

The 'Black-Blue' Coalition

National elections were held in October 1999. Polls indicated that the FPÖ party, led by Jörg Haider, was gaining popularity. This raised concerns within Austria and the international community. Peaceful anti-Haider and anti-racism rallies were held in the country. Foreign governments warned that an FPÖ government would not be accepted.

The electorate ignored the international threats. The Socialists won the elections but did not get an absolute majority. The FPÖ did very well, winning 27 per cent of the votes, up from 5 per cent in 1986. The ÖVP dropped to third place, although it won the same number of seats in the *Nationalrat* as the FPÖ. Political analysts argue that the FPÖ did so well because Austrians were fed up with the two main parties. During the campaign, Haider had spoken out against the *Proporz* system, the large number of immigrants in Austria and EU expansion to the east, while promoting the need to restructure the social security system. These were all highly sensitive issues. Not only did the party do well in the conservative Alpine regions, as was expected, but its popularity in Vienna grew as well.

The head of the Socialists, Viktor Klima, said that his party would refuse to form a coalition government with the FPÖ, and so entered into negotiations with the ÖVP, which dragged on for months. Finally in January 2000, the Socialist Party informed the president—who was opposed to an ÖVP-FPÖ coalition—that it could not form a government.

The ÖVP and the FPÖ immediately entered into talks, and an agreement was quickly reached. On 4 February 2000, the new coalition government assumed power, with the ÖVP ('Blacks') responsible for running the political portfolios, and the FPÖ ('Blues') managing financial and social issues. Many Austrians peacefully showed their discontent with the coalition: in February 2000, Vienna saw its largest postwar rally with approximately 200,000 demonstrators.

International Reaction

International reaction was swift and harsh. The other EU members imposed bilateral diplomatic sanctions; all diplomatic contact was to be kept to a minimum and there would be no support for Austria in international forums. France and Belgium were the staunchest opponents. Austria considered EU sanctions 'unjust and exaggerated'. Other countries, including Israel and the United States, also showed disapproval. Economically, only the tourism and conference sectors were marginally affected.

The Austrian government faced the immense task of legitimising itself. President Thomas Klestil agreed to accept the ÖVP-FPÖ government on the condition that party leaders sign a statement that promised to reject discrimination and intolerance, uphold European values, respect ethnic and religious minorities, accept Austria's role in Nazi crimes and promote EU expansion. This was achieved, but critics were not appeased. The government tried to fight the sanctions but met strong resistance. Finally, it was agreed that the president of the European Commission on Human Rights would name a group of 'three wise men', who would monitor the 'political nature' of the FPÖ and the conduct of the Austrian government towards minorities and immigrants. The commission's findings, although critical in many aspects, did not find the situation in Austria worse than in other European countries. Sanctions were eventually lifted in September 2000. Haider, who was once again elected governor of Carinthia in 1999, stepped down as head of the FPÖ at the end of February 2000.

In 2002, the government collapsed due to in-fighting. Elections were held in November 2002, and this time the Freedom Party came in a distant third, only getting 10 per cent of the vote, less than half of the support it received in the previous elections. The ÖVP, which received the most votes, formed another coalition government with a much weaker FPÖ.

RECENT DEVELOPMENTS

In April 2004, Heinz Fischer was elected president, the first Social Democrat to hold that position since 1986. He is very well liked. In the 2006 parliamentary elections, once again, the opposition SPÖ received the most votes. After weeks of negotiations, a SPÖ-ÖVP coalition government took power in January 2007. The new chancellor, Alfred Gusenbauer (SPÖ), promised to set a minimum monthly wage, address unemployment and illegal immigration.

The controversial Jörg Haider remains in the news. In 2005, the Freedom Party split and Haider formed the Alliance for Austria's Future. In the 2006 parliamentary elections, the Freedom Party came in third and Haider's party came in a distant fifth. As governor of Carinthia, a province with a historic Slovenian population, Haider ordered that signs with the name of the city in both German and Slovenian be removed. This led to protests, and under pressure from the constitutional court, he put up new bilingual signs. However, while the new signs have the German name in huge letters, the Slovenian name is so small that it can barely be read.

Domestic Issues
Immigration Reform

Increased calls for tighter regulations on immigration were a result of a jump in the number of foreigners living in the country. During the 1990s, the immigrant population doubled from 345,000 to almost 750,000. Austria has one of the largest proportions of foreigners in the EU. In fact, the percentage of foreign-born residents is higher than in the United States. Yet Austria does not see itself as a nation of immigrants.

The majority of immigrants are from the former Yugoslavia and Turkey. Following World War II, Austria instituted a guest worker policy, encouraging workers from Turkey to temporarily relocate to Austria. Of course, temporary immigration often turns permanent. The fall of the Iron Curtain led more immigrants to Austria, and then the outbreak of war in the former Yugoslavia brought refugees. Austria accepted a large number of displaced Bosnians; in fact, it welcomed the highest number of refugees per capita in all of Europe.

The arrival of so many people gave rise to calls for immigration reform, and, in part, increased the popularity of right-wing politicians like Haider. In response, the government changed immigration laws a number of times, limiting the number of work permits issued to foreigners and then placing restrictions on asylum seekers. The overall policy tends to focus on 'integration before immigration'. It remains a hot topic in domestic politics.

Environmental Issues

Austrians are very concerned with environmental issues, and have strongly supported progressive policies. In 1975, Austrians voted in a plebiscite against the use of atomic energy, launching the first such ban in Europe. Critics, however, argue that even though Austria does not produce nuclear energy, it buys it gladly from its neighbours. Yet, Austrians oppose the operation of 'unsafe' nuclear power plants by their former eastern bloc neighbours. At times, protestors have blockaded border crossings to the Czech Republic.

International Issues
EU Expansion

Austria is a committed member of the European Union. In spite of the sanctions imposed after the 1999 elections, the majority of Austrians never considered withdrawing from the union. There is, however, some disagreement on the terms and pace of EU expansion towards the east. Officially, the Austrian government favours EU expansion. It is believed that it would promote security and stability in the region. Moreover, proponents say that Austria could be one of the main economic beneficiaries of EU expansion because of its existing presence in eastern markets.

The biggest current issue is Turkey's potential membership. The majority of Austrians would prefer to see Turkey join the EU with something less than full membership. They cite Turkey's size, poverty levels and religious differences as reasons to limit its participation in the EU.

Austria's Military Role

Austria, a vital neutral presence during the tense days of the Cold War, wants to continue to be a key player between East and West. Yet, after so many years of neutrality, Austria must answer difficult questions regarding its involvement in multilateral security structures. This issue was brought to the forefront during the Kosovo crisis and the NATO bombing of Yugoslavia.

Having retained its neutrality, Austria can only participate in UN and EU humanitarian and peacekeeping missions. Being outside of NATO prohibits Austria from fully participating in an EU mission if sensitive NATO material is used. As a consequence, Austria is not considered an equal partner in EU security policy. The Socialists and the Greens are strongly opposed to joining NATO, as are a majority of Austrians.

The ÖVP and FPÖ are, in general, pro-NATO. Membership, however, would require a constitutional amendment revoking permanent neutrality.

Compensation for Nazi Crimes
Slave Labour

On 27 October 2000, an agreement was finally reached regarding compensation for 150,000 slave labourers under the Nazi government. Payments to victims, the majority of whom are from Central and Eastern Europe, come from a special reconciliation fund of US$ 415 million. Half of the funds come from the Austrian government and the other half from private businesses. The highest payments are made to former slave labourers in concentration camps. Smaller payments are made to other categories of victims. In return, Austrian companies will be safe from future lawsuits.

Stolen Assets

On 17 January 2001, an agreement was reached on the difficult subject of Aryanised property. A General Settlement Fund of US$ 210 million was established by the Austrian government and Austrian companies. The bulk of the fund is intended to compensate Holocaust victims who were robbed of businesses, property, bank accounts and insurance policies. The balance will be used for interest payments, insurance claims, social benefits, the restoration and maintenance of Jewish cemeteries, to fund Jewish organisations and to expedite the return of works of art. In return, the claimants must agree to drop their lawsuits. Payments were delayed, however, because there were legal actions against Austria pending in the United States. In November 2005, the last case was dismissed and the Austrian government began the process of making compensation payments.

A court found that Austria must return five priceless paintings by Gustav Klimt to the heirs of a Jewish family. The paintings were stolen by the Nazis and have since been on display in the Belvedere Museum in Vienna. Austria said it would comply but has proposed that the paintings remain on display as national treasures and have asked the heirs to loan the paintings. One of the heirs, Maria Altmann, who now lives in the United States, has said that they should be kept available for public display.

AUSTRIAN FOLK

CHAPTER 3

'A man should not strive to eliminate his complexes,
but to get into accord with them; they are legitimately
what directs his conduct in the world.'
—Sigmund Freud, founder of psychoanalysis

THE AUSTRIANS ARE AN INTERESTING but complicated people. Their day-to-day life is conservative and quite regimented. They are deferential to a fault, dress neatly and properly depending on the venue, and are always punctual. Frugal and moderate, they enjoy their children and retain close connections with family, and like to meet their friends at the local coffeehouse. For leisure, they enjoy the outdoors and sports related to each of the four seasons. But that's just the tip of the iceberg.

The Austrian personality is a paradox. Austrian humour and grumpiness are tied into one. Whether at home or at work, they complain about most things: colleagues, neighbours, their children and their health. However, they also yearn to make good and to be accepted, and their pliancy helps them achieve this. This manner of being makes them appear contradictory and inconsistent at times, and they end up saying yes and no to everything and everybody. Some believe that this ambivalence has roots in Austria's landscape, ethnic mix, history, attitude toward religion and mature civilisation.

Their sense of humour is not obvious. Austrians rely on wit and irony, rather than on pun. The wit shines through in their use of wonderfully vivid names. Nestroy, a comedian and playwright, employed the word *Lumpazivagabundus* in many of his works as a label for a scoundrel and vagabond. Irony, known as *Weltanschaung*, is where the Austrian tends to see the whole world in himself. Self-deprecation is

A jolly Austrian shows off his felt hat with *Gamsbart* (like a shaving brush).

a form of humour realised from the day-to-day world: it's much easier to see the negative and expect it than the other way around.

The bureaucracy may have a hand in the personality of the people. On the one hand, Austria has a well-structured social security system which takes good care of everyone's health, job security and pension; on the other hand, the government system can be extremely oppressive in that it keeps everyone mired in bureaucratic procedure.

A very good reason for Austrians' automatic compliance with rules dates back to the Metternich era (1814–48), when those who did not obey and conform were penalised. In fact, it was in this period that spying on the general population to keep it in line was rampant.

One shouldn't forget, however, that Austria is divided into nine federal provinces and that each province has its distinct personality and pride. Salzburg, for example, feels itself to be more German, whereas people from Vorarlberg think of themselves as more Swiss. The Carinthian is very macho and hot-blooded, and supposedly still dreaming of a greater Germany. The Burgenländers are farmers, and life in their part of the world tends to be simple.

Differences also exist between the urban and the rural populations, between the upper-income and lower-income groups and between families of different ethnic backgrounds.

All said and done, Austria is a wonderful place to live in. In a recent poll, Austria ranked highest in Europe as having the best political and economic situation, environmental standards, health and social security system and cultural and leisure activities. These standards do give a vivid account of life in Austria. The people are proud of their country and, in turn, try to maintain its beauty.

THE FAMILY

The family is important to Austrians. Parents try to establish a safe place for their children. Moving from town to town is quite unheard of and the children grow up knowing one town and the same people and friends their whole lives. The mother and father usually take equal share in the care of the children and do numerous activities with them. They often go to the many different parks, woods or mountains together. In turn, the children grow up with a considerable awareness of the natural environment. Austrian parents, although frugal,

Sunday dinner is a time for Austrian families to get together and share the week's gossip.

spend more money per capita per child on toys than parents in any other European nation.

School System
Even the school system is geared to having the children spend time at home. From kindergarten until about the 4th grade, children come home at around noon. The mother or grandmother is at home waiting to serve them lunch. After lunch, they go out to play, attend team practice, study another language or learn to play an instrument. The latter two activities are seen as a sign of good education and culture.

In Public with Mom and Dad
In public, children are extremely well behaved; in fact, one doesn't hear a peep from them. To an outsider, it seems a little harsh that the children cannot just 'be children'. A strict but loving upbringing molds them to fit neatly into society.

Having Fun Together
Parents also do many sports with their children—ice-skating, soccer, cycling, tennis, horseback riding and swimming. Skiing is by far the most popular sport; having the Alps

beckoning at the doorstep makes it the natural sport of choice. Children put on skis as soon as they learn to walk. By the age of seven or eight, they start resembling speeding bullets going down the ski slopes.

Getting to Know Everyone in the Family

The children grow up knowing each member of the extended family, including their grandmother and grandfather, or *Oma* and *Opa*. *Oma*, especially, takes on an important role. She is the one who babysits the children, takes them for walks, and, of course, spoils them silly. On Sunday afternoons, most families get together at *Oma* and *Opa's* in the afternoon for an early dinner followed by cake and coffee a little later on. This is a good time to catch up on the past week's happenings, but more importantly, it is a time to relax and enjoy each other's company.

The Weekends

The weekends are sacred to the average Austrian family. They value spending their time off with their family and don't believe in working after hours. That is why you will often find all stores closed on Sundays, and it is only in the last couple of years that stores have stayed open until

Austrians love outdoor activities and take advantage of their free time on weekends.

5:00 pm on Saturday. There is opposition to the idea of opening stores on Sunday, because many feel this would lead to the breakdown of the family.

Special Holidays Together

Families love to come together to celebrate special occasions, especially birthdays, Saints' Days, Easter and Christmas. Each celebration is a time for a nice family dinner, the opening of gifts, having friends over and making merry.

The Elderly

A great percentage of the Austrian folk are over the age of 60. You often see white-haired men and blue-haired old ladies on trams or doing their weekly shopping. Many are good-natured and friendly, especially if you have a baby or dog in tow, but some can seem grumpy and unhappy with you if you don't appear to be following the rules of good behaviour.

The social system is so good and the family situation so close that the elderly are very well taken care of by their immediate family. They usually enter nursing homes only when close medical supervision is required.

GETTING AWAY

Garden lots

Garden lots or small gardens (*Schrebergärten* or *Kleingärten*) became popular after World War I as a private source of vegetables in times of shortage. Later on, the garden became a summer retreat and a means of escaping from the crowds of the city.

Today, the garden lot has become a second home for many, who build small houses on the lots and either live in them permanently, or on weekends or in the summer. In most of the outer districts of Vienna alone, there are approximately 35,000 garden lots.

Inheriting a House

Many Austrians are lucky enough to inherit an apartment, house or farmhouse. The house can become the permanent home or, if it is located outside the city, the country home.

The much-loved *Kleingärten* (garden lot) is visited frequently in the summer or lived on year-round.

Families tend to stay in one place all their lives, which makes the passing on of a house or apartment more common than in more mobile societies.

Vacations

All Austrians believe in their vacation time, which is usually about five to six weeks a year. Depending on their interests, many go skiing for a week in February, go away for a week to ten days during Easter, take two to three weeks during the summer, and perhaps a week or so at Christmas time. Those with families tend not to leave Austria for their vacations. They would rather go skiing locally and spend the rest of their vacation time at their second home in the countryside or in the mountains. Of those who do travel, many go to the seaside in Italy, Croatia or even Spain (popular spots include Mallorca and the Canary Islands), especially in the summer. Other popular destinations include Greece, Tunisia and Turkey.

Singles and couples usually travel far and wide, from the Americas to Australia, Asia and Africa. They enjoy the exotic culture, new language and different food. One often sees billboards advertising documentaries on faraway lands, enticing people to travel more.

SAVING FOR THE FUTURE

Saving is a virtue in Austria. There is little debt and credit cards are used wisely. Many Austrians save to buy a car, go on family holidays, and, most importantly, build a home. When it comes to homes, parents' longer-term savings are usually needed, and fortunate are the children whose parents help them in times like these. Julie is married to an Austrian and when they built their own house, they turned to her in-laws for help. If it weren't for them, they would not have been able to afford it.

FRIENDS

Friendships are extremely important to Austrians. They value their friends and believe in staying in touch on a regular basis. Many, unless they have moved from the country to the big city, have had the same friends since childhood. They meet their friends in their homes or at a restaurant, *Heurige* (wine tavern), coffeehouse or *Beisel* (bar).

It is often easier to meet and befriend non-Austrians than locals. Austrian reserve hinders them from making friends quickly, and should you make a move to talk to them in a

Austrians enjoy socialising with family and friends at outdoor festivals year round.

class or meeting, they will usually be friendly but introverted. Friendships develop over a long period of time.

If you work among Austrians, you will get to know them eventually, although you may find that many Austrians who work together don't necessarily go out together. Studying in Austria makes it much easier to get to know Austrians, as students are more carefree and uninhibited. If you are neither working nor studying in Austria, being open and chatting with your neighbours and local shopkeepers will help you feel more relaxed and at home. Other ways of meeting people include joining art, dance or exercise classes or groups such as the American Women's Association (AWA), which is open to all nationalities, going to church, and just being outgoing yourself.

The Esoteric Side of the Austrians

Although reserved, many Austrians are drawn to the esoteric during their leisure time. Many love to take dance lessons not only to enjoy the ball season but also to add another dimension to their lives. Samba, mambo, cha-cha, tango, rumba, fox trot, waltz, jive and jitterbug are but a smattering of the dances taught at the many dance schools. Indian dance and belly dancing are popular among women, and country-and-western is popular among couples, with quite a few locations featuring live bands playing music for the two-step. Susan once went to a birthday party for an Austrian friend and one of the gifts was an Indian dance complete with full costume, performed by a guest—also Austrian—who had been taking lessons.

MOTHERHOOD

The Austrian woman is a very strong-minded individual. She takes care of her household, the budget and raises her children. Yet, many more women are going to work today than previously. About half the workforce is made up of women, as more and more are going back to work after childbirth to improve the family's standard of living. Children are well taken care of by the state. Women cannot work within eight weeks of giving birth; this gives them a compulsory 4-month break from work. After this period, either the mother or father (or both, in alternation) get 24 months paid leave from their work in order to raise their child. And until the

Austrian women take great pride in their appearance. No matter what their activities are for the day, they dress nicely and with care. Fashions are elegant and understated, never flamboyant. You will not see women dressed in sneakers or ratty jeans. Workout clothes such as sweat pants are only for the gym.

child is done with school, there is an additional payment from the government to help defray the cost of child rearing.

Single motherhood is also on the rise in Austria. The state takes such good care of the mother and child that many women choose single motherhood over abortion, adoption or marriage—a not unreasonable choice when one considers that half of all marriages in Austria today end in divorce.

Even with all the incentives to have children, the birthrate is equal to the death rate, resulting in a zero net birthrate. Austria has a low birth rate because women are having less children than before and are postponing motherhood until they are older. The implications of this statistic will be felt in years to come.

THE NEIGHBOURS

Neighbours can be important to you. Most of them are friendly and will always greet you. They are a good source of information and advice during your stay, and will also help out during emergencies. They often keep an eye on their neighbours' homes when their neighbours are on vacation. Julie moved around a lot in Vienna and always found the neighbours extremely nice. Once, when there was a medical emergency, the neighbours really went out of their way to help out.

It is also a good idea to always invite the neighbours if you are having a large party. Not only is it a goodwill gesture, but if you are intending to make a lot of noise, there will be no one to complain. This would also avoid the inconvenience of having to end the party early or toning down the noise by 10:00 pm, which is the law! There have been instances when the police visited our friends in response to a neighbour's complaint regarding the noise level. Then again, there are neighbours who go to the party out of courtesy, then leave at 10:00 pm and turn around and call the police. Figure that one out!

You might find your neighbours openly nosy. They seem to know everything that goes on in most of the neighbouring households, and if they are walking by a house, will blatantly stare into the windows without a hint of pretense.

Remember that Sunday is acknowledged as a quiet family day. So don't go disturbing your neighbour by mowing the lawn, working on the car or doing carpentry work. All of this should be done on Saturday or on weekdays during the day.

THE CELL PHONE

If at times the Austrian way appears old-fashioned and anachronistic, the cell phone or *Handy* revolutionised the Austrian way of life. From moms pushing baby carriages, to people walking their dogs, horseback riders, *Fiaker* (horse-drawn carriage) drivers, businessmen at lunch and the public transportation rider, everyone is carrying one. Austria has one of the highest densities of mobile phone users in all of Europe.

FARMING COMMUNITY

Much of Austria is made up of mountains, beautiful lush forests, and, most importantly, farmland. The farms produce a variety of plant and meat products, such as wheat, vegetables, fruit, wine, milk, eggs, pork and beef. The dairy products, especially, are thought of as truly superior.

Farming is hard work, and everyone in the family contributes. Working hours on a farm (*Bauernhof*) are from sunrise to sunset, and the women do as much as the men. Despite this, many farms, unless they are large, have difficulty making ends meet in spite of subsidies. Many have had to offer rooms to travellers in order to bring in an additional source of income. They are great vacationing spots, as children enjoy learning about and interacting with farm animals. The fresh milk, cheese, eggs and freshly baked bread are also a treat.

Generally speaking, people on the farms are much friendlier than city folk and much easier to talk to and laugh with. Certainly, the *Heurigen* (wine taverns) in the country are much more interesting because of the light-heartedness of the people. (Plus their wines are nothing to balk at!)

SAFETY

Austria is a very safe place to live and work in. One can walk the streets alone in the wee hours of the morning, whether in a small or large city, without fear of muggers, rapists or the like lurking around the corner. One does hear of the occasional pickpocket in large department stores or on the metro, and of home or car burglaries, but crimes are generally rare.

AUSTRIA'S UNCONVENTIONAL SIDE
Prostitution
If you think the average Austrian a bit too demure, take a drive late at night along the Gürtel or the Prater in Vienna, and you might be surprised at the scantily-clad women waiting for customers. Prostitution is legal in Vienna and the rest of Austria. Legalising prostitution could have begun with Emperor Franz Josef, as he did not have a blissful marriage and sought other women to satisfy his needs. Franz Josef also felt that prostitutes should be well taken care of and had a special health system instituted for them.

Saunas and Nude Bathing

Austrians are open and accepting toward nudity. Now and then, you will see nude or suggestive advertising. On warm summer days, many women go about braless. If you enjoy saunas, be prepared to wear just your towel. Some saunas have mixed days when men and women share the sauna. Women at the beach or the pool are often topless. Along the same lines, there is nude swimming, usually on Sunday evenings, at certain pools; nudist swimming areas can be found around lakes and rivers as well. While cycling or strolling by the Danube, don't be surprised if you spot one or two people with nothing but their birthday suits on!

> Nudity is a normal part of life and as such is prevalent in advertising and magazines. It is only natural that an ad for soap or shampoo would show a naked woman taking a shower. You'll also find nudity on the pages of glamour and fashion magazines; some layouts even border on the pornographic.

Sex

Austria seems to have no hang-ups about sex. Prudery and chastity were never very fashionable. Most also ignore the Catholic Church with regard to contraception and abortion. The unmarried person in a steady relationship is referred to as the *Lebensgefährten* or *Lebensgefährtin* (life companion); a married woman's lover is referred to as the *Hausfreund* (friend of the house).

LOVE THOSE DOGS!

Austrians love their dogs and they are integral members of the family. People openly demonstrate their affection for their canine friends. Dogs accompany their owners on outings and in stores and restaurants. They are not to be left behind at home. You'll see a lot of dogs in Austria and you'll enjoy your stay more if you are a dog lover.

The downside of having so many dogs in Austria, especially in large cities like Vienna, is having to clean up the 15 tons of fecal matter every month, deposited by those sweet, loving canine pets. Many dog owners don't feel in any way responsible for cleaning up after their pets as they pay a

Austrians revere their dogs and take them just about everywhere, not only for walks on the street but also to banks, stores and restaurants.

special dog tax. Helmut Zilk, a former mayor, tried to clean up the streets by hiring a French firm to vacuum up the waste using heavy motorised 'shit collectors'. The mayor even accompanied these trucks on their rounds. The citizens were not amused and the collecting machines were sent back to France. Therefore, until a street sweeper cleans up the mess on a sidewalk, one must tiptoe around it or endure messy, smelly shoes.

For all the love bestowed on these animals, the government has interesting ways of disposing of them once they are dead or out of the reach of their owners. Dogs cannot be buried. A law from 1919 states that all animal carcasses have to be collected and utilised, or burned. A pet owner has to call a special agency, TKW (Tierkörperverwertung), to remove its corpse; if he does not, a fine could result. Recently, it was revealed that bodies of dogs, cats and laboratory animals ended up being processed into animal feed for pigs and chickens. Many Austrians and environmental groups were aghast and are trying to make the Ministry of Agriculture change the outdated law.

Austria's Supreme Court upheld a law that fines drivers if they brake to avoid hitting smaller animals such as cats, lap dogs, puppies, hares and hedgehogs. Only wild boar and deer have the law on their side. Austria's animal rights groups are crying murder over the ruling, and some are even saying that the law gives drivers the legal right to murder animals on the roads. The government's Department for Traffic Safety holds that a driver should brake if the size of the animal endangers road safety, but drivers cannot stop for smaller animals even after they have run over them.

Cruelty to Animals

A new law against cruelty to animals not only makes it illegal to cage hens and rope cattle, but also prohibits dog owners from using choke collars or invisible electronic fences and from clipping their ears and tails.

DEATH
Preparing for Death

Austrians, particularly the Viennese, are said to have a fascination and special relationship with death. There is a general attitude that death is a part of life, not simply the end of it. Most Austrians are practical and buy a graveyard plot when they are in their 30s or 40s, both as an investment (graves are extremely expensive) and to secure a gravesite. Many older Viennese who do not come from wealthy families belong to a death association (*Sterbeverein*), to which they pay monthly dues that eventually pay for a decent burial and gravesite.

Elaborate funerals are known as a *schöne Leich'* (literally translated as a 'beautiful corpse'). Many people are given these expensive funerals, noted for having a large cortege, paid speakers and lavish meals. It is not uncommon for members of the Vienna State Opera to be asked to sing at the departing soul's grave, particularly at the Zentralfriedhof.

Mortuary Services

The mortuary service in Austria is one of the biggest funeral enterprises in the world. There are approximately 500 employees arranging 30,000 burials a year. They provide wreath-carriers, grand hearses and major paraphernalia.

The Zentralfriedhof

The Zentralfriedhof in Vienna is the second largest cemetery in Europe. It holds over 3 million people, or twice the population of the city. There are approximately 50 funerals a day, and it has special Jewish and Muslim sections. A number of famous Austrians are buried here as well.

The cemetery is quite beautiful and is reminiscent of a park, with green grass and trees everywhere. In fact, many go there to unwind or take a stroll. On 1 and 2 November, All Saints' and All Souls' Day respectively, the cemetery takes on a jovial atmosphere. *Würstelstände* (sausage stands) and *Maronistände* (chestnut stands) open up, friends and family gather and the dearly departed are remembered.

If you are interested in how the Viennese are laid to rest, head to the Vienna Funeral Museum. You can check out its collection of urns, coffins, shrouds, funeral vehicles and more.

The Japanese are especially keen to see this cemetery. Some say that it is the first place they visit. Julie was very surprised to see a chorus of Japanese women singing beautifully next to Johann Strauss's grave. The women were paying a most gracious homage to their favourite musician.

Suicide

At one point at the turn of the 20th century, it was commonplace to hear in Vienna of intellectuals dying by their own hand. The best-known suicide at the time was that of Prince Rudolf, the son of Franz Josef, who after killing his mistress put a gun to his head. The suicide rate is still high, some 17 per 100,000 according to the World Health Organization, with men more than three times as likely as women to do so. The reason is not certain. It is speculated that some people believe that in death, they will achieve the recognition denied during life. It has also been said that the warm winds that occur in the fall, the *Föhn*, have debilitating mental effects, causing some to kill themselves.

RELIGION

The main religion in Austria is Roman Catholicism. The Habsburgs made it the religion of their empire and fought many wars in its defense. Josef II made many religious reforms in the late 18th century and gave Calvinists, Lutherans and Jews more rights. He also gave Orthodox citizens the right to practise their religion and build churches. Today, about 73 per cent of Austrians classify themselves as Catholic. Slightly less than 5 per cent are Protestant and 4 per cent of the country are Muslim. About 3 per cent belong to other faiths and 12 per cent claim no religious identity.

Austria, and Vienna in particular, has always been at the crossroads of many nationalities and their respective religions, yet not until Austria became a sovereign country after World War II did the various nationalities openly practise their religions. As you drive through some of the larger cities, especially Vienna and Salzburg, you sees synagogues, mosques and Buddhist temples.

Paying into the Church
Belonging to any church in Austria requires you to pay a certain percentage (approximately 1.5 per cent) of your earnings into the church's account. A word of warning: if you don't wish to pay into a church, do not fill out the religion section of your initial police registration form (*Meldezettel*). You might then get a payment form (*Zahlschein*) and newsletters from the church, and you will be expected to pay. Getting out of this situation is extremely difficult and requires many phone calls and a letter or two in German stating why you do not wish to contribute toward that church.

Religious Classes for Children
Religious instruction is provided in public school for 12 years. Classes are offered for all of the officially-recognised religions. Parents can elect to have their child not attend these classes, and instead opt to have the child take private religious classes during the week. However, these are expensive and not very popular.

Catholicism
The vast majority of Austrians are considered to be Roman Catholic. The Catholic rituals, such as weddings and funerals,

are similar to those around the world, with a few exceptions. Only a small number of Austrian Catholics practise their religion and attend church. They have many beautiful churches to choose from, several fashioned in the Baroque style. There is usually daily mass. On Sundays, there are three masses: early morning, late morning (where the priest gives a sermon called a *Hochamt*, and a choir performs) and late evening.

THE JEWS

The Jews have always been in Vienna. In a commercial edict passed in AD 966, less than a century after the name Vienna first appeared on historic documents, the phrase 'Jews and other legitimate merchants' shows up. In the 1300s, a contemporary observer remarked, "There are more Jews in Vienna than in any other German city familiar to me." Vienna had become known in the Jewish world as a centre of learning, and rabbis and Hebraic scholars were often referred to as the 'sages of Vienna' (*Vienna and Its Jews*, page 29). The history thereafter is one of being exiled, then let back in, and so on and so forth. At one point, the Jews were the reason for the economic stability of the Austrian empire. Maria Theresa hated them and said, "I know of no greater plague on the state than this nation which, through deception, usury and cheating, brings people into beggary." She should have bitten her tongue, as her finance minister was a Jew. Her son, Josef, was a true son of the Enlightenment, and issued a Tolerance Ordinance in 1781 that protected many Jews.

The Jews came in great numbers to Vienna in the 19th century. In fact, at the close of the century, they accounted for 11 per cent of the population. Jews held a variety of positions at differing economic levels and many were very successful. Many of those positions were in the retail and wholesale trade, banking and in the press. In fact, 61 per cent of the doctors, 57 per cent of the lawyers and 86 per cent of the law clerks were Jewish.

At the turn of the 19th century, the population of Jews started dwindling. They were used as scapegoats during the 1873 stock market crash. Karl Lueger, Vienna's mayor from 1897 to 1910, was virulently anti-Semitic and caused approximately 120,000 Jews to flee even before the *Anschluss* in 1938. Over 65,000 died during the Holocaust. More left after World War II. In 1954, they numbered 11,224, but by 2002, their numbers had dwindled to around 7,000. Unlike in other countries, the Austrian Jewish community appears to be shrinking.

Today, feelings toward the Jews have changed dramatically. Catholics have spoken in defense of Jews and groups of Austrian Catholics have made pilgrimages to Israel. Parliament has disbanded organisations and limited events believed to have pro-Nazi overtones. A Sigmund Freud park was opened and the city has contributed generously to the maintenance of various Jewish institutions. Simon Wiesenthal set up a documentation centre in the former Jewish textile quarter. The Jewish Welcome Center keeps in contact with emigrants all over the world. There is a new Jewish school, Lauder Chabad Campus, with 400 students.

Recently, the Judenplatz (Jewish Plaza) was totally redesigned and is now a place of remembrance. The Judenplatz Museum, located in the Misrachi House, is run by the Jewish Museum of the City of Vienna. It houses three exhibition rooms on medieval Jewish life in addition to the excavations of the Or Sarua Synagogue. Built in the mid-13th century, this synagogue was later destroyed during the pogroms of 1420–1421 that forced the Jews out of Vienna.

The Holocaust memorial in Judenplatz was designed by British sculptor, Rachel Whitehead. It is a large concrete library that depicts books with their bindings facing inward. The locked doors and the fact that you cannot read the book titles represent the loss of those who died. Engraved around the base are the names of the places where Austrian Jews were killed by the Nazis.

The sheer size of the historical Jewish population is better understood after a visit to the Jewish section of the Zentralfriedhof. However, the oldest surviving Jewish cemetery, with gravestones dating back to 1540, is found in the 9th district on Seegasse 9–11. To visit it, one must go through the foyer of an old folks' home to the back of the building.

Eisenstadt, the capital of Burgenland, also has a significant Jewish population and museum.

MUSLIMS

Muslims have a significant presence in Austria. Numbering around 200,000, they account for about 4 per cent of the population. The majority are Turkish, about 120,000, and another 50,000 are Bosnians. The remainder are primarily Arabs. The Muslims have a long history in Austria and as a result they enjoy more rights here than in other European countries. The Austro-Hungarian Empire brought Muslim groups such as the Bosnians under their rule while other groups immigrated to Vienna. Religious freedoms were granted early on. In 1867, a law that guaranteed respect for all religions of the empire gave Muslims the right to establish mosques and to practise their religion. In 1912, the 'Law of Islam' was passed that made Islam an official religion. This gave Muslims the right to organise and manage their affairs independently.

In 1988, the 'Law of Islam' was amended to recognise Islamic theological schools, allow women to wear the veil at work and school and give Muslims the right to study Islam in public schools and in the army. The *Islamische Glaubensgemeinschaft* in Österreich is the organisation that trains these teachers and speaks for the Islamic community. Following the events of 11 September 2001, the Islamic community has noted a slight increase in offensive comments and threats, especially from the far right.

IMMIGRANTS

Immigrants, especially in Vienna and its suburbs, have always been a part of Austrian culture. In centuries past, Austria was a large empire with many different peoples interacting and trading within it. The turning point came toward the end of the 19th century, when, under the dual monarchy, many Hungarian aristocrats and artists came to seek a new life in the cosmopolitan city of Vienna. Many other groups, including Turks, Greeks, Macedonians and Rumanians, were also drawn to the metropolis, which was then at a major crossroads intellectually, artistically and politically. Vienna was Austria's centre, and it was a great mix of faces. A ditty was sung in the late 19th century epitomising the mixture:

> 'The Christians, the Turks, the Heathen and Jew
> Have dwelt here in ages old and new
> Harmoniously and without any strife
> For everyone's entitled to live his own life.'

In fact, no Austrian today could trace his roots in unbroken lines to his great-grandfather. Yet, most ethnic groups, except the Hungarians who formed part of the empire at one time, are not completely accepted. The Slavs, i.e. Czech, Croatian, Polish or Slovakian, are especially unpopular. The Turks and Yugoslavians have been working in Vienna for over 50 years and are still seen as outsiders and often treated badly. Recent immigration has come from the war-torn lands of the former Yugoslavia, Turkey and Nigeria. Many migrants are illegal aliens: some have sought political asylum, and others have gone through the proper channels to obtain residency permits or citizenship.

Many immigrants were brought in as *Gastarbeiter* or guest workers following World War II. Most of them are hardworking, pay their taxes and contribute to the social system. In fact, the Employers' Federation is one of their main supporters. Immigrants fill a variety of jobs: they are manual or hard labourers working on construction sites, some are custodians and maids, others sell newspapers and flowers, open up restaurants (especially the Chinese, Turks and Croatians) and shops, and yet more are taxi drivers. Some gain a good education and become professionals.

Some Austrians still deprecate Turks and other dark-skinned people because they look and act differently. Many are called

Most immigrants have settled in Vienna. In fact, 10 per cent of Vienna's population is foreign. Most live in the 2nd–6th, 16th and 22nd districts. Hungarians and Croatians live mainly in Burgenland, while Carinthia is home to many Slovenians. Muslim women from Bosnia or Turkey are easy to spot as they wear scarves and long dresses or long coats. They are often seen in the parks with their families, enjoying picnics or barbecues on warm summer weekends.

Tschuschen, which is an insulting term for the Balkan people. Some of Julie's dark-skinned friends have experienced bad treatment by Austrians in stores and other service-oriented areas.

Immigration has risen to the forefront of domestic politics. The government has had to address immigration problems, and in 1986, Austrian politics became a rational zone of compromise rather than an arena of conflict. However, the right-wing, anti-immigration Freedom Party led by Jörg Haider reared its ugly head in the late 1980s, when increases in Eastern European immigration followed the collapse of the eastern bloc. Concern even among moderates was exacerbated by the influx of refugees from the former Yugoslavia. Reforms were made that restricted work permits and asylum rights by limiting appeals and nations of origin. There has been opposition to the reforms and it remains a hot issue.

SOCIALISING WITH THE AUSTRIANS

CHAPTER 4

'*Zwischen zu früh und zu spät,
liegt immer nur ein Augenblick.*'
'Between being too early and too late,
there is never more than an instant.'
—Franz Werfel, Austrian novelist

SOCIAL CUSTOMS

Austria is built on 'the right way' of doing things. In the cities, customs haven't changed much since the time of the Habsburgs. The formalities are overwhelming at first. After a while, some become second nature and can be quite charming.

Greeting One Another

The greeting is essential in almost all social situations. When walking into a public area, whether a boutique, coffeehouse or doctor's office, an obligatory *Grüss Gott* (hello) is said. In some of the nicer boutiques, a woman may be greeted as *Gnädige Frau*, an old-fashioned term meaning 'most gracious woman'. When leaving, one would say *auf Wiedersehen* or *Wiederschaun* (goodbye). This greeting does not apply when out of confined spaces, unless you pass someone in your apartment building.

Grüss Gott!

Once Susan entered a small drugstore and saw no one at the cash register or in the aisles, so she remained quiet and started off to find her items. Immediately, she heard someone yell out "*Grüss Gott*" in a manner implying Susan's rudeness. She apologetically replied "*Grüss Gott*" and found the clerk hidden in an aisle stocking a bottom shelf. From that moment on, she made it a point to always yell out "*Grüss Gott*", even to a seemingly empty store.

You will notice that when walking or jogging about, Austrians will not go out of their way to greet you. This can be rather puzzling as they do it automatically in the shops. It is also understood that a younger person should greet a mature person, and not the other way around. This can change dramatically in villages or smaller cities around Austria, which tend to be friendlier and less inhibited.

Shaking Hands

Shaking hands is another important gesture for first meetings. Generally, the woman offers her hand to the man, and the older person to the younger. Handshakes are firm, with direct eye contact, and you usually say your last name without prefacing it with a greeting.

At a party or a dinner at a friend's house, wait until the host introduces you before you go around introducing yourself. The host will generally introduce you by your last name. While being introduced, you shake each person's hand accordingly. At large parties, the introduction seems to take forever. However, Julie finds it to be a wonderful way to break the ice.

Kissing Each Other's Cheek

Once you have become close to someone and are on a first name basis, you may kiss each other's cheek in greeting. If you are a woman, you have the privilege of kissing both women and men on each cheek: first right, then left. A man would only shake the hand of another man. If unsure what to do, go for the handshake and wait until the Austrian makes the next move.

Body language isn't excessive after kissing or shaking hands. Hugging is not done except with close family members or with a friend that you haven't seen in a long time. Gesticulating to put a point across is rarely done. Simply put, the Austrian way is reserved and calm unless driving on the Autobahn (freeway)!

Küss die Hand

A very Austrian male greeting is the one called *Küss die Hand*. It means to kiss the back of the hand, but the man never actually kisses the hand, merely the air above it. The custom is old-fashioned and very formal. You could envision Emperor Franz Josef doing it with his many women friends.

The greeting is used at formal events such as balls, weddings, special parties and among the supposedly defunct aristocracy. The male will normally be older and from an old Austrian family, or a younger man with savoir-faire who wants to make a good impression. We wouldn't suggest this practice to any non-Austrian.

MANNERS

Manners on Public Transportation

The public transportation system is a good example of Austrian civility. Before getting on the train, tram or bus, everyone waits for the people on board to alight. There is also special seating near the exit doors for the elderly, pregnant women, children and the handicapped. Lively discussions are rarely carried on between strangers, although these may take place in smaller cities more often than in larger ones. No one goes out of his or her way to make small talk, even about the weather.

Children are also well controlled on public transportation, and do not chatter, jump or run around. Our inference is that older ladies can stare so creepily at children who have made any untoward noise that they are dumbstruck forevermore.

Furthermore, even though eating and drinking are allowed on public transportation, passengers are seldom seen taking the privilege. Drinking coffee on the go is never done as it is considered a pleasure and a form of relaxation.

Table Manners

Table manners are similar throughout Europe. When invited to someone's home for a meal, start eating only after the host has begun. It is customary to say *Guten Appetit* or *Mahlzeit*, which means 'have a good meal', beforehand. The former is for more formal situations and the latter is used among friends and family. The napkin then goes on the lap, the fork in the left hand and the knife in the right. The hands are above the table at all times. Elbows are close to the body and never put on the table. While pausing to drink or talk during a meal, put one piece of silverware on either side of the plate facing downward. Close your mouth when chewing, and please, no slurping while eating soup. Only take what you can eat. When the meal is finished, the knife and fork are put together on the right side of the plate.

Smoking

Austrians love to smoke. As a consequence, cigarettes are ubiquitous. The sad truth is that cigarette smoking is on the rise among women and teenagers. While other EU members have started a debate on the subject and have introduced smoking bans, Austria remains far behind. If you come from the United States and its anti-smoking bias, Austria will be quite a shock. You may not be appalled at people lighting up in train stations and restaurants, but we were when we saw patients at the AKH hospital smoking in the lounge with an IV in their arm. In general, non-smoking laws in Austria are very lenient and even a 2005 law that banned smoking in public buildings is rarely enforced. There is hope, though.

Workplace bans on smoking are slowly taking hold as more and more employers comply.

Most likely, restaurants, bars, discos and coffeehouses will be the last to fall. Several restaurants now have non-smoking sections, but most often the smoking section is so near that it really doesn't make much of a difference. It may be hard to find a well-ventilated restaurant. Windows are closed in winter and air-conditioning is non-existent in the summer. Sometimes, an option is to eat outdoors (weather permitting) or at off-peak hours. But not too many restaurants serve dinner early, especially outside of the cities. Hopefully things will improve over time, but don't expect any major changes to happen overnight.

Noise

Noise levels are kept at a minimum in general. In fact, while driving, it is against the law to use the horn except in extreme emergencies.

In public dining or drinking areas, it is common courtesy not to talk above a certain pitch, as it would disturb other customers. There are also signs up in outdoor eating areas that warn the public to keep their voices down, in order not to disturb those nearby. Julie and her friends have occasionally been told by maîtres d' to please keep the noise down, much to their embarrassment.

Children rarely make noise in public. The only places you notice them are at playgrounds or amusement parks. They, too, have been conditioned not to disturb others.

At home, in your house or apartment, noise is also kept at a minimum. You never hear music blaring out of any home, and there are in fact apartment rules prohibiting it. Private parties are usually toned down past 10:00 pm. Remember that Sunday is a quiet day. Also, what you might find to be an acceptable level of noise could be too noisy to someone else. A rule of thumb is to keep your ears open, and try to blend in.

Obscene Gestures

Austria isn't a country that uses its hands to express anger. However, put an Austrian behind a wheel, and, well, things

Austrian children are well behaved and respectful of adults.

are slightly different. Here you might see hands or fingers doing strange things. The standard middle finger is used when someone is cut off, but pointing to the head with the middle finger repeatedly is also common. The latter means that you are crazy or that you have '*einen Vogel im Kopf*' (a bird in your head).

THE DRESS CODE

The dress code varies from one occasion to the next, but the Austrian is generally conformist and will never wear something ostentatious.

When attending a theatre or concert performance, Austrians will always dress up in formal wear (long gowns are usually only worn for balls but they can be worn for the opera as well). Julie has known young people who were not allowed into the Opera House for a performance because they were wearing jeans.

Dinner at a restaurant requires semi-formal wear: no jeans, beach sandals or shorts. It is extremely embarrassing when you are thrown out for improper attire. However in the summer, the *Schanigärten* and *Heurigen* do not care what you wear.

When going for walks in the country, people sometimes opt to dress in *Trachten* or traditional Austrian clothing (many

It is not uncommon to see Austrians dressed from head to toe in modern *Trachten* outfits every day of the year

stores carry a modern, affordable version): *Lederhosen* for men (usually older men) and boys; short-walking *Loden* jackets (buttons can be made out of bone or plastic) for men, women and children; checkered or plain white shirts for men, women (sometimes with frilled collar and cuff) and children. Walkers often wear pants of linen or denim, with flowers stitched on the pockets for women; traditional *Dirndl*, or dresses, for women and girls; scarves with *Edelweiss* (mountain flower) for women and children; sturdy shoes for men and children with *Edelweiss* decoration, and similarly decorated high-heeled versions for women; and green or grey felt hats worn with a *Gamsbart* (like a shaving brush). Even if you don't get into the Austrian style of dressing, you should still dress quite nicely, meaning no jeans, T-shirts or tennis shoes.

AN INVITATION TO LUNCH OR DINNER

If you are invited to an Austrian home, be punctual, not 10 or 15 minutes late! Always bring a small gift of flowers for the hostess and a bottle of wine for the host. While these are standard, chocolates and special gifts would also be appreciated.

After you enter the home, offer to take off your shoes unless told otherwise. Most homes have a myriad of slippers to be doled out if necessary. Julie often brings her own as she can be sure they will fit, and perhaps even match her outfit. Men should stand the first time a woman enters or exits a room, but not each time thereafter.

If you are at someone's house for dinner, aperitifs are usually served beforehand. Campari soda seems to be the classic drink, but sparkling wine on its own or mixed with fruit juice is also popular. Appetizers will sometimes be served, but they are an exception.

Tips on Socialising

- Always be punctual.
- Greet people with a handshake.
- Address people by their last name until invited to use their first name.
- Use the formal 'you', *Sie*, until otherwise indicated.
- Bring a small gift for the hostess.
- Be prepared to take off your shoes upon entering someone's home.
- Wait to be introduced to other guests.
- Do not begin eating until the host says *Mahlzeit* or *Guten Appetit*.
- Never drop by unannounced.
- Do not be loud.
- Dress nicely and conservatively.
- Expect there to be heavy smoking.
- Call or send a thank you note the following day.

Before beginning to eat, a toast of '*Prost, zum Wohl*' is said by the host or hostess. The company then toasts one another, looking directly at each other, clinking glasses, and saying '*Prost*'.

It's always nice to call the day after the event. The host will welcome it. Some people write thank-you notes as a gesture of gratitude.

SPECIAL OCCASIONS

Austrians celebrate special events with family and close friends. If you're lucky enough to get invited to a festive occasion, there are a few things you should know.

Wedding

An Austrian couple can choose to have either a civil court marriage or a religious ceremony. The civil court marriage is quick, short and inexpensive. Setting up a date and bringing all the necessary paperwork to the civil court is all a couple needs to do. If a couple chooses to have a religious ceremony, they first must go to a civil court, register and get the necessary paperwork. Then they need to talk to the religious official of their church, temple, mosque, etc. If they have been paying into their religious institution, they will have no problems and can set a date for the ceremony.

At the wedding, the bride and groom usually have a bridesmaid and best man who stand by them during the ceremony. The exchange of rings is performed and the ring is worn on the ring finger of the right hand, which is believed to be closest to the heart. Then there is a mass followed by an *Agape* (meaning love in Greek), where canapés are served with champagne and other drinks. A couple of hours later, close friends and family of the newlyweds will go to a restaurant or special hall to celebrate with dinner and music.

If you are invited to a wedding and don't know what to give, money is always acceptable (there is special stationery where banknotes can be inserted). It is also appropriate to ask if the couple is registered with any store. There, one may choose to buy something on the couple's pre-selected list.

Baptism

The baptism of a child requires a godmother only. If the godmother belongs to the church, there should be no problems in getting your baby baptised. A fee must be paid to the church and a date set. On the day of the baptism, the child will be blessed on the forehead with holy water, a prayer said and then a mass held.

Grandparents on both sides are invited, together with some uncles and aunts close to the family. Afterward, there is a small get-together for lunch at a nice restaurant, where gifts for the baby are presented. Gifts vary from baby silverware to jewellery, and even money in a card or a savings account voucher.

Funeral

When there is a death, an official funeral announcement (*Parte*) is delivered immediately to family and friends before they have time to find out from a different source. It is usually on black-bordered stationery and gives details of the memorial service. Once the announcement is received, one can choose to go to either the church or cemetery service, or to both. The standard practice is to meet the grieving family, shake hands, and say '*Mein Beileid*' (my condolences). Then one would follow the mourners to the gravesite and cast a scoop of dirt onto the coffin as it is being lowered into the grave. Sometimes, three red roses may be cast along with the dirt. Today, instead of bringing or sending a special flower arrangement to the grieving family, it is common to make a contribution to the favourite charity of the deceased. This information is available on the announcement.

The Wake

There are also traditional wakes after the burial where family members and friends get together at a relative's home to mourn the passing of a loved one. It is customary to eat and drink at this event.

UNIVERSITY STUDENT CUSTOMS

Austria has a number of traditional universities such as the University of Vienna, founded in 1356, the University of

Salzburg and the University of Graz. It is also full of music and fine arts universities, and many young musicians dream of training here. For those who are going to Austria as a student, there are certain marked differences between studying in your home country and abroad. Not only are there differences in the system, but in the students themselves as well.

University education is quite cheap for Austrians (and other EU nationals), costing about € 700 per year. Students from outside the EU pay roughly twice that amount, although citizens of some developing countries are exempt. Foreigners are welcome to study at Austrian universities, but must have the special diploma called the *Matura*. Up until recently, higher education in Austria was free. This meant that an Austrian could be a student until the end of his or her life. It is said that the high school years are particularly stressful as the students try to get into university. Once in, the students slow down and the pace becomes more relaxed. The new fees are meant to encourage students to finish their studies in a more timely fashion and to cut down on the number of students who register for class but never show up. Most students finish their studies at about the age of 24, depending on their discipline. But nothing prevents them from spreading their education out over a long period of time or resuming their studies after an interval.

Students must be self-motivated as the system is impersonal, with classes having up to 100 students. Attendance is usually once a week for each class, but is not mandatory. The only thing that you must do is take a written or oral exam, which is given either once a semester or once a year. The oral exam is in front of the whole class, which can be rather nerve-wracking.

The idea of a university campus is non-existent in Austria. In the case of the University of Vienna, for example, the main building is in the 1st district, while myriad other academic buildings are located in nearby districts. At the end of a class or lecture, students knock on their desks to show their appreciation for the professor and the quality of the presentation.

Austrian students do not belong to fraternities or sororities like in the United States. The push to drink to excess or to perform odd rituals to be accepted into a group is non-existent. Undergraduates don't feel the need to conform or prove themselves. Privacy is important to them. If you are athletically inclined, there is no outlet for your abilities; a university education is structured for the intellectual. The dress code is reserved and dark colours reign supreme. American-style baseball caps, shorts, sweatshirts and pants are not the norm.

GAY LIFE

Although Austria is a predominantly Catholic country and its people tend to be traditional, when it comes to sex, nudity and homosexuality, Austrians are somewhat liberal. Yet, politicians seem to lag a bit behind the general public. There is an anti-discrimination law, but legal same-sex partnerships have yet to be legalised. However, now that it is a member of the EU, many believe that gay marriage will eventually become the norm. There are thriving gay communities in Vienna, Graz, Innsbruck and Linz. The Homosexual Initiative Vienna (HOSI), founded in 1979, has come to represent the community in the political arena.

The Rosa Lila Villa at 102 Linke Wienzeile in the 6th district provides a number of services, such as coming-out groups and support groups for the gay, lesbian and transgender communities. The Café Willendorf on the first floor is a good place to get your bearings and meet people. Many other gay establishments are in the same neighbourhood. Within Austria, you can find gay-friendly hotels, restaurants, bars, clubs, discos, saunas, cinemas, travel agencies and stores. The *Vienna Gay Guide* also lists gay groups, hotlines and health centres. There is an AIDS organisation (AIDS Hilfe Wien) on Gumpendorferstrasse at the Mariahilfer Gürtel in the 6th district. Every May since 1993, Vienna has hosted the Life Ball in front of the Rathaus. Organised by Aids Life, this is Europe's largest annual AIDS charity event. The money raised goes to help various groups working with HIV positive people and those living with AIDS. The Life Ball is a lively event that showcases wild and wonderful costumes and a sense of open-mindedness and acceptance.

TIPPING

Tipping is normal in restaurants and bars, and for taxi drivers and porters. There are many others who also look forward to a tip.

Blue-collar workers who do something special often get a tip. For example, the repairman who fixes your heating would get € 5; the postman who delivers a package up three flights of stairs € 2; and a mover € 10 per day. The tips aren't mandatory, and are appreciated all the more for it.

During the Christmas season, it's also nice to remember the people who often provide services to you. Money, alcohol or gifts are graciously accepted; the first is the most welcome. The people you shouldn't forget are your cleaning lady, the trash collectors (if you live in a house), the postman, the building superintendent (*Hausbesorger*, if you live in an apartment) and your hairdresser.

SETTLING IN

CHAPTER 5

'I was cut off from the world.
There was no one to confuse or torment me,
and I was forced to become original.'
—Joseph Haydn, composer

MOVING TO A NEW COUNTRY can be a tremendous enterprise unless you have travelled before or have an adventurous heart. Austria is easier to adjust to than some other countries, as many Austrians speak English, and each of the large cities has an established international community which can be a great source of information and help. Moreover, the country offers a quality of life that is quite high.

Of course, there are problems that cause frustration for newcomers, including short opening hours for stores, banks, post offices and government offices; the bureaucracy and cranky civil servants; occasional chauvinism; poor to adequate service in some stores and restaurants (although changes have been noticed); and having to deal with the intricacies of the German language.

Yet relocating to Austria means you can look forward to less stressful working conditions, a relaxed pace of life, a safe and family-oriented environment, a rich cultural atmosphere, beautiful and unpolluted landscapes, good medical care and an excellent public transportation system.

HOUSING

If you are working for a consulate, embassy or international organisation, your employer may help you find a nice apartment or house and bear the partial or full cost of your rent. If you are searching for an apartment on your own, look through advertisements in the Saturday editions of local newspapers such as *Kurier*, *Die Presse* and *Der Standard*. The *Bazar* is an advertisement paper that contains listings not only of apartments and homes to rent, but also furnishings, cars and other useful amenities. *Falter*, a paper for the trendy, lists entertainment events in addition to apartments.

In your search for an apartment, it is useful to know how the floors in a building are named. Generally, the first floor is the *Erdgeschoss*, and the second floor is the *erste Stock* (first floor). If you are in an old-fashioned building, you may encounter other floor levels including the *Mezzanine*, *Tiefparterre* and *Hochparterre* floors before getting to the first floor! Large apartment complexes have different buildings or stairwells, known as *Stiege*. For example, if your address is Juliagasse 38/12/17, this will translate to: Julia Street, street number 38, building or stairwell 12, and apartment number 17.

Tenants Assistance Hotline

Wohnservice Wien was established in January 2000. This partnership between the Vienna Land Procurement and Urban Renewal Fund and the City of Vienna offers free information on available housing, subsidies, financial assistance, rental agreements and tenants rights and helps resolve complaints and other problems. It is open weekdays from 8:00 am until 8:00 pm. Most requests are dealt with immediately. For more complex matters, they will contact the relevant authorities. The hotline is (1) 4000-8000 or (1) 245-030.

Using a Realtor

If you have cash to spare, use a realtor (*Makler*). The cost can be alarming: for a rental of up to two years, the commission is one month's gross rent; for two to three years, it is two months' rent; and for leases of more than three years, the commission is three months. There is no harm in trying for a cheaper fee, so ask! There are also relocation services advertised in the *Yellow Pages* that help you not only in finding an apartment, but also with moving in. If you choose

not to use a real estate agent, be prepared to do all the legwork yourself and to take responsibility for each and every minute detail.

Where to Live in Vienna

Vienna is the largest city in Austria and made up of 23 districts or *Bezirk*. Some of the ritzier areas to live in are the 1st, 13th, 18th and 19th districts. (Be aware that especially in the first district, street parking is very difficult to find.) More affordable—and still central—districts are the 2nd to 9th. The closer you live to the city centre, the more likely you will be living in an apartment. Depending on your budget, they can be small renovated apartments, every inch of which is used wisely. Many apartments on the top floor have sloping ceilings that make the actual living space even smaller. If you have a healthy budget, you can find a large luxurious apartment. Also, be aware that many apartment buildings do not have elevators and you will have to lug your groceries up the tightly curving flight of stairs. If you really prefer to live in a house, you will have to move much farther away from the city centre. In general, the further away you get from the centre, the cheaper the housing. Nevertheless, nothing in Vienna is really inconvenient, as public transportation is excellent. Furthermore, there are no slums or bad neighbourhoods, so one feels safe all the time.

> **Essential Documents**
>
> Bring:
> - Passport
> - Birth certificate
> - Marriage/divorce certificate
> - Children's school records
> - Diplomas/degrees
> - Medical records
> - Vaccination history
> - Proof of health insurance
> - Driver's licence
>
> Obtain in Austria:
> - Visa (*Sichtvermerk*)
> - Temporary Residence Permit (*Aufenthaltsbewilligung*)
> - Permanent Residence Permit (*Niederlassungsbewilligung*)
> - Work Permit (*Arbeitsgenehmigung*)
> - Police Registration (*Meldezettel*)

The Perfect Landlord

Having a good landlord is an advantage, but no matter how perfect your landlord, make sure you have a city approved rental contract. Each lease is written up individually and the tenant must abide by the terms of the contract. In the contract, the rent will be divided into three categories: *Hauptmiete* (net rent), *Betriebskosten* (maintenance costs, such as garbage collection) and *Umsatzsteuer* (taxes). This tax is not paid if the tenant is a diplomat and there is tax-exempt reciprocity between Austria and the respective country.

You may rent your house or apartment furnished or unfurnished. Be aware that unfurnished may mean that it lacks kitchen appliances, wardrobes, light fixtures, etc. If the house or apartment comes furnished, inspect the furniture and fixtures and take pictures of anything that is marked or damaged, and be sure to append a list of such flaws in the contract. You can repaint the apartment and make changes only if the landlord agrees to it. There may be extra costs (*Ablöse*) before you move in, including renovation expenses and furniture left behind by a previous owner. If something breaks down, such as the refrigerator, oven or heating, the renter is usually responsible (unless the contract says otherwise). Many of the older houses have only one phone line and phone outlet. It is wise to ask the landlord to install a second outlet, especially if you want to use a computer or keep a second phone upstairs.

Utilities

Make sure that all the utilities are in your name and be prepared to put down deposits for them. Gas and electricity usage is billed quarterly. The total due may take you by surprise as it is based on the previous year's consumption—a shock if the previous tenant had six kids! Unfortunately, the meter is read only once a year, so wait for the yearly itemised bill or *Jahresabrechnung*. Either a credit or a debit will show up on the next quarter's bill based on your usage of gas or electricity, so don't despair.

Your phone bill comes bimonthly. There will be a base charge from Telekom Austria (which provides the telephone line), and an itemised list of your calls by area from the telephone company of your choice. If you want a breakdown of the telephone numbers called, you will need to contact the telephone company personally.

A chimneysweep comes four times a year to clean out the gas or coal heating system. His schedule is posted in your apartment building or in your mailbox if you live in a house. You must be available to let him in one of the four times, or have an explanation handy for the fire police. The rat man usually comes every two months. If you merely say a few words to him, be prepared to pay up to 15 minutes of his time; the price can be hefty. Instead, answer your door only twice a year with, hopefully, good news.

The electricity/gas man (*Strom/Gas*) will also send you notice of when you must be home to let him in to read the meter. Houses built after 1930 have the meter outside; for these, meter inspection does not require the presence of the occupant.

Registering with the Police

If you are living in an apartment or house, you should register with the police at a police station or municipal office within three days of arrival by filling out a *Meldezettel* (registration form). If you are staying in a hotel or hostel for up to 60 days, the hotel or hostel reception will fill out the necessary forms; if you are staying longer than 60 days, you must register personally. A form can be purchased at any *Tabak-Trafik*. (Originally a smoke shop or tobacconist, it now carries a variety of goods besides.) Unless you read German, find someone to help you fill out the form, and make sure your landlord signs it too.

In the form, there is a section regarding your religion. If you don't plan on paying into a church, do not fill out this section, or write 'O.B.' (*Ohne Bekenntnis*).

Bring the form with your passport to the police station in your district (*Bezirkspolizeikommissariat*, signified by a blue and white shield on a map of your district). At the police station, look for a sign on the directory that says *Meldeamt* (registration office). Take a number and wait your turn. Remember to arrive between 8:00 am and 1:00 pm (the earlier the better), Monday through Friday. If you don't have a visa in your passport and plan on staying longer than six months, make sure you go back to the *Meldeamt* and show them your visa or residence permit when you get it.

VISA

If you plan on staying in Austria for a while, remember that a visa is not necessary if you are from an EU country or the European Economic Area (EEA). Citizens from other countries who are going to Austria to work or study for a finite period of time need only apply for a Temporary Residence Permit (*Aufenthaltsbewilligung*) if they intend to stay longer than up to two three-month periods during one calendar year. Those who wish to live in Austria for a long period of time need to apply for a Permanent Residence Permit (*Niederlassungsbew illigung*). You should apply at the Austrian consulate in your home country before departure. Hours are limited, so check before going. Also, expect to wait about a month for your visa to be approved. If you decide to apply for residency after your arrival, go to the local magistrate (*Magistrat*), district office (*Magistratisches Bezirkamt*) or regional district office

Getting Your Visa

Below is a list of documents needed for a visa. Documents must be professionally translated into German:

- Current passport
- Copies of previous passports
- Application form
- One passport-size photo
- Birth certificate (original or notarised copy)
- Certificate of good conduct/criminal record (from police station)
- Proof of health insurance
- Proof of income or sufficient funds
- Proof of lodging in Austria
- Photocopies of all documents

Additional documents as applicable:

- Work permit
- Marriage certificate
- Original letter of admission to Austrian school
- Copy of round-trip ticket

(*Bezirkshauptmannschaft*). Once the six-month period is up, you are required to leave the country. For more information on all official documents, visit http://www.austria.org/govsite. htm on the Internet or contact your consulate or embassy.

Temporary Residence Permit

To get a job, a temporary residence permit is required. To obtain the permit, you must provide proof of health insurance (*Unfall- und Krankenversicherungsnachweis*), proof of accommodation (rental contract or *Mietvertrag*) and financial means, police record certificate (*Leumundszeugnis*) and working papers (*Arbeitsgenehmigung*) issued by the Labor Office (*Arbeitsmarktservice*).

Diplomats (United Nations, foreign embassy and consulate staff) and their families are exempted from *Meldezettel* and residence permit requirements.

BANKING

Banking in Austria is as simple as pie. The hardest part is getting there while the bank is open, as the hours don't fit the working person's schedule. Vestibules open during banks' hours of closure allow you to withdraw cash, make payments or print out a statement. In the main cities, one has several banks to choose from, including Die Erste Bank, Bank Austria Creditanstalt, Volksbank, Raiffeisenbank, Österreichische Postsparkasse AG (P.S.K.) and Bank für Arbeit und Wirtschaft (BAWAG). There are also regional banks in small cities.

Banking Hours

Mon–Wed, Fri:	8:00 am–12:30 pm, 1:30 pm–3:00 pm
Thurs:	8:00 am–12:30 pm, 1:30 pm–5:30 pm
Sat–Sun, holidays:	Closed

Banking Services

Depending on the service you are looking for, you may have to go to a special counter or speak to one of the representatives (banks are one of the few places in Austria where the customer is king). If you are just changing money, go to the window labelled *Geldwechsel*; all other transactions are done at the *Kassa* window. Austrians have a tough time standing in line. That's why you'll often see footprints in yellow on the ground more than 2 meters away from the window, signalling that the next person in line must wait at that point.

Standing Payment Orders

To make banking easy for yourself, open up as many standing orders as necessary. If you have fixed amounts to be paid on a certain date, the orders you want are called *Dauerauftrag*. If the amount and date vary from month to month, open an *Einziehungsauftrag*. Regular payments to doctors, dentists, etc. can be made using the *Erlagschein* (product of the postal bank) or *Zahlschein* (product of the regular banks), account-to-account transfer forms which will be given to you by the payee. You may also receive a letter from the payee (*Honorarnote*) with his or her bank's information. You can do all of these payments at the bank. There is an area set up telling you exactly how to fill out and stamp the forms and to put one in the box and keep the other for your records.

Bankcards

Bankcards, or debit cards (*Bankomatkarte*), and automatic teller machines are widely available in Austria. Some words you should know in order to use the ATM:

- Confirm amounts with the green button marked *BESTÄTIGUNG*
- Correct a mistake with the yellow button marked *KORREKTUR*
- Cancel the transaction with the red button marked *ABBRUCH*

Once you have your money (take the card first, then the money), don't wait for a receipt, as none will be given. You can withdraw up to € 400 per day.

Bank Credit Cards

Bank credit cards give you a one-month grace period before the total amount you charged is due. They are not set up to charge a monthly minimum amount, so beware! They can be used in any teller machine with your PIN number for cash withdrawal.

Personal Checks

Personal checks are non-existent. Instead, one can use Eurocheques, which are also valid in bordering Mediterranean countries. However, one must be extremely careful while using these checks, as there is no section marked for the payee. Once filled out, the checks are like cash. For this reason, banks only issue ten at a time and charge a fee. If stolen, report the loss immediately to the nearest police station and then to your bank. If you do not, expect to be held responsible for 10 per cent of the total amount.

Savings Accounts

Regular savings accounts, such as the simple savings book, earn very little (1.5 per cent interest). Fixed deposits earn more, the percentage increasing with the investment duration.

Anonymous Accounts

Anonymous savings accounts used to be extremely popular because the owner had to declare only the interest earned for tax purposes, and not the principal. In response to pressure by the European Union and the Financial Action Task Force on Money Laundering, Austria drew up legislation in 2000 bringing about the end of the traditional anonymous accounts.

Monthly Statements

You don't have to wait for your monthly statement (*Kontoauszüge*) to come by post. You can get a daily reading from an account statement machine at your bank simply by putting in your bankcard and waiting a few seconds (a special ring binder to hold the statements is available from the bank). Another benefit is that you can overdraw up to twice your monthly income, if you request this facility. Be careful as there is daily overdraft interest, charged on a quarterly basis.

Online Banking

Online banking is a great alternative if your time is at a premium. Your bank will provide you with the necessary information.

POST OFFICE

Post office locations and hours are listed in the *White Pages*. The hours are generally Monday–Friday, 8:00 am–noon and 2:00 pm–6:00 pm (sometimes 7:00 pm at the main offices). Post offices located at major train stations are open 24 hours a day.

The post office experience can be quite daunting in the bigger cities. One may have to choose from between ten and 20 different counters. The following terms should help you decide where to go:

Counters	
Auf u. Abgabe	mailing of packages
Briefaufgabe	posting, mailing
Ein- und Auszahlungen	deposit and withdrawals
Fax	fax
Gebühren Eilsendung	cost for express item
Kleine Inlandspakete	small domestic packages
Massensendung	mass mailing
Pakete-EMS	express mail service
Postanweisungen	money transfer
Postlagernde	in care of general delivery
Produktverkauf	sales
Radio- und TV-Anmeldung	radio and television payments
Sondermarken	collector's stamps
Telegramme	telegram
Telekom/Mobilkom Beratung	advice on phone and mobile
Wertzeichen	postage stamp
Wertzeichnen Und Grossen	cost for bulky items

Counters	
Zeitung	mailing newspapers

Terms	
Absender	sender
Anschrift	address
Aufgabeschein	postal form
Bestimmungsort	destination city, country
Bezugszahl	reference number
Brief	letter
Briefmarke	stamp
Buchstaben	letters
Detaillierte Inhaltsangabe	detailed contents
Empfänger	addressee, recipient
Nachnahme	cash on delivery
Päckchen	small package
Postleitzahl	postal/zip code
Unterschrift	signature
Wert/Wertangabe	value
Ziffern	numbers

The cost of sending a priority letter weighing 20 grams or less is € 0.55 within Austria and the EU, and € 1.25 outside of Europe. Further postal rates or *Postgebühren* are listed in a small booklet called *Das kleine Postbuch*, which is left in your mailbox every December. Rates are also listed in the introductory section of the *White Pages*. When sending a small package (at the letter window), make sure that it is not sealed if going outside Austria, nor tied with string, and that it does not contain a letter. Don't forget to fill out the appropriate forms for registered mail. Tape-sealed packages weighing more than 2 kilograms require a customs declaration form or international customs form (*Zollerklärung*). There are three categories of mail: Airmail / *Luftpost* (ten working

days), Surface Air Lifted Mail / SAL (slower than airmail but faster than surface), and Surface Mail / *Gewöhnlich*) (up to ten weeks).

Postal Codes

When sending mail within Vienna, remember that the city has 23 postal codes. When addressing a letter, make sure the postal code is written correctly. In the postal code 1010, for example, the first digit refers to Vienna, the middle two digits refer to the 1st district, and the last digit refers to the post office in that district. In the telephone book, however, the address is written with the district first; for example, '1, Fleischmarkt 8', which means door number 8, on Fleischmarkt Street, in the 1st district.

All other cities and towns within Austria have postal codes that are much easier to figure out.

Telegrams

Telegrams are sent through the local post office. The forms can be found at the *Telegramme* counter. You can also send a telegram by phoning 190. You can speak in English, making sure that your telegram is longer than seven words. Rates are listed in the *White Pages* under *Telegrammentgelte*.

TELEPHONE SERVICE

Applications for telephone service are found at your local post office at the *Fernmeldedienst* counter. You can also apply by phone at 0800-100-100, or through the Internet, at http://www.telekom.at. There is a one-time installation fee of € 167 and a six-day waiting period for the line. It is much easier to take over the telephone number of the last tenant. This requires filling out a form entitled *Übertragung* and a payment of € 47.

Telephones at the Post Office

You can make international phone calls from the post office. At the telephone call (*Telefongespräche*) counter, you will be directed to a telephone booth. After your call, return to the counter and pay your charges.

Telephone booths are also conveniently located throughout the cities. A booth accepting coins is usually placed beside one that accepts telephone debit cards (*Telefonwertkarte*). The cards may be bought at post offices and most *Tabak-Trafik*.

Mobile Phones

Austrians are attached to their *Handys* (mobile phones.) There are numerous mobile phone companies to chose from, some offering contracts, others that provide pre-paid cards. Try Telekom or A1 (Mobilkom Austria), T-Mobile, One, Drei (H3G), Telering, Tele2 or Bob (discount service provider from Mobilkom). Yesss is among the cheapest mobile phone service providers. The prepaid SIM card is only available at the discount store Hofer. Another cheap alternative that uses a prepaid SIM card is eety (http://www.eety.eu).

Telephoning Long Distance

Country and city codes can be found in the *White Pages* of the telephone directory. The Austrian telephone monopoly was broken and there is now an overabundance of telephone service providers. Please see the Resource Guide for names.

Call-Back Telephone Services

US-based call-back services for international phone calls are available. Once you have registered with a call-back service provider, you dial a phone number, hang up and wait for a call back, which gives you an open US line. The call made with that line is charged at US rates. International companies such as Kallback (http://www.kallback.com) and GlobalTel (http://www.globaltel.com) provide such services.

INTERNET

Internet access is easy to get in Austria. A number of companies now bundle services, like Telekom Austria (http://www.aon.at) and http://www.tele2.at. Other providers include http://www.chello.at, http://www.eTel.at, and http://www.inode.at.

RADIO AND TELEVISION

If you own a radio or television, you must register them at the post office at the *Radio- und TV-Anmeldung* counter and pay a bimonthly fee to use them. Many newcomers are unaware of this fee and could be fined by the police if found out.

DRIVING

Having your own car is a big plus if you intend to travel around Austria and Europe. Driving can be fun and delightful, but there can also be problems along the way.

Austrians have a tendency to get aggressive while driving, and will often go on the offensive. Some might get angry and flash their lights if they are made to wait behind you, or get flustered if you don't seem to know what you are doing. On the freeways, they will go exceedingly fast, even in rain, snow and fog. Drivers now use their headlights during the daytime as a means to prevent accidents, especially in mountainous areas.

One of the scariest situations to be in is to be driving along a freeway and having a *Geisterfahrer* or 'ghost driver' coming head-on. These are people who drive on the wrong side of the freeway. Austria, unfortunately, has one of the highest frequencies of ghost driving in the European Union.

These large signs are posted in strategic locations to prevent the recurring problems of the 'ghost driver'.

It has been a problem for years, and officials reported 233 incidents in the first half of 2005, a 10 per cent jump from the same period the previous year. Often, the outcome is the tragic death of many innocent people.

There are many reasons for ghost driving, but the most common factors are drunken driving and obscure traffic signs at the entrances and exits of freeways. Authorities have tried many different solutions. In addition to the big signs posted at highway exits and entrances, some states put up fluorescent yellow warning lights. On the A9 freeway in southern Austria near Graz, authorities have installed the country's first highway alarm system designed to alert wrong-way drivers before they can cause a fatal accident. This digital system automatically emits high-decibel sounds when a motorist ignores warning signs and enters the wrong way. It is always a good idea to have the radio on when driving on the freeway because they will always interrupt their programming to warn of a ghost driver.

Bringing Your Own Car

Cars are expensive in Austria. If you decide to import your car from outside the EU, you must submit a permission form beforehand. Shortly after the car arrives, you should get the necessary inspections done. Your car must comply with Austria's environmental standards, which will likely cost you

If You Get into an Accident

Accidents happen and it's always best to be prepared for one. Here are some basic tips:

- Stop your car immediately, turn on your hazard lights and set up your red warning triangle 50 metres ahead of the accident area.
- Administer first aid or call an ambulance if necessary (tel: 144 for ambulance, or tel: 133 for police).
- Always exchange names, addresses and telephone numbers with the other party.
- Take note of details, such as the make and model of the car(s), licence plate number(s), driver's licence number(s), insurance company(ies) and policy number(s).
- Don't claim responsibility. Instead, call and talk to someone from your insurance company.
- Fill out the accident form (*Europäischer Unfallbericht*) provided by your insurance company.

some time and money. In order to drive the car duty-free, it must have been in one's possession at least six months beforehand. Check with the Austrian consulate in your home country for further details.

Rental Cars

Car rental facilities (*Autovermietung*) are available at all international airports in larger cities and in most major train stations (e.g. Bregenz, Graz, Innsbruck, Klagenfurt, Linz, Salzburg, Seefeld, Zell am See and Vienna's Westbahnhof and Südbahnhof). Reservations at any of these stations can be made through any railway ticket office in Austria or through a travel agency. All major international car rental firms have offices in Austria.

Automobile Clubs

There are two automobile clubs: Austrian Automobile, Motorcycle and Touring Club (Österreichischer Automobil-, Motorrad- und Touring Club/ÖAMTC) and Austrian Auto, Motor and Bicycle League (Auto-, Motor- und Radfahrerbund Österreichs/ARBÖ). Members receive free road service and towing, but even if you aren't a member and need such a service, you can call for help and pay for the membership on the spot.

Car Insurance

All owners of Austria-registered cars must have recognised third party or liability insurance. All EU countries have the same requirement so they don't need green insurance cards (except for Italy). The green insurance card is proof that you have insurance and must be specifically requested from your insurance provider. If you are travelling outside the EU, you are expected to present the green insurance card at the border. Further insurance can be bought. Full comprehensive insurance (*Vollkaskoversicherung*) adds collision and vandalism damage. A letter from your previous insurance company stating that you have had no recent liability claims may get you a discount of up to 50 per cent on your premium.

Driver's Licence

For those who will be staying in Austria longer than a year and are neither diplomats, nor citizens of the EU or the EEA, you will have to apply for a driver's licence. Driver's licences from the EU or the EEA are accepted in Austria. Plan on needing a lot of patience. It is conceivable to end up with an Austrian licence, but many steps must be followed.

Once you arrive in Austria, you have six months from the date on your *Meldezettel* form to apply for a driver's licence. If you miss the six-month limit to apply for your licence, you will have to take the driving test, which may cost as much as € 2000. You need a certain amount of hours for theory and practical class, and if you fail, you must repeat the class and pay again.

These are the steps to take:

- If your licence is not in German, go to an automobile club such as ÖAMTC or ARBÖ to have your licence translated. The fee is likely to be less than that charged at your own consulate.

- Go to the *Bundespolizeidirektion* (Federal Police Headquarters) or, in cities without federal police, to the *Bezirkshauptmannschaft* (District Administration) or *Magistrat* (Municipal Authority), and in Vienna go to the *Verkehrsamt* (Department of Motor Vehicles). Get an application form for a driver's licence at the entrance.

- Fill out the application form (*Führerscheinantrag*) and present along with the following documents: current driver's licence, German translation of your driver's licence, passport, birth certificate, police registration form (*Meldezettel*), two passport-sized photos and proof of at least one year's driving experience (a letter in German from your company or a friend verifying that you have been driving for one year will suffice). There is a fee of € 55.

- Once your application has been accepted, you will be notified by mail as to where and when you will need to undergo a medical examination.

- Once all the above is completed, you can pick up your licence! Remember that you will have to give up your current licence. (You will most likely get it back. However, you should get another one from your home country beforehand just in case.)

For more detailed information, go to http://www.help.gv.at.

Road Information

The roads in Austria are well maintained and very well marked. The freeways (*Autobahn*) are all over Austria and lead to all surrounding countries. Be careful when driving along the mountain roads, as there are many turns and the grade is steep at times. Major border crossing points are open 24 hours a day. Those served by minor roads are open between 7:00 am and 9:00 pm, give or take an hour.

Austria's freeways and high-speed roads are subject to a road tax or *Vignette*. The tax is paid through the purchase of a sticker, which has to be affixed to the middle of the windscreen. The annual road tax is € 72.60 for automobiles and vehicles (up to 3.5 tons), and € 29.00 for motorcycles. For vacationers, two-month (€ 21.80 for cars / € 10.90 motorcycles) and ten-day stickers (€ 7.60 cars / €4.30 motorcycles) are available. Compliance is overseen by both the police and the *Mautsheriffs* (Toll Enforcement Officers). A heavy fine of € 110 is charged if you don't have a *Vignette*, or € 220 if the *Vignette* has been manipulated in anyway. The road tax stickers may be purchased at automobile clubs (ÖAMTC or ARBÖ) in Austria and abroad, at petrol stations and stores close to the border, and at post offices (*Postämter*), tobacco shops (*Tabak*) and gas stations (*Tankstelle*).

> ### Traffic News
> Information on road conditions and the traffic situation is available in English daily from 6:00 am to 8:00 pm (including weekends) from the Austrian Automobile Club; call 711-997 in Vienna, or (1) 711-997 from anywhere else in Austria.

Radars are becoming more and more obvious throughout Austria. They are large, grey metal boxes located on the side of the street. If you are going over the speed limit, a picture of your car is taken, the licence plate number looked up, and a traffic ticket sent to you by mail. So if you are in a rush going through the city, make sure you smile!

Rules of the Road

Traffic regulations in Austria are similar to those in other European countries.

- For driving during the winter months, winter tires are essential; in extreme cases, snow chains have to be used. These can be rented at all major border crossings.
- The minimum driving age in Austria is 18.
- Wearing seatbelts is compulsory. The driver is responsible for the safety of his passengers, and will be held accountable if anyone is injured while not wearing his or her seatbelt.
- Children under the age of 12, or shorter than 1.5 metre, are not allowed to sit in the front seat. Infant seats are mandatory for babies under the age of nine months. The seats must go in the back as airbags pose a potential danger to babies and small children.
- Buses and trams have the right of way. Always yield to a bus leaving a bus stop. Be careful not to block tram tracks as trams are silent, heavy and will hit you, as they have nowhere else to go. Some tramlines cross roads and always have the right of way coming from the left. Stop where trams stop (the stop is always in the middle of the road) to allow passengers to get on and off safely.
- The speed limit is 100 km/h on highways, 130 km/h on freeways, 50 km/h in built-up areas and 30 km/h in residential areas.
- Mobile phone use is only allowed with a hands-free headset or loud speaker.
- Drunken driving (the permissible alcohol limit is 0.5 per cent) is punishable and can lead to confiscation of your driving licence.

Demerit Points System

On 1 July 2005, the Austrian government instituted a system for recording driving offences. The first offence will be recorded in the local driving licence register for two years. The second offence requires some type of action, such as a driving course. The third offence results in your licence being suspended for at least three months.

Parking

You can park your car on the street either in or against the flow of traffic. This can be handy if you are in a hurry and don't want to make a U-turn to get in the right direction.

Limited parking zones (blue zones) allow you to park for 1 ½ to 3 hours. Read all parking signs. In some cities, such as Vienna, Graz, Linz, Klagenfurt and Innsbruck, there is a charge for parking. You either buy parking vouchers from a *Tabak*,

What to Bring with You in the Car

The following are extremely important items that you should have at all times, either on your person or in the car:

- Driver's licence—on your person.
- Car registration (*Zulassungsschein*)—on your person. Be careful not to leave this in the car or glove compartment. Thieves can register your car, and insurance companies may invalidate your theft claim.
- Automobile inspection sticker (*Pickerl*), plus documentation showing that this annual test has been performed. (The documentation, which is carried with you at all times, is required in order to show what minor damages need repair.)
- Country identification sticker (*Internationales Autokennzeichen*).
- Road tax sticker (*Vignette*). Must be displayed while travelling on expressways or freeways.
- Insurance papers.
- Radio registration.
- First aid kit.
- Red reflective warning triangle (*Pannendreieck*).
- Fog lights. Use only when visibility is low—turn them off when visibility improves or risk paying a fine.
- Reflective warning clothing must be worn in case of accident or breakdown. Failure to wear this clothing may result in a fine.

or display the receipt you get from a coin-operated machine located nearby (only in some parking areas). If you are parking for ten minutes or less, you can get the required vouchers at *Tabaks*, banks, hotels and some gas stations. Whatever your situation, display the vouchers or receipts clearly on the inside of the windscreen or risk getting a parking ticket.

PUBLIC TRANSPORTATION

If you live in a major city, having your own car is not a necessity as Austria's public transportation system is one of the best in Europe. It is safe, clean, reliable, reasonably priced, and, surprisingly enough in this day and age, practises the honour system.

Variety of Public Transportation

In Austria, you can ride the underground (*U-Bahn*, found only in Vienna), buses, trams (*Strassenbahn*) and quick train (*Schnellbahn*, only in Vienna and its surrounding zones). The underground and bus systems are reliable, quick and easy to figure out. There are also night buses, available only on weekends after midnight. Old trams, though reliable, are slow and inconvenient for the handicapped or people with strollers. New trams are lower to the ground, making access much more convenient. The fast train is a bit of a misnomer: it is only fast if you catch it at the right time (usually four times per hour—the times are posted on each platform). The waiting time in between can be long, but the ride is quick, hence the prefix *Schnell*.

Honour System

Since the honour system is practised on public transportation, no gates or turnstiles bar your entry. But remember to buy a ticket to avoid the embarrassing and far more costly experience of having a plainclothes transportation officer check your ticket. If caught riding 'black', there is a fine of € 62, which is higher than the monthly pass. If you do not have the money, you will have to show a photo ID, take a payment form (*Zahlschein*) and pay within three days. If you don't have a photo ID, you could be taken to the police station to sign a sworn statement. Either way, you must pay the fine within three days or be forced to pay additional fees.

Myriad of Tickets

There are a variety of tickets (*Fahrschein*) to buy, depending on how frequently you will use the public transportation system. When travelling in Vienna, the tickets are strictly for the 100 zone (the area within the city limits). If you travel to the far suburbs, you pay a supplement. You can buy a one-way ticket (which does not have to be validated if bought on the bus), a 24-hour pass, a 72-hour pass or an 8-day pass. Remember that the ticket with a date and time, called a Time Ticket (*Zeitkarten*), is good only for the specified day. There are special tourist tickets for travel of up to three days in some of the larger cities. Anyone using public transportation regularly would want a weekly, monthly or yearly pass that allows them unlimited rides in the specified period. The pass requires bank information and a picture, and is only available at a pre-sale ticket window or *Vorverkaufstellen*.

Tickets can be bought at a *Tabak-Trafik*, on the bus or tram (one-way tickets only), at an automatic dispenser found outside most metro stations or at the pre-sale ticket window at the bigger metro stations.

Unless you bought your ticket on the bus or tram, don't forget to validate it in a cancelling machine (*Entwerter*). These small machines are usually found on the bus or tram, at the entrance of *U-Bahn* stations and on the platforms of the *Schnellbahn*.

Fares for Children

Children up to the age of six ride free year-round, and children up to the age of 15 can travel free on Sundays, public holidays and national school holidays. Children over the age of sx must always carry their student identification card (*Schülerausweis*).

Taxis

With taxi stands throughout the city, it isn't usual to hail a taxi, although they have been known to stop if empty. Pay what the meter reads, based on a per kilometer charge and a small transportation levy. On Sundays, public holidays, and from 11:00 pm to 6:00 am, both charges go up. Tip 5–10 per cent of the fare. If calling in advance for a taxi, the dispatcher will ask for the district (if in Vienna) and house address. If you are going away and have lots of luggage or have children, ask for a large wagon (*Kombiwagen*). If you are going to the airport, call a taxi service the night before and you will get a discounted rate.

INTRA-CITY AND INTERNATIONAL TRAVEL
Trains

Austria has excellent rail connections to major European destinations. Trains are efficient, safe, clean and reliable. It is best to reserve a seat if you intend to travel on a holiday or in the summer.

Stops are usually announced via loudspeaker. Sometimes, especially when going through some mountain resorts, there is a chance your stop won't be announced. Julie was in such a situation, and had to run and throw herself and the bags out the door at her stop.

The *Bundesbus* (federal bus) network supplements the rail service, and is used for local trips, or to get to out-of-the-way places, rather than for long-distance travel. The *Bundesbus* travels to some ski resorts in Tyrol and Vorarlberg.

If you are going on a cycling trip, most trains have a compartment for bicycles. Check before your trip.

Boats on the Danube

Boat services on the Danube are slow and expensive, and geared to scenic excursions rather than functional transport. Fast hydrofoils skim between Vienna, Bratislava and Budapest in spring and summer, but are not cheap. Steamers travel between Vienna and the German border town of Passau from May to late September.

Airports

Vienna is Austria's main air transport hub, but there are also international airports at Linz, Graz, Salzburg, Innsbruck and Klagenfurt. The closest airport to Eisenstadt is the Vienna airport. Tyrolean Airways, the main domestic carrier, operates several flights a day between Austria's larger cities.

The airports are modern, well maintained and easily accessible. Short- and long-term parking are available for a reasonable fee.

MEDICAL SERVICES

The medical services in Austria are good and efficient, and it will not be difficult to find a doctor or dentist who speaks English. Vienna has one of the biggest hospitals in Europe, the Allgemeines Krankenhaus (AKH). Although most Austrians are part of the public health care system, private doctors and specialists are in practice throughout the country.

Emergency Telephone Numbers (For All of Austria)	
Ambulance or *Rettung*:	144
Police or *Polizei*:	133
Fire or *Feuerwehr*:	122

Austrian National Health Insurance

The Austrian national health insurance is the *Krankenkasse* (KK). It is part of Austria's huge social security system. Health insurance is mandatory for all Austrian workers and as soon as a person is employed, they are automatically covered. Insurance protection extends to school and university students as well as pensioners. Insurance contributions are calculated on the basis of a person's income. Half the premium for coverage is a set percentage paid out of a person's salary; the other half is paid by the employer. Any permanent resident can become part of the KK by applying at the health insurance agency (*Gebietskrankenkasse*). You can also apply for self-insurance (*Selbstversicherung*) if you are self-employed or unemployed.

Once a part of the KK, all insured persons and their family members will receive the so-called e-card. The e-card replaces the health insurance certificate that was issued in the past. The e-card is used to verify insurance coverage and you should have it with you every time you visit a doctor. It will also be used to retrieve and/or add information. You don't need to apply for the e-card because it is automatically sent to you by mail.

Once you have found a doctor, expect a long wait as doctors are paid a minimum sum per patient, and the system is there to serve everyone. Be prepared with all of your questions ahead of time and you will not be disappointed. If further consultation with a specialist is necessary, your doctor will give you a referral voucher (*Überweisungsschein*). If you are unhappy with your doctor, you may opt for a change at the end of the quarter. If your doctor is on vacation, you can obtain information from his or her office as to which doctors in your neighbourhood have a similar practice.

The *Krankenkasse* is a wonderful system and protects you generously. Some of its highlights include maternity leave, annual physicals, paid sick leave and treatment in other countries (make sure you have a certificate or *Auslandsbetreungsschein* for care in a foreign country to exercise this privilege).

Private medical insurance (*Nebenversicherung* or *Zusatzversicherung*) is for those who require special services in a hospital or treatment by doctors who do not have contracts with the *Krankenkasse*. There are numerous plans to choose from, some of which might be available through your employer.

Doctors

You can find an English-speaking doctor through your employer, private insurance provider, embassy, consulate or friends. The *White Pages* have a listing by district under *Ärzte*. Be aware that during a doctor's appointment, the chances are high that if you must disrobe, there will be no gown for you to wear.

Pharmacies (Apotheken)

Pharmacies proliferate as most drugs need a prescription, and common items such as aspirin and cough syrup must be bought at a pharmacy and not a drugstore (*Drogerien*).

Pharmacies take turns staying open during lunch and after hours. A notice of the next pharmacy open is posted on each pharmacy door. In some cases, the pharmacy remains closed and you make your purchase through a small window. There is an extra charge for medicine purchased after hours.

Immunisations

Austrians are big on having both regular and incidental (for travel) immunisations. An important shot for anyone living in Austria is the tick shot, which guards against *Meningoencephalitis*, an inflammation of the brain and meninges. The threat is especially great for those living near the Vienna Woods, the Wachau, Burgenland, Styria and Carinthia. The series of shots is given in the following sequence:

- First injection: late winter/early spring
- Second injection: after an interval of 2–8 weeks (protection starts)
- Third injection: 1–12 months later (protection complete)
- Booster injection: every 3–4 years thereafter

Go to the District Health Office or *Bezirksgesundheitsamt* for your tick shots. They can be obtained cheaply at certain times of the year.

EDUCATION

The Austrian educational system is well thought out but complex. It begins with kindergarten at about three years of age. Children start primary school (*Volksschule*) at about age six and stay for four years. Then there is a choice between four types of schooling to create a well-trained workforce of young adults.

- Vocational school—five years regular secondary school (*Hauptschule*) followed by three years vocational training with salary.
- University path—eight years upper-level secondary school (*Gymnasium*) followed by final exams for the diploma (*Matura*).
- Trade school (secretarial, bookkeeping)—four year *Gymnasium*, then five years trade school.
- Electronic school (*Höhere Technische Lehranstalt*)—four years *Gymnasium* or *Hauptschule*, then five years electronic study, followed by final exams for the diploma *Matura*.

Religion is taught in the public schools for 12 years. The children attend classes for their specific faith as long as it is an officially-recognised religion. However, the classes are not mandatory and some parents choose not to have their child attend. Public schools usually register students in early March. Children cannot be turned away based on gender, income, language or religion.

International Schools

There are a number of private schools in Vienna. The American International School (AIS) provides American-style education from pre-kindergarten up to 12th grade. The Vienna International School (VIS) provides British-style education from kindergarten up to 12th grade. The Danube International School (DIS) has a similar programme and as with the other schools, offers an International Baccalaureate Diploma Programme. The Vienna Christian School is a private religious English-language school that goes up through high school. More and more Austrian schools are providing bilingual education, or instruction in a foreign language. The Vienna Elementary School offers a comprehensive programme in English from kindergarten through fourth grade. There is also the Lycée Français de Vienne. Other private schools are the Japanese, Arab, Jewish and Swedish Schools. The American International School in Salzburg is a boarding school for students in grades seven through 12, as is the Saint Gilgen International School near Salzburg. The Graz International Bilingual School functions in German-English.

School Registration

Private schools:

- Previous school transcripts
- Birth certificate
- Immunisation records
- Application form
- Passport photos
- Some may require an exam or interview
- Application fee

German Classes

German classes for foreigners are easily available. In Vienna, most classes are held in the 1st district. In other cities, most universities and adult schools (*Volkhochschule*) have special German classes for foreigners (see Resource Guide). If you already know some German, you can take a placement test to ascertain the level you should start at. Classes meet once or twice a week and intensive classes are available as well. Private tutors can also be easily found.

SHOPPING

Shopping in Austria is quite an experience. First, shops are not open seven days a week, unlike in some other parts of Europe. Second, cash payment is still popular, although grocery stores and some shops have bankcard or debit machines. Third, if you head out in jeans, you'll have the distinct feeling of being underdressed. Most Austrians 'dress up' to shop, and you will get better service when well dressed.

When entering or leaving small stores, it is customary to say hello or *Grüss Gott*. This is a sweet formality which makes one feel welcome. The owner or clerk will automatically ask if you need help. You can then ask for what you want, or if you are only browsing, say, "*Ich schaue nur*". It is mainly in the smaller boutiques that the help can be a bit overwhelming, if you are not used to it. Of course, there are large department stores in most cities where you can browse to your heart's content without being followed about by a salesperson.

Clothing

Fashion in Austria is conservative and elegant. Some well-known women's stores are Fürnkranz and Maldone and traditional Austrian clothing stores such as Loden and Geiger. For men, there are Teller and Tlapa. For the teens and 20-year-olds, there are fun stores such as H&M, Zara, Esprit, Mango, Mexx, Vero moda, Promod, Pimkie, Schöps, Street One, Orsay, Turek and Sisley. Children's clothing stores in the large cities are part of big chains like H&M and C&A, and of smaller ones like Dohnal and Mary for Kids. The popular department stores for just about everyone in the family are C&A (budget), Gerngross and Peek and Cloppenburg.

Household essentials like kitchen utensils, linens, toys and casual clothing can be purchased at theTschibo/Eduscho stores or Interspar. Housewares, baby items, simple furniture, etc. can be found at Kika, Leiner and Ikea.

In addition to the streets lined with stores like Mariahilferstrasse in Vienna and the main street of any town, Austria does offer large modern shopping centres. Near Vienna, you can head to Shopping City Süd in Vösendorf, the largest shopping centre in Europe. With 10,000 parking spots and 300 shops, you'll be able to find just about everything you're looking for. On the northern outskirts of Vienna, you can shop at Shopping Centre Nord. This complex includes shops, restaurants, a modern movie theatre, a childcare facility and ample free parking. It is easily accessible by car and public transportation.

Many other shopping complexes can be found in the capital city such as Donauzentrum, Millennium City and the Gasometer, gas holders built in 1869 at the Simmering Gasworks that were renovated and now house a mall, restaurants, businesses, apartments and a movie theatre.

What to Bring from Home

Pretty much everything you'll need will be available in Austria. Many international food items are found at the bigger, and sometimes even local, grocery stores. Electronic appliances from home may not be compatible. Clothing and shoes are reasonably priced. There are even a number of English bookstores. Our advice is to bring any item or brand that you absolutely cannot live without, for example a friend had to have her favourite toothpaste. Also, bring any decorations or other items used to celebrate a holiday that Austrians do not observe. Finally, although books in English are sold in Austria, you might find a larger selection at home with lower prices.

Near Wiener Neustadt, you can shop at Fischapark. This shopping centre was built in accordance with ecological

Pricey boutiques and souvenir shops line Vienna's premier shopping street, Karntner Strasse.

guidelines and in character with its natural surroundings. The Traisenpark in Saint Pölten has many speciality stores and a childcare area. The McArthur Glen Designer Outlet in Parndorf, Burgenland, is a true paradise for bargain hunters. More than 70 shops feature a total of 320 brand names at low prices.

Upper Austria's largest shopping centre is Plus City, just outside of Linz. Shopping City Seiersberg in Graz is Styria's largest and Austria's third largest shopping mall. This mall combines stores and various eateries, from trendy cafes to fine dining. Südpark in Klagenfurt is that region's largest mall.

In Salzburg, you can visit the easily accessible Europark, located on the A1 Motorway. Founded in 1970, DEZ in Innsbruck was Austria's first shopping centre. It has over 110 stores and receives an average of 18,000 visitors per day. In addition to the stores, it offers free childcare and hosts interesting events. If you are in Vorarlberg, you can head to Messepark in Dornbirn.

Specialty Stores

Austria produces its own ceramics in the town of Gmunden, in Upper Austria. The patterns are well known among Austrian households, but the most popular are green swirls or blue polka dots on a white background. Ceramics are sold in household stores.

The Augarten in Vienna produces fine china. The popular pattern is fine pastel flowers on white. The decoration is beautifully painted in a very delicate manner. Special tours can be arranged by contacting the Augarten factory.

The Wiener Werkstätte (WW) produces an assortment of objects for the kitchen and dining room. Its heyday was at the turn of the 20th century during the Jugendstil period. The WW believed it could make anything a household could want. When the materials used proved to be too costly for the average family, it ended up making specialty objects for a select clientele.

Also popular is the Dorotheum, fondly called 'Aunt Dorli's', an auction house, pawn brokerage and store that opened in 1707. The Dorotheum proper is located in Vienna's 1st district, but smaller branches are found throughout Vienna. One can get anything from furniture and china to jewellery, paintings and fur coats. Auctions are held almost daily, with a special viewing time before the event to allow prospective bidders to check out the merchandise.

Let's not forget the famous Flea Market which borders the Naschmarkt. It is open every Saturday, from the wee hours until sunset. There is an assortment of everything from junk to real treasures. Mind your purse or wallet as the place is crowded.

Claiming a Tax Refund

If you are a non-resident and spend more than € 75 on any one item, you may claim a tax refund. The forms are available at most stores. The item must be taken out of the country within three months of purchase. When leaving the EU, customs officials at the airport or train station will validate your items. Cash your refund check at a refund office after you have cleared passport control. You may also be able to mail your validated refund check to an address provided at customs (if you can't find your receipt) and have your credit card account credited.

Food

Shopping at grocery stores (*Lebensmittelgeschäfte*) or supermarkets (*Supermärkte*) can be a shock if you are used to huge grocery stores. Many stores are expanding, and it is common to find two stores of the same name a small distance apart, one selling food and the other toiletries. The aisles can be extremely small and it requires a lot of patience and good humour to make shopping a pleasant experience. The common grocery stores are Billa, Zielpunkt, Mondo, Hofer, Spar and Eurospar. Interspar, Metro and Merkur tend to be large but not very accessible, as they are located on the outskirts of large cities. Metro is extremely large and sells in bulk, but only to customers who have the membership or diplomatic card necessary to gain entrance. Zielpunkt, Mondo and Hofer tend to be much cheaper as they are wholesale stores that also sell overstocked merchandise at low prices.

The produce section usually carries a wide selection of goods, with more variety now than ever before, due to trade within the European Union. A word of

When you go grocery shopping, bring your own shopping bags or a shopping wagon, as you have to pay for shopping bags. Once you are at the store, remember to have either a € 1 or € 2 coin to get a cart. Withdraw the coin or token at the end of your shopping trip by attaching the chain at the end of the cart line to your cart.

warning: always weigh the produce you buy if it is not sold on a per piece basis. With very few exceptions, this is not done by the cashier. It can be embarrassing when the cashier has to leave her register and weigh an item you have forgotten, while there are customers waiting behind you.

The meat and cheese section is wonderful, offering a great variety from all over Europe. Everything is priced by the kilogram. However, one doesn't break down the amounts by 100ths (100 gram) but by 10ths (decagram). So, if you want 200 grams of cheese, you say, "*zwanzig deca Käse, bitte.*" ("Twenty decagrams of cheese, please.")

Many bottles and some plastics carry a deposit (*Pfand*). You usually go to the back of the store, where a conveyor belt will accept your empties, then spit out a credit receipt (*Flaschenzettel*). Present this ticket to the cashier when you check out and she will credit the amount to your grocery bill.

Bankcards (*Bankomatkarte*) make it easy to pay for your groceries. You just insert your card and type in your PIN. Remember to keep your *Bankomat* card current.

The most shocking part about the grocery stores is the small area, sometimes non-existent, in which to gather the groceries you have bought. This means that once the items have been scanned, you have to gather them all at Olympian speed and put them back into the cart. Then you go to a special packing counter to pack the groceries. If you go to a larger grocery store with your car, you can bring the grocery cart to the car and unload it directly.

If you like the royal treatment and have a penchant for fine foods and wine, go to Julius Meinl on the Graben in Vienna. The employees will greet you and make you feel quite at home. The ambience is refined and ultramodern. There is also a cozy coffee shop on the first floor, and a gourmet restaurant located behind the store. The best thing of all, however, is that when you leave the store, someone will bag your groceries, even without you having to pay for the bags!

Some grocery stores are trying to make life a bit easier on the customer. Merkur, for example, has an order and delivery service available from 6:00 am until midnight.

Tabak-Trafik

An important little store is the *Tabak-Trafik* or just *Tabak*. These were originally small tobacco shops, but now the extent of their wares is mesmerising. *Tabaks* stock transportation tickets, cigarettes, magazines, newspapers, greeting cards, stationery, maps, stamps, registration forms (*Meldezettel*), lottery tickets, parking tickets and small toys, for a start.

During your stay in Austria, the *Tabak-Trafik* will prove indispensable.

Keep in mind the hours of operation: 5:30 am–noon, and 3:00 pm–6:00 pm.

Shopping Hours

The hours for shopping can sometimes be annoyingly inconvenient, but changes are taking place, and now stores are opening later and later. Generally, the hours at department stores and boutiques are Monday–Friday 9:00 am–6:00 pm, Saturday 10:00 am–5:00 pm. Some popular shopping areas have extended their hours on Thursdays until 9:00 pm and on Fridays until 7:30 pm. Grocery stores are open weekdays 7:30 am–7:00 pm and Saturdays 7:30 am–5:00 pm.

Plan to have enough food to get you to Monday, but don't despair if you find yourself with nothing in the fridge. You can always head out to one of the main train stations and gas stations which carry foodstuff and other necessary items.

RECYCLING

Austria is well known for its fastidiousness about keeping the environment free of pollutants and piles of trash. It recycles 65 per cent of all its paper, and is the third largest

The Austrian's love affair with recycling is obvious on most streets.

paper recycler in the world. The recycling bins found at every second street corner are receptacles for plastic, glass (green and clear), metal, compost and paper. Make sure you read what you are allowed to throw in. Also, to keep within noise level restrictions, throw out your bottles during working hours only! You can also recycle batteries at most supermarkets by depositing them in a small box near the exit.

FREE TIME
Movies

Austria receives a good selection of international films, although most American films arrive well after they have premiered in the United States. Most Austrian cinemas show films that have been dubbed in German. Check movie listings for the following categories: OmU, original with subtitles in German; OV, original version, no subtitles; and OmeU, original version with English subtitles. Not many movies fall into the last category.

Cinemas that show movies in their original language and usually have English-speaking staff are English Cinema Haydn

Most *Kinos* (cinemas) show movies dubbed in German. Look for movies in the OV (original version) or OmU (original with German subtitles) categories at select theatres.

on Mariahilfer Strasse, Votiv Cinema near Schottenring, Artis International Cinema near Hoher Markt and Burg Kino on Opernring near the Hofburg. The last runs the Graham Greene classic, *The Third Man*, every Sunday. This black and white mystery was filmed in occupied Vienna at the end of World War II and provides a glimpse into Vienna during that period. The Film Museum in the first district shows foreign films with English subtitles.

In Graz, check out the English Royal Cinema and KIZ–Kino im Augarten. In Linz, head to the City Kino or the Moviemento. In Salzburg, try Das Kino or Elmo Kino. If you are in Innsbruck, look for Leokino or Cinematograph Innsbruck. Klagenfurt has the Volkskino and Bregenz has the Filmforum in Metrokino.

DVD Rental

DVD rental stores are everywhere, but once again, most of the movies are dubbed in German. You may be able to find an English-language section, but more often than not it will be very limited. In Vienna, for a small membership fee, you can rent English-language movies from Pickwicks in the 1st district, Alphaville in the 4th district and Video International in the 19th district. For expatriates who work at the United Nations, there is a video rental store within the UN complex that offers movies in a number of different languages.

Television

Regular Austrian television has two channels, ORF 1 and 2, each presenting a mixture of news, sports, local programmes and shows and movies from other countries dubbed in German. Local programmes consist of soap operas, talk shows, variety shows and game shows. If you don't want to be limited to two channels, or are unable to understand German, consider installing cable or a satellite dish. A wide range of channels from many different countries are on offer (practically every country in Europe has a cable or satellite channel). If you are looking for English programming, there is news on CNN from the United States and Sky News and BBC World from Great Britain. Televisions operate on the

PAL system; if you bring an NTSC television from the United States, it will not work.

Radio

Austria has a number of radio stations. Stations like Hitradio Ö3 focus on pop music from the 1980s onwards. FM4 at 103.8 in Vienna plays alternative music, and broadcasts mainly in English until 2:00 pm. From 6:00 am to 7:00 pm, the news is read in English at the top of the hour. The Morning Show provides general information from 6:00 am to 10:00 am. FM4 Update, a service-oriented programme, is on from 10:00 am until noon. From 12:00 pm until 2:00 pm, news and features are discussed on Reality Check. For classical music, tune in to Ö1 or Radio Stephansdom. The latter is linked to the Catholic Church and broadcasts mass live from the cathedral every Sunday morning. Each province has its own radio station, where local news and issues are presented and discussed. On most stations, news, weather and traffic reports are given for the entire country.

English-Language Bookstores

It is not all that difficult to find books in English in Austria, especially Vienna, which has a good number of English-language bookshops. Best known is The British Bookshop, which has a large selection for adults and children, and a very good section for instructive materials teaching English as a foreign language. The staff of primarily native English speakers can help you with any inquiries. Their main store is in the 1st district, but they have a couple other locations. Shakespeare & Co. is smaller and concentrates on the classics and academic works, with a focus on political science and history. It also has a nice selection for children and second-hand books. There are German-language bookshops that offer some English-language books. The Buchhandlung Kuppitsch store on the old Allgemeines Krankenhaus (AKH) campus offers books in several different languages. Gerold & Co. on the Graben in the 1st district also carries a number of English-language books. The large chain Libro has a small English-language section in its stores all across the country. Amadeus (part of the Libro group) is a chain of large multimedia stores that also carry English books. Do not count on native English-speaking staff in these stores.

Borrowing Books

If you prefer to borrow books, you can find English-language and other non-German language books throughout the country at the *Städtische Büchereien* (city public libraries), but be aware that the staff may not speak English. The public can also borrow books from the American International School Secondary Library (Salmannsdorfer Strasse 47, 19th district, tel: (1) 401-3222). It has an extensive collection of American periodicals.

English-language Newspapers

Austria Today, issued weekly, publishes good articles on politics, business and sports. You can subscribe to the on-line publication at http://www.austriatoday.at. You can also read interesting articles at http://www.austrianews.co.uk.

German-language Newspapers

Although the newspapers claim to be independent, some tend to lean in a certain direction. *Neue Kronen Zeitung* has the largest circulation. It is published in Vienna, Graz, Klagenfurt, Linz and Salzburg, and is somewhat populist and right-wing. The *Kurier* is published in Vienna and appeals to the masses. *Der Standard* is linked with the Social Democrats and *Die Presse* is a conservative newspaper tied to the People's Party (ÖVP). Both are read by businesspeople and the better educated. The *Wirtschafts Blatt* is a financial newspaper. *Österreich*, a new newspaper, is nice, very neatly done and has a smaller, easier to handle format. As with the Metro system, you can pay for your newspaper using the honour system.

Other papers include the regional publications such as the *Niederösterreichische Nachrichten*, *Oberösterreichische Nachrichten*, *Tiroler Nachrichten* and *Salzburger Nachrichten*.

AUSTRIAN CUISINE: MAHLZEIT!

CHAPTER 6

'When you are worried, have trouble of one sort or
another—to the coffeehouse!
When she did not keep her appointment,
for one reason or another—to the coffeehouse!
When your shoes are torn and dilapidated—coffeehouse!
When your income is four hundred crowns
and you spend five hundred—coffeehouse!'
—Peter Altenberg, Viennese poet,
from his poem 'To The Coffeehouse'

IT IS AN ACCOMPLISHMENT if you leave Austria the same size as when you arrived. Not only are the main dishes hearty and filling, but the pastries are so delicious that you won't be able to refuse them. Main courses are meat-oriented, consisting primarily of pork, but chicken, veal, beef and turkey are also eaten regularly. As if these large portions of meat aren't enough, potatoes, dumplings or sauerkraut often accompany them, with green vegetables in short supply.

Austria's neighbours have heavily influenced its cuisine, although by now, favourite dishes are considered truly Austrian. Regional influences become evident once you begin to look at provincial specialties. The food of Burgenland, for example, reflects the Hungarian taste for paprika and sour cream. *Gulasch* is perhaps Hungary's most important contribution to Austrian stomachs. Bean soup with *scipi*, a kind of small dumpling, is the 'national dish' of the Croatian community of Burgenland. Upper and Lower Austrian and Viennese dishes include many Czech staples. Bohemia, in the Czech Republic, is the birthplace of the dumpling, which Austrians have made their own. Sausages arrived via Germany and Poland. Italian, Slavic, Middle Eastern and even Asian cooking have also influenced the Austrian menu.

REGIONAL CUISINE
While you can order most dishes throughout the country, each region is particularly proud of its own delicious specialties.

Vorarlberg, which in many aspects is closer to Switzerland than Austria, is a major producer of cheese. The region is noted for *Käsespätzle* (egg noodles covered in cheese and topped with onions). Tyrol is famous for *Nocken* (small dumplings) that are mixed with berries, cherries or apple. *Tiroler Gröstl* is a very tasty dish of sautéed sliced meat and boiled potatoes (similar to hash browns). *Speck*, ham that is cured high up in the fresh mountain air and found in a variety of dishes, is another trademark of the region.

Salzburg is famous for the *Salzburger Nockerln*, a light dessert soufflé dusted with vanilla sugar. Carinthians love *Ritscher(t)*, a meat dish made with white beans, barley, vegetables and herbs. They also eat a variety of *Nudeln* (noodles) that are stuffed with different fillings such as cheese, meat, poppy seed or pears. Styria is known for the hearty *Steierisches Wurzelfleisch*, beef cooked with carrots and other root vegetables. The province is also known for its *Sterze* (mashes made from different grains).

Upper Austrians have invented a number of different types of *Knödel* (dumpling). Many dumplings are made from potatoes (*Reiberknödel*), although there are also semolina dumplings (*Griessknödel*), flour dumplings (*Mehlknödel*) and bread dumplings (*Brotknödel*). To the basic dumpling, you

can add bacon (*Speckknödel*), meat (*Fleischknödel*), crackling (*Grammelknödel*) or white cabbage (*Krautknödel*). A favourite among the farmers are *Mühlviertler Hackknödel*, made with leftover meat. *Mostbraten*, pork marinated in *Most* (semi-fermented grape juice), is extremely popular. For something sweet, they like *Strauben*, fried dough.

Lower Austrians prefer *Buchteln*, a sweet bun filled with plum marmalade and served warm with vanilla sauce. The Wachau valley is a major producer of apricots, also found in a number of sweets. The Waldviertel region of Lower Austria uses lots of poppy seeds (*Mohnsamen*) in many dishes, both savoury and sweet, such as noodles, dumplings, breads, cakes and strudel.

The not particularly healthy *Grammelpogatscherl*—fried pork fat baked in dough and served with sour cream—is a favourite in Burgenland. Of course, Vienna is known for its *Schnitzeln* and other meat dishes like *Tafelspitz*, *Lungenbraten* and *Rostbraten*. Perhaps, it is most famous for its pastries and coffee.

ENTRÉES

If you find yourself living in Austria, you'd better be a fan of pork, because it is eaten everywhere. It comes as cutlets, ham, sausages, pork chops, etc., and tends to dominate menus and the meat section at the supermarket.

Perhaps the dish most closely associated with Austria, and Vienna in particular, is *Wiener Schnitzel*, a veal or pork cutlet that is pounded paper thin, dipped in egg, flour and breadcrumbs and fried. *Schnitzel* refers to the thinly pounded piece of meat. It is often served with potato salad. The menu will specify if the meat is veal, and if it doesn't say *Wiener Schnitzel von Kalb* (veal) it is most likely made with pork (*Schwein*). If you are dining in an upscale restaurant, it should be veal. After you've been in Austria a while, you should be able to guess which it is just from the price.

Putenschnitzel (turkey *Schnitzel*) and *Hühnerschnitzel* (chicken *Schnitzel*) are prepared in exactly the same manner as *Wiener Schnitzel*. *Pariserschnitzel* is *Wiener Schnitzel* minus the egg. Not all *Schnitzeln* are breaded:

Champignonschnitzel is a thin slice of grilled pork served with a mushroom cream sauce and rice; *Rahmschnitzel* is covered in a thick gravy; and *Zigeunerschnitzel* (Gypsy *Schnitzel*) comes with mild to hot peppers in a spicy tomato sauce.

> *Tafelspitz*, boiled beef served with potatoes and vegetables, was Emperor Franz Josef's favourite meal (he ate it every day), and its name translates as 'the head of the table'. *Schweinsbraten* is juicy roast pork.

Zwiebelrostbraten is a thin steak that is fried and then smothered with sautéed onions.

Gulasch originated in Hungary but is a staple of Viennese fare. Served as a soup or stew, often with dumplings or bread, it is made with large pieces of meat in a strong paprika sauce. *Fiakergulasch* comes with a hardboiled egg and is said to be the favourite of drivers of *Fiaker*, the horse-drawn carriages seen throughout Vienna.

Laibchen are tasty little meatballs, and *Fachiertes Fleisch* refers to ground beef. For the adventurous, there is *Beuschel*, or lung. *Backhendl* is a young stuffed chicken that is breaded and fried. *Grammelknödel* are delicious rich dumplings stuffed with pork and fried lard.

If you can't decide what to order, get *Bauernschmaus*, a sampler of smoked ham, roast pork, sausage, sauerkraut and dumplings.

Fish

Freshwater fish comes from the lakes and rivers of Austria and is commonly eaten in towns and cities outside of Vienna. However it is prepared, the fish is usually very good. Commonly eaten fish are *Karpfen* (carp), *Kabeljau* (cod), *Scholle* (sole), *Heilbutt* (halibut), *Flunder* (flounder), *Zander* (perch or pike), *Lachs* (salmon), *Forelle* (trout) and *Thunfisch* (tuna).

Vegetarian Food

Vegetarians do not have an easy time in Austria, although the situation is improving. Many menus list at least a couple of meatless entrées, like fried Emmenthaler cheese or dumplings. Some restaurants do offer large salads, although many are topped with chicken, tuna or seafood.

Other restaurants provide salad bars, but be advised that you are permitted one trip only. The number of vegetarian restaurants in the cities is steadily growing, however, and more options are becoming available. When travelling through rural areas, though, you'll have to make do with a limited menu.

SOUPS

Perhaps because winters can be so cold and long, soups are popular. One of the tastiest ways to start off a meal is with *Fritattensuppe*, a clear beef broth with thin slices of crêpe. Other clear soups are *Leberknödelsuppe*, with a large liver paté dumpling, and *Griessnockerlsuppe*, loaded with small gnocchi-style dumplings. *Hühnersuppe* (chicken soup) is always a safe and delicious choice, as are *Nudelsuppe* (noodle soup), *Knoblauchsuppe* (cream of garlic soup) and *Erdäpfelsuppe* (potato soup).

BEILAGEN

In most restaurants, *Beilagen*, or side dishes, are ordered separately. Unless the description of your entrée specifically mentions an accompaniment, it will come à la carte. The *Beilagen* section consists of a number of *Kartoffel* or *Erdäpfel* (both words mean potato) dishes. *Gröstl* or *Röstkartoffeln* are fried potatoes with onions. *Petersilkartoffeln* are parsley potatoes. The term *Pommes Frites*, borrowed from the French, is used for French fries. *Kartoffelsalat* is cold potato salad made with a vinegar and sugar dressing. *Reis* (rice) is another option, or you may choose the heavy but delicious *Knödel*, large dumplings. These are made from either bread or potato dough and boiled.

You may notice that vegetables are lacking on the side dish menu. In fact, most meals are not accompanied by anything green. This can be traced back to medieval days when vegetables were in short supply and considered luxury items. Even though the price of vegetables is no longer prohibitively expensive, they have failed to become an integral part of the Austrian diet, with the exception of asparagus in season.

SALADS

If you are a big salad eater, you'll have to alter your expectations while in Austria. Most salads, especially the *gemischter Salat*, are a combination of tasty marinated vegetables. These commonly include beets, green beans, cucumbers, sauerkraut, potato salad, carrots and *Rettich* (a large white radish that is thinly sliced and mixed with vinegar and oil). If you prefer a lettuce salad, be sure to ask for a *Grünersalat* (green salad). This is a leafy salad with a number of different types of lettuce.

BREADS

If you enjoy eating bread with your meal, or even on its own, Austria is the place to be. There are so many different types of bread that it would be impossible to list them all here. What follows are just the highlights. For a better idea of what's available, visit your local bakery or the bread section at the supermarket. If the entire loaf is too much for your family, you may ask for a half (*Halbes*) or a quarter (*ein Viertel*). A *Semmel* is the average white roll. *Stangerl* are long rolls and come in different varieties like *Salzstangerl* (salted). *Hausbrot* (housebread) is a mixture of wheat and rye. *Roggenbrot* is rye bread and *Schwarzbrot* is black rye bread. Be sure to sample the bread when you travel around Austria because there are many different regional breads. Of course, if you must have white sandwich bread, that is available too.

DESSERTS
Pastries

The wonderful flavours of the pastries are difficult to describe. The best way to fully appreciate this aspect of life in Austria is to force yourself into a pastry shop and start eating. *Strudel* is the most popular dessert. Many layers of phyllo dough surround a warm filling, usually *Apfel* (apple) or *Topfen* with raisins. *Topfen* has been translated as sweet cream cheese or sweet curd, but it does not exist outside of this part of Europe. It should not be confused with cheesecake; *Topfen* is less sweet and has a delicious yet distinct flavour. A dash of lemon is sometimes added to heighten the flavour.

Whipped Cream

If you love rich desserts, all of the above can and should be ordered with *Schlagobers*, or fresh whipped cream, on the side. No self-respecting Austrian would eat the light and airy pre-made whipped cream. *Schlagobers* is heavy unsweetened whipped cream that, in our opinion, is one of the advantages of living in Austria.

Sachertorte is Austria's most famous dessert. Sampled by practically every tourist, *Sachertorte* is chocolate cake covered in chocolate icing with apricot jam. Although it sounds heavy, it actually has a very delicate flavour. Herr Sacher, Prince Metternich's personal pastry chef, baked the first *Sachertorte* in the mid-19th century. The chef's son opened the Hotel Sacher in 1876, and the son's wife built up the hotel's reputation. This hotel claims to have the original secret recipe and legally won the right to spell it as one word. All other restaurants, coffeehouses and pastry shops must spell it as two words—*Sacher Torte*.

Linzertorte is made with apricot jam and almonds. *Esterhazytorte* is a delicious cake consisting of many very thin layers of dough with vanilla cream between the layers. *Mohntorte* is a poppy seed cake, and *Nusstorte* is walnut cake.

As you've probably guessed by now, *Torte* means cake. *Schnitte*—cut or slice—refers to a piece of pastry cut from a large sheet, the most famous being the *Kardinalschnitte* or Cardinal's cut. This rich but light dessert consists of meringue, yellow cake and either chocolate, strawberry or raspberry mousse. If you are lucky enough to find homemade *Kardinalschnitte*, you are in for a big treat. *Imperialschnitte* is a personal favourite of ours, and consists of chocolate and marzipan.

More Desserts

Kaiserschmarrn is an omelette/soufflé made from eggs and raisins. *Mohr im Hemd*, which means 'Moor in a shirt', is a must for any chocolate lover: it is chocolate cake covered in warm chocolate sauce and topped with whipped cream. *Gugelhupf* is reminiscent of a bunt cake, but smaller. *Krapfen* are fried donuts filled with jam (often apricot jam).

Another big favourite is *Palatschinken*, a delectable plate of crêpes with a variety of fillings. *Marmaladepalatschinken* are filled with apricot jam, and *Schokonusspalatschinken* have walnut filling and are topped with warm chocolate sauce. The crêpe can also be filled with Nutella, ice cream or fruit.

Chocolates

Austria is famous for *Mozartkugeln*, little round chocolate balls covering a nougat and marzipan center. Several boxes of these are all you need to take home as souvenirs! Not quite as well known, but every bit as delicious, are the candies named after Princess Sissi and Johann Strauss.

Ice Cream

As much as the Austrians love their pastries, Italian style ice cream (*gelato*) is also a favourite in summer. Many people have their favourite *Gelateria* and intense rivalries have arisen. With a few exceptions, most ice cream parlors close from October to March. The opening of the local *Gelateria* in the spring is a day for celebration. Once

you taste the creamy ice cream, you'll understand why. We promise that you'll return again and again to try each and every exotic flavour. If you want more than a simple ice cream cone, the selection of ice cream dishes and sundaes is so broad that it'll take you at least one summer to sample them all. A popular dish is *heisse Liebe* (literally 'warm love'), creamy vanilla ice cream smothered with warm raspberries and garnished with loads of whipped cream. Not to be missed!

HEALTH AND DIET

The average Austrian diet, which is high on meat, fats, starches and sweets, and low on fish and vegetables, may be blamed for the high rate of circulatory disorders and heart disease. It used to be quite common to compliment an overweight person by saying, "You're looking healthy." This attitude probably arose out of the years of hunger and hardship characterising the world wars. Today, however, the younger generation is more concerned with body size, although not necessarily with their health.

MEAL SCHEDULE
Breakfast

Breakfast is usually eaten very early in the morning, between 6:00 and 7:00 am, as most Austrians are early risers. A typical breakfast consists of a few of the following: bread, butter, marmalade, cold cuts, paté, softboiled egg, cheese, yogurt, müsli, coffee, tea and hot chocolate.

Gabelfrühstück

For many people who work, this is an important part of the day. Work schedules are such that many people start and end work early. For those who return home in the early evening, a big dinner awaits. Therefore, they pass up the traditional afternoon coffee break with pastry. But rather than go a whole day without something sweet, they stop for *Gabelfrühstück*, literally 'breakfast eaten with a fork', around 10:00 am. This snack, consisting of coffee and a pastry, tides them over until lunch.

Lunch

Lunch can be a formal or informal affair, and is usually eaten between noon and 1:00 pm. For many busy workers, a quick bite from a *Würstelstand* (kiosk selling a variety of sausages), sandwich shop or pizzeria is all they have time for. Since their clientele are often in a rush, most of these eateries do not offer seating, but rather tiny-topped, tall tables for customers to stand around. Every *Stehcafe* is usually packed at lunchtime. Don't worry if this is not how you want to spend your lunch hour. Traditionally, lunch used to be the biggest meal of the day, and there are a large number of restaurants available where you are invited in to sit and take your time to enjoy your meal. Many restaurants offer a set lunch menu, which includes soup, entrée and dessert. For those on a budget, this is the best option. If the day's special doesn't appeal to you, the menu will have all the usual dishes.

Jause

Jause is a short coffee break taken in mid-afternoon, around 3:00 to 4:00 pm, primarily by those who either do not eat a big dinner or who eat much later at night. It provides people with an opportunity to relax and enjoy something sweet. The cafés and *Konditorei* begin to get very crowded with retirees and students around this time of day.

Dinner

Dinner is eaten between 7:00 and 8:00 pm and is quite a substantial hot meal. This is especially true for workers who eat a quick lunch. Restaurants offer the same hearty meals served at lunch. For those who have had a substantial lunch or a particularly filling *Jause*, dinner may be ham or cold cuts, served with pickles, a salad and one of the many delicious breads.

WHERE SHOULD YOU EAT?
Beiseln

Beiseln are neighbourhood pub-restaurants that offer low-priced, simple home-style food and beer. They are warm and cozy, and can be easily recognised by the chalkboard outside which describes the daily menu. The pace is slow and each *Beisel* has its share of regular customers.

International Restaurants

If you want a change from Austrian fare, there is an abundance of international restaurants. Italian restaurants serve good pasta dishes and pizzas. If you like Asian food, Chinese restaurants are quite common throughout the country, but they do use MSG. In Vienna, you can find Japanese, Thai, Indian and Korean restaurants, among others. There are many French restaurants to choose from as well. Central and Eastern Europe and the Balkans are well represented, and the many Turkish and Greek restaurants are particularly good. Austria is relatively free of American chain restaurants, except for fast food giant McDonald's. Middle Eastern food is also available. Another tasty option is Latin American food, including Mexican, Brazilian and Argentinian cuisine.

The Würstelstand

If you need to grab something quick to eat, your best option is a *Würstelstand*. They are virtually everywhere and offer some very tasty snacks. There is such a wide variety of sausages that it's easy to become confused. However, don't take the easy way out and only order a hot dog, because you will deprive yourself of the more savoury offerings. A *Bratwurst* is a fried sausage. A *Burenwurst*, on the other hand, is boiled. A *Weisswurst* is a fat white sausage containing herbs. A *Debreziner* is a spicy paprika sausage, and a *Käsekrainer* has chunks of cheese inside. *Currywurst* is yet another option. If you prefer something less spicy, order a hot dog, which is just that, a hot dog stuffed into a delicious long roll; or a *Frankfurter*, also similar to a hot dog, but served on a plate with some mustard and a roll on the side. *Leberkäse* is a common item on the *Würstelstand* menu, even though it is not a sausage. It is sliced from a loaf of meat that is a mixture of liver, meat, bacon, onions and spices, and served on a roll. Be sure to specify whether you want it *vom Schwein* (pork) or *vom Pferd* (horse). You may be asked if you want your order with ketchup, *süssen Senf* (sweet mustard) or *scharfen Senf* (hot mustard).

Würstelstände, which offers a wide array of sausages, can be found on almost any street corner.

Fast Food

Although eating out in Austria is generally not cheap, there are several options for cheap fast food. In addition to the *Würstelstände*, you can buy pre-made cold sandwiches (usually different forms of ham sandwiches) at the bakeries Anker and Ströck. Open-face sandwiches are sold at Der Mann, Duran and Trzesniewski. In fact, many Austrians buy open-face sandwiches from these stores to serve at home for lunch and special occasions. You can also have sandwiches made at the meat counter in a supermarket. You could try Nordsee, a fast food chain specialising in fish and shellfish, although the prices are not low. A few fast food restaurants from the United States have made inroads into Austria. Be forewarned, though, that you will be charged for ketchup at McDonald's. Also, dirty trays are left behind for the staff to collect. A nice change of pace are the tasty *Döner Kebabs* (pita bread stuffed with lamb and vegetables) sold at Middle Eastern kiosks and restaurants. In winter, little stalls offer *heisse Maroni* (roasted chestnuts) and *Kartofelpuffer*. The latter are similar to hash brown potatoes and are smothered in garlic.

DINING OUT

Because most restaurants and *Beiseln* are family-operated, they observe a *Ruhetag* one day of the week, when the restaurant is closed so the owners and employees can 'rest'. Many restaurants have Sunday and holidays as their *Ruhetag*, yet this is not necessarily the norm. Some restaurants may close for a break between lunch and dinner, and you'll be pushed out the door as closing time approaches. Even if they remain open, you may find your options limited during non-peak hours. Susan and her mother sat down to eat lunch at 3:00 pm once and were forced to order the same meal so that the cook wouldn't have to dirty too many pans. Most restaurants and *Beiseln* close at around midnight, but tend to empty out well beforehand.

Etiquette

If you are dining with Austrians, be sure to say *Mahlzeit* before digging in. To start eating before wishing everyone else at the table a good meal would be rude. In several restaurants, dishes are served in the order in which they are prepared. Wait for others at your table to invite you to begin eating before you dig in. Also, keep in mind that Austrians eat with their knives and forks, even for pizza.

Once you've arrived at your chosen restaurant, seat yourself, making sure the table you select is not reserved with a card reading *reserviert*. Not every restaurant has a non-smoking section, and if it does, it may be so close to the smoking section that it makes little difference. So if cigarette smoke affects you, try more spacious restaurants, dine during off-peak hours, or sit at outdoor tables in summer.

The server will appear relatively soon to take your order. Water does not automatically come with your meal, so ask for *Leitungswasser* if you want tap water, or *Mineralwasser* if you want mineral water. Once served, the waitstaff tends to leave the customers alone to eat in peace; there is no checking every five minutes to see if you need anything. It may take a long time to get your waiter if you need another drink or even when you want the bill. When clearing away your meal, the waiter or waitress will ask if you enjoyed your meal ("*Hat's Ihnen geschmeckt?*"), and if you've left food on your plate, they'll ask you if you didn't like it.

Paying

When you are ready to leave, request the bill. Restaurants that cater to the tourist market and upscale restaurants will accept credit cards, but be advised that many restaurants do not take plastic. The first time you visit, you should always have enough cash on hand to avoid an embarrassing situation. *Beiseln*, *Heurigen*, *Gasthäuser*, small restaurants and coffeehouses definitely do not accept credit cards. If you are travelling through small towns and villages, rest assured that irregardless of size of restaurant, you can only pay with cash. However, if you are travelling on the freeway, there are very good and affordable restaurants (many are part of a chain) that will accept credit cards. Several offer incredible buffets with a very good selection of quality food.

Normally, you will be asked if the bill is *zusammen* (all together) or *getrennt* (separate). When paying, you may be asked to repeat everything you ordered as the waiter jots down the price for each and mentally calculates the total. Remember that you have to pay for each roll or piece of bread, so you will be asked how many were eaten.

When presented with the final bill, round the figure up, normally to the nearest Euro. Either give the server the total amount (bill plus tip) and say "*Das stimmt*", or, if you don't have the exact amount, tell the server the total and wait for your change. For example, if the bill is € 25.30 and you only have € 30, tell the waiter "*Sechs-und-zwanzig* (26)." In upscale restaurants, you can leave a tip of 5 to 10 per cent. Waiters are paid an average wage and don't rely on tips as a significant portion of their income. Avoid leaving a tip on the table.

Stammtisch

Austrians continue to uphold the longstanding tradition of the *Stammtisch*. This is a table reserved for regular customers. Often, friends choose a night of the week for the *Stammtisch*, and they meet regularly without having to call the restaurant first or organise the evening among themselves. It provides a place and an opportunity for friends to sit down together, drink a glass of beer and chat.

Most Austrian restaurants and cafes are small and cosy and are great places to meet up with friends.

SCHANIGÄRTEN

As the first warm breezes are felt, Austrians jump at any opportunity to be outside after a long winter indoors. Patio tables and chairs are brought out of storage and street cafés and *Schanigärten* emerge. *Schanigärten* can be small gardens with soft lighting or candlelight, or larger patios with large benches that are shared by a couple of restaurants. These tables fill up quickly while the indoor seats tend to remain unoccupied.

In Vienna, the Donauinsel (Danube Island) and the Am Kai area along the Danube between Schwedenplatz and Friedensbrücke are lined with outdoor restaurants. The university campus at the Allgemeines Krankenhaus (AKH) has a number of open-air beer gardens and restaurants open until 2:00 am, where you can take in a cultural event while dining. Another option is to spend a warm evening in front of the Rathaus (City Hall), watching filmed opera on a giant screen for free while eating and drinking. The Rathaus square is covered with stalls that offer food from over 17 countries.

KAFFEEHÄUSER

Although coffeehouses can be found throughout Austria, they are a Viennese institution. The Viennese linger reading, writing, thinking and discussing, much as their ancestors did. According to popular history, the first coffeehouse was opened in Vienna shortly after the Turkish siege of 1683. Beating a hasty retreat, the Turks left behind bags of coffee beans. A Pole, Georg Franz Kolschitzky, is said to have requested the beans as a reward for his military achievements. Only he knew how to process them into coffee, and the story goes that he opened the first Viennese coffeehouse, the Sign of the Blue Bottle, near Stephansdom. Yet, evidence suggests that coffee was already being drunk in Vienna prior to this time.

Coffeehouses played an important role in society, especially in *fin-de-siècle* Vienna, up until 1938. As the arts flourished, intellectual life centred around the coffeehouses. Many of the most creative and brilliant Viennese had their *Stammcafé*, or regular coffeehouse, where they spent a good portion of their

Biergartens open all across Austria with the arrival of warm spring weather.

day. Here they met with others to debate the issues of the day. Among the more prominent guests at the Café Central on Herrengasse were authors Arthur Schnitzler and Hugo von Hofmannsthal. Even Leon Trotsky was known to have frequented the café. Gustav Mahler regularly visited the Café Imperial. Sigmund Freud liked the Café Landtmann, and the composer Franz Lehár spent much time at Café Sperl. Artists such as Oskar Kokoschka, Gustav Klimt and Egon Schiele, and the composer Alban Berg, could all be seen at the Café Museum. Sadly, all of this ended with the annexation of Austria by Hitler, and this aspect of Viennese life never fully recovered after World War II.

Coffeehouses tend to be a bit formal. The waiters dress in tuxedos and even the clientele take care to look nice. In fact, before or after the theatre or a concert, you might see patrons in tuxedos and sequined gowns. Even though the waiters may not be the friendliest servers you'll ever encounter, they will not push you out. You can stay for hours, even if you've only ordered one cup of coffee. Newspapers and magazines are put out to help you while away the time. Other customers may play chess or cards. In the past, coffeehouses only offered a small selection of pastries. Today, however, many not only offer pastries, but also alcohol, savoury snacks and sometimes even a full menu.

KONDITOREI

If you like pastries, visit one of the countless *Konditorei*. There are two types of *Konditorei* found throughout Austria, the elegant and the utilitarian. The elegant offer luxurious surroundings and make you want to linger for hours. In Vienna, Demmel is the most famous and clearly ranks among the best. Other elegant *Konditorei* can also be found within the 1st district, primarily on Kärntner Strasse, Graben and Neuer Markt. Other *Konditorei* offer the same high quality pastries, but their lower prices reflect the cramped, stark surroundings. You won't find any cozy plush furniture here, and in fact most have only a standing section. The most common *Konditorei* is the Aida chain. *Konditorei* are easily recognised by the elaborate marzipan figurines and other sweets in the windows.

BEVERAGES
Non-alcoholic Beverages

Perhaps the best way to quench your thirst is with *Apfelsaft* (apple juice) or an *Apfelsaft gespritzt* (apple juice mixed with sparkling mineral water). Soft drinks are very popular, including *Soda Zitrone*, a lemon soda, and *Almdudler*, a soft drink made with herbs that closely resembles ginger ale. The Austrians are proud of their water, which is just about the best in the world. It comes from the Alps and is so clear that it is better than bottled water.

Coffees

Ordering a cup of coffee in Vienna is not as easy as it may seem, as there are several types to be had. Because coffee is made with Italian espresso machines, it can be very strong. *Mokka* is black coffee, a *kleiner* (small) or *grosser* (large) *Brauner* is coffee with milk, and café latte is espresso with lots of steamed milk. Other choices are:

- *Melange*, coffee mixed with steamed milk
- *Kapuziner* or cappuccino, served with whipped cream

- *Einspänner*, black coffee topped with a heaping serving of whipped cream and served in a tall glass
- *Fiaker*, black coffee with rum or brandy served in a glass
- *Kaffee Johann Strauss*, a large black coffee served with whipped cream and apricot liqueur
- *Wiener Eiskaffee*, cold coffee poured over vanilla ice cream topped with whipped cream
- *Türkischer*, very strong Turkish coffee

Coffee is always served on a silver tray with a glass of water.

You can enjoy a coffeehouse even if you don't drink coffee. If you want a cup of tea, ask for *ein schwarzen Tee* and specify if you want it with milk or lemon. You could also try *Früchtetee* (fruit tea) or *Grüner Tee* (green tea). There is also a wide array of herbal teas such as *Fenchel* (fennel), *Kamille* (camomile) and *Pfefferminz* (peppermint). For those with a sweet tooth, hot chocolate is always a good choice.

Austrian Wines

Unlike many of their neighbours, Austrians drink a substantial amount of wine. Wine cultivation and drinking have their roots in the Celtic and Roman periods. Sixty per cent of all wines are cultivated in Lower Austria, in the Wachau valley and the Weinviertel. The Wachau is a scenic valley of terraced vineyards climbing up the hills, alongside the Danube River between Krems and Melk. The Weinviertel (wine quarter), located in the northern part of Lower Austria, is the largest wine-growing region in Austria. Much of the famous *Grüner Veltliner* is produced here. One of the most popular white wines, it has won awards for the best wine grown in Vienna. The province of Burgenland, known primarily for its red wines, produces 32 per cent of all wine. Styria contributes 7 per cent, and the remaining 1 per cent is grown on the hills surrounding Vienna.

Head into Lower Austria, Burgenland or Styria if you enjoy wine tasting. You can then buy your favourite right on the spot. Most Austrian wine is consumed locally, with only about 20 per cent exported. Overall, when compared with wines from other countries, the quality of Austrian wine ranges from average to very good. Most of the vintages are best when they are young, and this is the reason behind the *Heurigen*.

Heurigen

For centuries, local wine producers have served wine to their customers right where the grapes are grown. A pine branch hung on a pole outside a house in the wine villages surrounding Vienna informed passers-by that the year's wine was available. Emperor Josef II legalised the practice in 1784. Originally, these locales were only allowed to sell what had been produced on their own land, so people brought along picnics to enjoy with the wine. This continues today at certain out-of-the-way *Heurigen*. The word *Heurige*, which refers to a place where you can buy and drink new wine, comes from the Austrian term for 'the current year', or *heuer*. Thus, *Heurige* also means 'this year's wine'. The wine becomes 'old' after Saint Martin's Day on 11 November and can no longer be called *Heurige*.

A refreshing way to enjoy the wine, which may seem odd at first, is to drink it *gespritzt*: carbonated mineral water is ordered separately and mixed with the wine.

In the autumn, shortly after the grape harvest, *Most* and *Sturm* are available at *Heurigen* and jugs are sold to take home. *Most* is semi-fermented grape juice with a very low alcohol content, and *Sturm* (or storm) is fermented grape juice that is not yet wine. *Sturm* may not appear to be strong at first, but drink it in moderation because it can hit you without warning. For those who do not drink wine, non-alcoholic beverages are limited in certain *Heurigen*. True to their original purpose, some *Heurigen* serve only grape juice. Others, however, also offer apple juice, lemonade and *Almdudler*.

Many people visit the *Heurige* just to have a glass or two of wine, but if you don't sample the food, you'll be missing a real part of Austria. While wine and other drinks are ordered from the waiter, you must head to the food counter if you want to eat. Certain cuts of meat, like *Wiener Schnitzel*, are not on display and must be ordered. Unlike the drinks, which are paid for at the end of the evening, you must pay immediately at the food counter. Meat is priced according to weight.

The dishes available vary with each *Heurige*, but can include cooked meats, sandwich meats, cheeses, salads and breads. Some favourites are *Kümmelbraten*, a delicious if somewhat fatty pork roast with caraway seeds. *Schweinsbraten* (roast pork), *Schinken* (ham) and *Laibchen* (meatballs) are also good. A *Knödel* (dumpling) and sauerkraut can accompany these. There are several varieties of *Auflauf* (soufflé), and a whole array of tasty salads, including *Kartoffel* or *Erdäpfelsalat* (potato salad), *Schwarzwurzelsalat* (an excellent salad made with a vegetable similar to asparagus, in a dill cream sauce), *Fisolensalat* (green bean salad), *rote Rübensalat* (beet salad) and *Krautsalat* (cabbage salad). There are several types of bread and rolls available and you may choose to top them off with *Liptauer*, a cream cheese, paprika and chive spread. If you would like *Senf* (mustard), for which there is an extra charge, specify *süss* (sweet) or *scharf* (strong). Most *Heurigen* do not serve desserts, and others only *Strudel*. Not all *Heurigen* serve coffee or tea either.

The Joys of a Heurigen

You really must visit a *Heurige* if you are in Vienna or are passing through a little wine village. Although the wine is the main reason to visit, non-drinkers can enjoy the scenery, atmosphere and food. Most *Heurigen* have beautiful gardens where you can sit for hours and enjoy the warm summer weather. In winter, the festivities move in to warm and cozy surroundings. Several *Heurigen* have lovely views of the nearby vineyards. The atmosphere is relaxed and it is a good place for children. In fact, a few *Heurigen* have play areas in the gardens. Often, traditional Viennese songs sung to the accompaniment of an accordion and violins make the *Heurige* experience complete.

Most guidebooks will direct you to Grinzing and Sievering in Vienna for your *Heurige* experience. This area, however, is flooded with tourists. If you want a more authentic experience, or just a more peaceful one, head to Neustift am Walde, Hietzing or Nussdorf. (You can take a 40-minute tour of the vineyards north of Vienna on a quaint railway that begins and ends in Nussdorf.) *Stadtheurigen* (city *Heurigen*) can be found throughout the 1st district. If you are really interested in partaking in Austrian culture, go into

Perchtoldsdorf, south of Vienna, or Stammersdorf, north of the city in the 21st district. Outside of Vienna, there are wonderful *Heurigen* in the Wachau valley, Weinviertel, Styria and other wine-producing areas.

Other Alcoholic Beverages

Salzburg is famous for its Stiegl brewery and beer. Another popular beer is *Gösser*. However, it is not ranked among the best in the region. If you are a beer drinker, you might prefer the excellent *Budweiser* (the original Budweiser beer, not to be confused with the beer made by Anheuser-Busch in the United States), or *Pilsen* from the nearby Czech Republic. If you do want to try the local beer, be sure to specify if you want it *vom Fass* (draught) or in *eine Flasche* (in a bottle). When ordering beer *vom Fass*, you will be asked to decide between *ein kleines* (small) and *ein grosses* (large).

> **Toasting**
> A toast is commonly made before the first drink. Most toasts are simple—a few nice words to honour a friend, family member or special guest, or to celebrate a certain holiday. When the toast has been made, glasses are lifted and everyone clinks everyone else's glass, looking the person directly in the eye and saying '*Prost*'.

Austrians do drink hard liquor, and *Schnaps* is by far their favourite. *Schnaps* is incredibly strong liquor made from just about anything from fruits to herbs. The most popular are made from apples, plums, pears and apricots. *Schnaps* are normally served after a hearty meal and should not be sipped but downed quickly.

SUPERMARKETS

There is no shortage of supermarkets. Traditionally, Austrians purchase groceries in small quantities daily, so every neighbourhood has at least one small store. This turns out to be very convenient because the opening hours are limited. Supermarkets close between 6:00 pm and 7:30 pm on weekdays, and at 5:00 pm on Saturdays. They are closed on Sundays. Exceptions are made for stores located in transportation centres. Technically, they are only allowed to sell food to be eaten on the road, so you may find certain sections closed off. The Billa at Bahnhof Wien Nord is open on Saturdays from 7:00 am till 7:30 pm, and on Sundays from 8:00 am until 7:30 pm. The Billa at the airport is open daily from 7:30 am until 10:00 pm. If you are in a hurry, you can find staple goods in the convenience stores of some large gas stations. (See Chapter Five for a detailed explanation of shopping habits.)

Grocery stores in Austria, and especially in Vienna, usually carry a wide range of products. If you are looking for something particular, there are a few specialty stores in Vienna. Bobby's near the Naschmarkt has a good selection of products from Britain. Nearby are stores that carry Italian foods and Asian goods, like Piccini and the Asia Shop respectively. Europa Delikatessen, Neli Malkov and Rebenwurzel & Co. in the 2nd district sell kosher products.

NASCHMARKT

In Vienna, you can buy fresh produce at the Naschmarkt in the 6th district. This is a huge outdoor market made up of many different stalls selling an incredible variety of items. The produce here is usually cheaper and fresher, although Susan once returned home with a bagful of rotten tomatoes from an unscrupulous vendor. Generally, you place your order by weight or pieces, and the vendors select and bag the items. If you prefer to pick out your own produce, demand that you be able to do so. As with supermarkets, you should bring a heavy canvas bag to carry everything home in.

The Origins of Naschmarkt

The Naschmarkt is not merely a grocery market. Many stalls sell prepared snacks and sandwiches. In fact, this is one version of how the market got its name. The word *naschen* means to nibble, and it is said that the name evolved into Naschmarkt because everyone walks around nibbling on something. Another story is that the name is derived from shouts of '*An aschen*' or '*Eine Asche*', meaning 'ashes', which were sold in the market as detergent. Yet another version states that in very old German, the word *Asch* used to mean 'milk pail', and the name comes from the fresh milk sold at the market.

In addition to the usual fruit, vegetables, fresh meat and seafood, the Naschmarkt is the place to go for special items such as sweet potatoes, tropical fruit, exotic spices, cheeses, nuts, olives and *halal* meat (ritually cut and blessed by an Islamic cleric). Other stalls sell flowers and clothing.

There are additional indoor markets on the Landstrasser Hauptstrasse near the Wien Mitte train station in the 3rd district, at the Sonnbergplatz in the 19th district, at the Nussdorfer Halle in the 9th district and at the Karmelitermarkt in the 2nd district. A free shuttle bus runs between Rotenturmstrasse in the city centre and the latter.

HOLIDAY MEALS
Fasching and Lent
Fasching begins on 11 November and continues until Ash Wednesday. Fasching is a time to eat, drink and be merry before Lent arrives on Ash Wednesday. It is a festive season when deep-fried pastries and *Krapfen* (donuts filled with apricot jam or vanilla cream) are especially common.

For Roman Catholics, Lent is a time of sacrifice and fasting as they prepare for Easter. In fact, the German word for Lent is *Fastenzeit*, or 'a time of fasting'. Ash Wednesday begins the Lenten season when Catholics are not allowed to eat meat. In keeping with the rules, but somewhat contrary to the spirit of the order, many Austrians begin Lent by enjoying *Heringsschmaus*, a huge herring feast.

Easter
The days preceding Easter Sunday have religious significance. On Gründonnerstag, Maundy Thursday, some people eat spinach and green coloured eggs. *Grün* stems from an old German word for 'weeping', but also means green, hence the green food. On Good Friday, a holy day, many people fast. On Easter, a day of celebration, Austrians indulge in food and sweets.

Coloured hardboiled eggs representing life and fertility are identified with Easter, but their use predates Easter to pagan festivals honouring spring. *Osterstriezel* (braided white bread) and *Pinze* (sweet white bread) are also eaten at breakfast. Most Austrians feast on an Easter dinner of ham, *Schinken im Brotteig* (ham baked in dough) or turkey. Cakes, chocolates and marzipan are shaped into bunnies, lambs, chicks and eggs.

Spargelzeit

You know spring has arrived when *Spargel* (asparagus) makes its appearance. During asparagus season, the delicate vegetable is featured in special dishes on many menus, and is promoted by every supermarket. It comes in both the white and green varieties.

Pilzwochen

Just as asparagus signals the arrival of spring, *Pilzwochen* lets us know that autumn is here. During 'mushroom weeks', restaurants serve special dishes containing several varieties of fresh mushrooms. You will also see a wide variety on sale.

Martinigansl

Saint Martin's Day, 11 November, is celebrated with a heavy but delicious meal of *Martinigansl* or Saint Martin's Goose. To many Austrians, Saint Martin is an important saint. Born

Fresh green and white asparagus appear in various dishes during Spargelzeit.

in the 4th century, he was a humble man who became a monk. According to legend, when he found out that he was to be named bishop, he hid to avoid taking the position. A honking goose gave him away, and now the bird is sacrificed in honour of Saint Martin.

The goose is served with red cabbage (which helps with digestion), dumplings and a hearty red wine or a full-bodied beer. If you are invited to someone's house at this time, expect *Martinigansl* to be served. This special meal is also available in many restaurants.

Game

Austrians have always enjoyed hunting, as evidenced by the decor of many eating establishments. During hunting season in autumn, wild game is often found on menus. You can choose from *Hirsch* (venison), *Ente* (duck), *Fasan* (pheasant), *Hase* (hare), *Kaninchen* (rabbit) and *Wildschwein* or *Eber* (wild boar). If you would like to prepare some at home, wild game can be bought at stands in the Naschmarkt and the Landstrasser Markt.

Christmas

Traditionally, Austrians eat carp on Christmas Eve. These fish can live to a ripe old age, and it was once believed that if you ate carp, you could also live a long life. Some Austrians have broken away from this tradition and prefer to eat goose, chicken or turkey for Christmas.

Like Easter, most of the special treats served at Christmas are sweet. *Stollen* (sweet bread) and *Kletzenbrot* (Christmas fruit bread) proliferate. There are several varieties of Christmas cookies. Some of the better-known are *Husarenkrapferl* (Husar Rounds), cookies flavoured with almonds and a dab of apricot jam in the centre; *Vanillekipferl* (vanilla crescents); *Kokosbusserl* (coconut kisses); *Zimtsterne* (cinnamon stars); and *Ischler Nussbusserln* (nut kisses). *Lebkuchen*, spice cookies flavoured with cinnamon, cloves and honey, are also a favourite. These cookies date back to the Middle Ages when sugar was difficult to come by. The *Christkindl* markets are also full of tempting sweets such as *Negerküsse* (chocolate-dipped marshmallow confections), red candy apples and cotton candy.

Blattlstock, from Tyrol, is a cake with layers of filling made out of stewed pears, ground poppy seeds, sugar, lemon peel, cinnamon and cloves. Also called *Stephansstock*, a piece of this cake is eaten at the end of every meal starting on Saint Stephen's Day on 26 December. As children eat a bit of the cake on 1 January, they make a wish for the coming year.

New Year's Eve/Silvester

As in many other countries, the New Year is rung in with *Sekt* (sparkling wine). Because many people celebrate midnight outside in freezing temperatures, *Glühwein*, a hot spiced wine sold at outdoor markets throughout the winter season, and *Punsch* are very popular. Little marzipan pigs, mushrooms, clovers and chimneysweeps are given to friends and family as good luck charms for the coming year; they also decorate pastries and cakes. Superstition has it that lobster and crayfish are not to be eaten, because they walk backwards, making them counter to the New Year spirit of looking to the future.

ENJOYING THE CULTURE

CHAPTER 7

'To each Age its Art, to Art its Freedom.'
—Motto of the Secessionists

A FRIEND OF JULIE'S was coming to live in Vienna. A key item on his 'to do list' was to learn to play the piano. "Why piano?" she asked. "It only makes sense to learn to play an instrument and play beautiful classical music in the city that made it so famous," he replied.

Austria is known the world over for its music, opera and composers such as Mozart, Haydn, Beethoven, Schubert, Strauss, Mahler, Bruckner and Schoenberg. The architecture, fine arts and applied arts are also well known and much admired. The country's accomplishments in the arts are attributed to Austria's history under Habsburg rule. The Habsburgs developed into a dynamic and effervescent force throughout Europe that directly influenced the social, political and artistic development of their empire.

Consequently, new and different artistic styles were created: Baroque with its exuberant forms, Biedermeier with its cozy snugness, Historicism with its cornucopia of artistic influences from centuries gone by, and Jugendstil with its sinuous ornamentation.

HISTORY OF LITERATURE AND DRAMA
Austria's literary history extends back to the 12th century, going by a collection of poetry found in an abbey in Styria. Courtly poetry also surfaced in the 12th and 13th centuries. Emperor Maximilian I (1459–1519) was himself a poet who supported theatre and dramatic arts. Operas,

which often involved the whole court, gave rise to popular religious drama. During the Baroque period, Austria became the centre of dramatic art, and its influence is still felt in today's theatres.

BAROQUE ERA (1685–1780)

Buildings on a grand scale, sumptuously decorated palaces, marbled and gilded churches and monumental curvaceous statues are all depictions of the 17th and 18th century Baroque art style. The three Baroque monarchs—Karl VI, his daughter Maria Theresa and her son Josef II—each played

When walking through the streets of the major cities, be sure to look up so as not to miss the beautiful details, such as this caryatid.

a part in forming the era. The monarchy held absolute power, Catholicism reigned supreme after the defeat of Protestantism, the threat of a Turkish invasion was gone, and the wealth of the empire shone through in all forms of art at that time.

Architecture

Without a doubt, the Baroque era left its most profound mark on architecture. Artists knew of the wealth of the empire, and its frenzy to build was a means to showcase the strength of the Church and State. They came from far and wide to exhibit their talents. The most famous architect was Johann Bernhard Fischer von Erlach. Some say he was the true inventor of Austrian Baroque, adapting it from the Italian style, which others before him had merely copied. In Vienna, he designed the Karlskirche (Saint Charles Church), National Library, State Chancellery, Royal Stables and palaces for the nobility. He died in 1723 and his son Joseph Emmanuel completed many of his projects.

Johann Lukas von Hildebrand designed the Belvedere and the winter palace for Prince Eugene of Savoy, palaces for the nobility, and the Federal Chancellery, Peterskirche (Saint Peter's Church) and the Piaristenkirche (Piaristen Church) for the court. He also designed the Mirabell Palace in Salzburg. Joseph Prandtauer can also be grouped with these two architects, but because he spent most of his time working on the glorious Abbey at Melk, he was not as prolific.

Baroque architecture can be found across the country. Salzburg boasts many Baroque buildings, such as the 17th century cathedral and the Altes Residenz. One of the architectural gems of Innsbruck is the Heblinghaus, a 15th century house that was redone in the rococo style. Maximilian's palace was also transformed in the 18th century when it became the Hofburg.

Sadly, many Gothic churches and monasteries were redone in the Baroque style. The Minoriten Church in Vienna suffered this fate, but thankfully was returned to its original Gothic style in 1784. Maria am Gestade, also in Vienna, is one of the few beautiful Gothic churches in Austria which escaped

Johann Fischer von Erlach, the most distinguished Baroque architect, designed many parts of the Hofburg, like the Michaelertor and several smaller palaces in Vienna.

the renovations. Of course, the best-known Gothic building is Stephansdom, Vienna's magnificent cathedral.

When Maria Theresa married Franz Stephan from Lorraine, a number of advisors followed him back from France. Thus, the city was slightly influenced by the French style, especially in its architecture. The best example of this style is the imperial summer residence, Schönbrunn Palace, commissioned by Maria Theresa.

Paintings from the Baroque Era

The effervescent frescoes of Johann Michael Rottmayr are found at the monastery in Melk, and again at Karlskirche and Peterskirche, in Vienna. Daniel Gran's ceiling frescoes at the Annakirche and the Prunksall at the National Library are magnificent in their colour and detail.

Music
Haydn, Franz Joseph (1732–1809)

Haydn is known the world over for laying the foundation of the classical style. After leaving his home in Rohrau, Burgenland, he started his career in Vienna as a choirboy at Saint Stephen's Cathedral. Besides spending 29 years of his life working for the Esterházy royal family in Eisenstadt, Burgenland, he was known throughout Europe and even in North America. London, especially, loved him. He wrote to a friend after arriving in London, 'My arrival caused a great sensation throughout the whole city and I was mentioned in all the newspapers for three successive weeks.'

Haydn was a slow worker but a consummate artist, who worked tirelessly in many different realms of musical composition. He was often affectionately called 'Papa Haydn', as he was a fair conductor compared to his dictatorial contemporaries. His masses included the *Missa in honourem Beata Maria Virgine*, *Nelson Mass* and *Maria Theresa*, and his most famous oratorios were *The Seasons* and *The Creation*. He loved opera and composed and directed about 20 of them, generally Italian comedies and classical tragedies, among them *Lo Speziale*, *Il Mondo della Luna*, *La Vera Constanza* and *Armida*. Haydn lost interest in composing operas after recognising Mozart's superiority in this field. Of his 100 symphonies, the most popular are *La Passione*, *Trauer*, *Farewell*, *Toy Symphony*, *The Surprise* and the *Paris Symphonies*. He also wrote numerous concertos, marionette operas, string quartets, piano trios, keyboard sonatas, songs and 377 arrangements of Scottish and Welsh airs.

The Great Composers

Haydn knew both Mozart and Beethoven well. He loved Mozart like a son and commented after the production of *Don Giovanni*, "Mozart is the greatest composer the world possesses at this time." Of Beethoven he said, "(he) will eventually attain the position of one of the greatest composers in Europe, and I shall be proud to call myself his teacher." To Mozart, Haydn became a surrogate father, and to Beethoven, a mere teacher whom the latter would later criticise.

Mozart, Wolfgang Amadeus (1756–91)

Mozart played before Empress Maria Theresa as a child and before her son, Josef II, a few years later. The Viennese nobility soon courted him, and Emperor Josef II commissioned a dramatic musical or *Singspiel* entitled *The Abduction from the Seraglio* or *Il ratto dal seraglio*. The piece pleased both the king and his court, and Mozart went on to compose other operas.

After his first success, he wrote *The Marriage of Figaro* (1786), *Don Giovanni* (1787) and the *Magic Flute* (1791). These operas were more popular with the common man. Part of the reason that Mozart failed to win the court's approval was that he decided to work on his own as a freethinking, 'freelance' composer, instead of under the patronage of the court. This defiant and independent attitude caused him financial difficulties and the loss of his popularity among the aristocracy.

The sad truth is that Mozart was a musical genius unrecognised in his day. He was a mastermind as a composer and a keyboard virtuoso who wrote popular music with astounding alacrity and ease. His works often combined both Classical elements in their perfection of formal balance, and Romantic elements in the intensity of their expression. He also wrote chamber music, piano sonatas and church music, including the *Requiem*.

If Mozart ever reflected on his life, he must have thought it an incredible disappointment and fraught with hardship. Acclaimed a child prodigy at six, by 11, he had written three symphonies; but by his early 30s, he was widely condemned and mired in poverty and ruin. He was never able to afford an adequate living, and he and his wife, Constanze, were hopeless in administering financial and household affairs. He died lonely and exhausted, and was buried as a pauper in a mass grave at Saint Marx in Vienna's 3rd district. His bones were never recovered, but there is a memorial stone bearing his name. The rest of Europe has mourned his loss more than Vienna ever did at the time.

Beethoven, Ludwig van (1770–1827)

Beethoven impressed Mozart with his talent and later became a student of Haydn. From a young age, Beethoven was extremely arrogant, self-confident and aware of his own genius. Like Mozart, he lived off his compositions under the sponsorship of many aristocratic patrons. His music was brand new and popular. Although he lacked social graces and had a profound contempt for many of his fellow men, he was able to act professionally when necessary. The onset of his deafness redefined him, and his compositions became more spiritual. For all his social defects, J W Sullivan writes about Beethoven's spiritual development, 'he was a composer unique not only for his depth, importance, and number of his inner states but also the power to realise them and give them expression.' He was one of the first composers to be appreciated during his lifetime. Twenty thousand people, or about 10 per cent of Vienna's population at that time, attended his funeral. It was a lavish *Schöne Leich'* (pageant): eight singers of the Court Opera carried his coffin, famous musicians were pallbearers, and Franz Grillparzer, Schubert, Czerny and other well-known figures held torches.

Beethoven was responsible for the opera *Fidelio*; 32 piano sonatas including the *Apassionata*; 16 string quartets; the *Mass in D* or *Missa Solemnis*; a violin concerto and a piano concerto; and nine symphonies, of which the *Eroica* (Third), *Victory* (Fifth), *Pastoral* (Sixth) and the *Choral* (Ninth) are best known.

BIEDERMEIER ERA (1780–1848)

The large, ostentatious buildings of the Baroque period gave way to the simple, smaller, purposeful buildings of the Biedermeier era. *Bieder* translates to 'respectable', and *Meier* was a common surname that symbolised the perfect citizen. At this time, democratic sentiments were on the rise after the American and French revolutions, but the economic situation was bleak as the state finances were being drained by the Austrian military's unsuccessful campaigns. State Chancellor Metternich created a secret police, began a policy of censorship and caused the loss of many civil rights.

People withdrew to their private interests. At home, it was commonplace for music to be performed, literature to be read and games to be played in private salons among friends and family. Musical evenings known as *Schubertiades*, where Schubert's *Lieder* (songs) were played, were popular. Theatres, concert halls and other venues were becoming more accessible to the middle class. The salons were decorated in a pleasant yet simple style. There were fine paintings decorating the walls, comfortable lightwood furniture to lounge on, charming clocks on the mantelpiece and delicate china and silverware adorning the dinner table. Biedermeier decor is still popular in many homes today.

Painting

Paintings of the Biedermeier period reflected the need to capture a realistic image of nature. Known as Austrian Realism, the style focused on forests, lakes, mountains and idyllic rural landscapes. The movement was toward the impressionistic idea of capturing a single moment in time. Ferdinand Georg Waldmüller, Friedrich Gauermann, Friedrich von Amerling, Rudolf von Alt, Moritz von Schwind and Peter Fendi all contributed to finding this realism in art.

Music
Franz Seraph Peter Schubert (1797–1828)

Schubert was thought to be the epitome of a Biedermeier artist. Although he never attained the recognition of virtuoso performers like Mozart and Beethoven, his music was lyrical

Baden, south of Vienna, is the centre of Biedermeier style: simple, two-story buildings marked by straight lines.

and melodic, and his 600 *Lieder* were in the spirit of early Romantic poetry. For one who died so young, he composed numerous symphonies, masses, quartets and sonatas.

Johann Strauss the Elder (1804–49)

Also popular during this time was Johann Strauss the Elder, who sought a different, livelier music than Schubert's. He started and conducted his own orchestra. With its rhythmic and tuneful melodies, his music appealed to people of all social classes. Along with Josef Lanner, an associate and rival, he popularised the three-quarter-time waltz. His most famous tune is the *Radetsky March*, which is always played on New Year's Eve at the Musikverein (concert hall of the Society of the Friends of Music).

Playwrights and Poets

The playwright Johann Nestroy (1801–62), who wrote *Freedom in Krähwinkel*, is famous for shattering the Biedermeier idyll with unforgiving skepticism. In his 80 farces and parodies of dramatic works, he became the king of psychological insights, and a mirror for society in his portrayal of his fellow citizens.

His best-known dramatic devices were language twists, name invention and Viennese dialect.

Ferdinand Raimund (1790–1836), author of *The King of the Alps and the Misanthrope*, is also representative of the golden age of the Viennese popular comedy and Viennese dialect theatre.

Franz Grillparzer (1791–1872) was Austria's foremost poet and dramatist. His work, described as being ahead of its time, is a mixture of Austrian and Spanish Baroque drama and artistic devices borrowed from Vienna's popular theatre traditions and from classical drama.

HISTORICISM (1848–1897)

Great social change followed the oppressive police state of Chancellor Metternich. Its culmination was the popular revolution of 1848, which demanded reforms guaranteeing free speech, free press and free universities. Emperor Franz Josef took over the empire at the tender age of 18. In a few short years, Austria had suffered debilitating war defeats, lost much of its empire and had major domestic worries. The country was ready for change and renaissance.

Building the Ringstrasse

Among Franz Josef's missions was to beautify his residence at the Hofburg, create a connection linking the outer districts with the inner city and enlarge the city centre. He ordered the removal of the medieval wall, which consisted of gates and fortifications around what is now the 1st district, and in its stead built a street, the Ringstrasse. Unparalleled in grandeur, the Ringstrasse was lined on both sides with beautiful palaces for the aristocracy, government buildings, parks, museums and theatres. Renowned architects came from all over Europe to compete for the honour to build on the Ringstrasse.

Architecture

Architecturally, Historicism was a mixture of past styles: Ancient Greek and Roman, Romanticism, Gothic, Renaissance and Baroque. The buildings on the Ringstrasse reflect the diversity of Historicism. The Staatsoper (State Opera

House) was the first building to go up, designed by August von Siccardsburg and Eduard van der Nüll in 1861–69 in the French Renaissance style. The Rathaus (City Hall) was designed by Friedrich Schmidt in a Flemish Gothic style in 1872–83. Carl Hasenauer designed the Kunsthistorisches (Art History) Museum and the Naturhistorisches (Natural History) Museum with Italian Renaissance style features in 1866. (Gottfried Semper later redesigned the facades.) Heinrich Ferstel redesigned the Universität (University) in the Italian Renaissance style in 1873–83. The Burgtheater (National Theatre) was designed by Semper (exterior) and Hasenauer (interior) in the Italian Renaissance style in 1874–88. The Parlament (Parliament) was designed by Theophil Hansen, a Dane from Athens, who chose the Hellenic style for the home of the imperial council and to honour the birthplace of democracy. Hansen also designed the Börse (Stock Exchange) in the Italian Renaissance style in 1874–77.

Music
Johann Strauss, Jr (1825-99)

Johann Strauss junior is known the world over for his engaging waltzes, polkas and operettas. He took over his father's orchestra after his death and travelled far and wide with it. His life, however, was unlike his music. He married three times and had a rather dark and driven demeanor.

His most memorable waltzes are *The Blue Danube* and *Tales of the Vienna Woods*. He also composed operettas such as *die Fledermaus* (The Bat) and *The Gypsy Baron*. When Julie took a tour around Vienna, the guide called Strauss one of the first modern pop stars. He inspired the masses to forget their troubles, be happy and dance!

Johannes Brahms (1833–97)

Brahms brought new life to the art song. He followed the classical approach like Mozart and Beethoven, concentrating on absolute music as opposed to composing programme music or opera. Although considered a traditionalist, Brahms is said to have invented the use of variations, from classical to modern compositions, in his music.

Anton Bruckner (1824–96)

Bruckner had served as an organist at the cathedral in Linz, and came to Vienna at the age of 44. Bruckner's main goal in life was to write for God. In fact, many people referred to him as 'God's musician'. He spent much time revising his powerful symphonies and masses, which encompassed great blocks of sound. He was best known, however, for his improvisation abilities on the organ. Mahler was a great fan of his and would often conduct his work.

Gustav Mahler (1860–1911)

In his music, Mahler captured the stormy changes within society and the monarchy toward the end of the 19th century. He was interested in a new path for modern music and experimented in polyphony—the immense use of sound—and employed a wide variety of percussion instruments. As a conductor, he brought discipline to the singers, musicians and audiences. He also improved the position of the orchestra pit so that the musicians' lights would not bother the audience. After ten years at the Vienna Opera House, he left for the United States, tired of gossip about rivals wanting to get him out because of their anti-Semitism or their opposition to his modernism. His talents were well received in New York City where he became the New York Philharmonic's conductor until he died.

> Mahler composed nine symphonies in the Romantic style, including the *Resurrection Symphony* and *Symphony of a Thousand.*

JUGENDSTIL AND THE SECESSION (1897–1918)

Jugendstil is a variation on art nouveau. The name is derived from the periodical *Jugend*, which debuted in Munich in 1896. It was a flattened, stylised form of the abstract where designs were exuberant and jubilant, with decoration and ornamentation outlining the figures. The smallest element of graphic detail was as important as the ground plan to establish a flow and movement to the whole piece.

Secession

Secession, or *Secessionstil*, and Secessionism are often erroneously associated with Jugendstil. Secession was not an art form, but the ideology or school of thought behind Jugendstil. Members of the Secession had belonged to the old school *Künstlerhaus*. Wanting to establish a modern approach to exhibitions, with less focus on commercialisation and more attention on a purified view of art, they drew the term Secession from the Roman *Secessio plebis*, whereby the plebs withdrew from the patricians due to the latter's misrule.

The men who first joined to form the Secession were Otto Wagner, Gustav Klimt, Josef Maria Olbrich, Kolo Moser, Carl Moll and Rudolf von Alt. They had a museum built, designed by Olbrich, and called it the Secession. Its golden laurel dome became known as the 'cabbagehead'. Inside the museum sat a statue of Beethoven, a symbol of misunderstood artists. During that time, they also published a magazine, *Ver Sacrum*, which publicised Jugendstil art and provided a mouthpiece for their artistic and political demands.

Architecture
Otto Wagner (1841–1918)

Wagner was one of the foremost leaders of the Secession, but he also became known as the father of modern Viennese architecture and the educator of an entire generation. Wagner believed that new styles in art and architecture usually followed great social change. However, the social changes of the end of the 19th century happened so fast that the development of art could hardly match them. Instead, artists were copying styles of days gone by in a movement called Historicism. He condemned the style and pushed instead for something that fit modern man's need, something utilitarian. In his book *Moderne Architektur*, he says, 'Modern forms must correspond to new materials, contemporary needs, if they are to be found suitable for mankind today. They must embody our own development, our democracy, our self-confidence, our idealism. They must take into account the colossal technical and scientific advances of our age, as well as the practical requirements of society.'

Wagner worked assiduously to achieve his goal. He ended up designing the entire railway system (all 36 stations), which connected the inner city to the suburbs. He was also responsible for major city and traffic planning, especially the regulation of the Danube Canal and the Wien River. He designed the Postal Savings Bank, where space was used economically for 2,000 workers. The Steinhof, or the Golden City on the hill, is a church that Wagner designed with function in mind as it was to be used for the mentally handicapped. The Majolica House, its exterior decorated with coloured ceramic, faces the Naschmarkt; it was built to fulfill sanitary requirements, with materials that made it easy to maintain.

Adolf Loos (1870–1933)

Loos also wanted to modernise the Viennese. He preferred clear-cut lines to ornamentation. Defending the aesthetic principle that usefulness is elegance and ornamentation is a form of ostentation, he paid more attention to the interior of buildings. He believed that designs should only reflect the feel of a place: a bar should be comfortable, a prison should show strength, and a bank should have the look of safety. His buildings were space-saving, economical, useful and had a comfortable style. His thrift influenced him to use sunlight to illuminate interiors. Many of the apartments he designed offer highly original solutions to severe spatial problems, using materials thoughtfully and with as little expense as possible. The stores he designed used brass, linoleum, marble and glass to form interiors that have been described as having 'geometric elegance and clinical precision'. His most famous works in Vienna are the American Bar, Cafe Museum and the House on Michaelerplatz (now a bank).

Painting
Gustav Klimt (1862–1918)

Klimt was revered by his Secessionist friends as one of the best painters of his time. He was so popular that he was elected the president of the Secession. Like many of his contemporaries, he initially painted in the Historicist style. His greatest desire was to be part of the great building frenzy on the Ringstrasse. He worked on ceiling paintings at the Burgtheater (National Theatre) and was also commissioned to decorate the Kunsthistorisches (Art History) Museum. Soon thereafter, changes in his style occurred and are best viewed in his painting *Schubert am Klavier*. Here he departs from the naturalist rendering of space and light, into more muted, impressionistic characters. Even then, Klimt's style did not yet portray the inner turmoil he was feeling. Through the use of the female figure, he was able to portray the future and femininity, which was his answer to the tension between patriarchal culture and chaos.

Der Küss

In *Der Küss* (The Kiss), Klimt's most famous work, he used the same decorative elements of geometric shapes and flowers on gold background as in his *Beethovenfrieze*. He avoids any sense of depth, putting the emphasis on ornamental structure and rendering the body abstractly. The meaning, therefore, is seen in form and material rather than content. *Der Küss* is the model for the Jugendstil philosophy; the lovers are shown as 'universal, cosmogonal and in tune with nature'.

Egon Schiele (1890–1918)

Schiele's work was initially influenced by Klimt and Jugendstil. He paid Klimt an unconcealed homage in both the *Watersprites* and *Zug der Toten* (*Procession of the Dead*). The themes that chiefly concerned him were love, life and death. Schiele was often accused of drawing pornography, and in fact did live at one time off his more explicit drawings. He also went to jail for 24 days for supposedly seducing a minor. Like Klimt, he used nudity as a source of inspiration. Unlike Klimt, his nudes, and people in general, expressed ugliness, misery and pain. Toward the end of his life, he married and his work changed. Gone were the emaciated nudes; in their stead, feelings of belonging and security were expressed, as in the painting *The Family*.

Oskar Kokoschka (1886–1980)

Kokoschka's talent was obvious to his teachers from the beginning. As a student, his work was so admired that he ran some of the preparatory classes in his school. His artistic life thereafter was cause for much verbal abuse by his critics, although his work was much appreciated by artists such as Loos, who became one of his dearest friends and supporters.

Kokoschka's paintings today rank among the masterpieces of early Expressionist painting. He pushed for a constant search for inner meaning and, like Freud, for the important role which nightmare, dream and fantasy played in one's life. He was always probing the inner essence of the personalities he drew.

Man of Many Talents

Apart from painting, Kokoschka was a talented writer. He wrote a children's poetic fairytale, *Die Träumenden Knaben* (*The Dreaming Boys*), illustrating it with beautiful colour lithographs. He was also deeply interested in every aspect of book production and lectured on the subject. His literary achievements included *Sphinx und Stromann* and *Mörder Hoffnung*, two dramas in the Expressionist style.

Applied Arts
Josef Hoffman (1870–1956)

Hoffman was a gifted architect and designer who believed in the simplification of forms. He is known throughout Vienna for designing both the interior and exterior of numerous buildings. Along with Moser, he headed the Wiener Werkstätte (Vienna Workshop).

Koloman Moser (1868–1918)

Moser was the most universal artist of his time. He worked with all kinds of materials in many different mediums: painting, graphics, commercial and industrial design, glass painting, furniture and state and costume design. Moser is responsible for the transition in Jugendstil art from the use of flowers to geometric forms as decorative elements.

Wiener Werkstätte (1903)

The aim of the Wiener Werkstätte (WW) was to have contemporary art for contemporary society, and its slogan was 'quality before quantity'.

Designers Josef Hoffman, Koloman Moser and a wealthy young businessman, Fritz Wärndorfer, led the workshop. Their aim was to design exclusively by hand without the use of machinery, out of pure materials such as ceramic, glass, leather, enamel and metal. The Biedermeier era motivated them, as its focus was on the home; therefore it was a means to manufacture products for domestic purposes with style and function. Their inspiration, however, came from Scottish designers Charles Rennie Mackintosh and his wife Margaret MacDonald.

The main aims of the group were to establish contact between the public, designers and craftsmen to create simple and elegant articles for household use and objects with a purpose and need; to gain recognition for the value of work or ideas; and to unify art, architecture and design. However, the high cost of WW designs placed them out of reach of all but the wealthiest patrons.

Music

Arnold Schoenberg (1874–1951), Alban Berg (1885–1935) and Anton von Webern (1883–1945) represented the Wiener Schule (Vienna School). They made use of atonality and invented the 12-tone technique. Schoenberg's compositions reflected the mystery of stillness and the curiosity of the subject in his own instinctual being.

The music of the Wiener Schule has been described as an 'emancipation of dissonance' that destroys harmonic order and cadence and allows for clusters of tones and enlarged rhythms and themes. Different and new, the music was shocking to the Viennese, such that at a performance of it at the Musikverein, fighting erupted on the floor.

Literature

The Secession also opened doors for new expression in literature. Arthur Schnitzler (1862–1931) was one of the most popular and frequently performed playwrights in the German-speaking countries. His psychologically subtle works, such as *Liebelei* and *Anatol Cycle*, depict the angst and hedonism of an affluent sector of Viennese society. *Der Weg ins Freie* (*The Road to Freedom*) is a vivid portrayal of Viennese society and various Viennese Jews at the beginning of the 20th century. This book is ironic and prophetic; some of the best academicians were living in Vienna during the rise of anti-Semitism.

Hugo von Hofmannsthal (1874–1929) was a poet and a librettist. He was a good friend of Schnitzler's, who thought him a true genius. His librettos were mainly written for the composer Richard Strauss and include *Ariadne auf Naxos*, *Elektra* and, his most famous, *Der Rosenkavalier*, in which he glorified the Viennese Baroque. In his book *Brief des Lord Chandos*, he explores the duality of the relationship between the individual and the world and social and moral chaos. Hofmannsthal also wrote *Jedermann*, a revival of the medieval mystery play which is so popular that it is performed every year at the Salzburg Festival.

Stefan Zweig (1881–1942), like Schnitzler, was interested in the subconscious world and wrote *Die Welt von Gestern* (*Yesterday's World*), the evocation of a Europe that no longer existed. He also wrote the biographies of Marie Antoinette, Mary Stuart, Fouche and other historical figures.

Karl Kraus (1874–1936) provided more reflections of the times in the critical periodical *Die Fackel* (*The Torch*), which urged truth and simplicity. Later, he wrote about the period between the wars in the revealing play *Die Letzten Tage der Menschheit* (*The Last Days of Mankind*), whose style brought about many changes in theatre.

CONTEMPORARY ARTS
Music
Folk Music

Folk music has a long history, and its popularity is as strong as ever. One trip to a music store with its endless rows of folk CDs will prove it. If you want to truly immerse yourself in Austrian culture, folk music provides a great introduction. One of the best ways to familiarise yourself with the various musical groups is to watch one of the several folk music shows and contests televised throughout the country. Always in traditional dress, folk groups sing upbeat songs. Some groups have mixed these songs with elements of rock and blues. Favourites are Peter Alexander, Die Knödel, the Broadlahn, Hubert von Goisern und die Original Alpinkatzen and Attwenger.

Schrammelmusik

Heurigen, best known for their wine and hearty food, are the natural setting for *Schrammelmusik*—well-loved traditional Viennese songs accompanied by accordion, violin and many of the guests. The very first ensemble to play such music was formed by Johann and Josef Schrammel in the late 19th century. Many of these songs tend to deal with death and other life tragedies and are somewhat morbid.

Pop Music

Much of the contemporary music played on the radio is in English. Many international popular music acts include Vienna in their world tour schedules, and some big names also play in Salzburg, Innsbruck, Graz and Linz. In Vienna, many play at the Stadthalle, Kurhalle Oberlaa, Austria Centre and Libro Music Hall.

This does not suggest that Austria doesn't have its own pop music industry. Though small, it has produced internationally famous stars. Austrians are extremely proud of Falco, who had a Number 1 hit on the US charts in 1986 with 'Rock Me Amadeus'. He also scored hits with 'Der Kommissar' and 'Vienna Calling'. In 1998, at age 40, he was killed in a car accident while on vacation in the Dominican Republic. Yet he remains a part of the Austrian music scene with over a dozen CDs and videos to his name, and is honoured in musical tributes. There is even a cyber musical about him.

The ORF's (Austrian Broadcasting Corporation) Radio Café on Argentinierstrasse in Vienna has live performances that range from jazz and folk to literary readings. Because it is associated with FM4, which has many English-language on-air programmes, a significant number of performances are in English. Nonetheless, do check before going.

Udo Jürgens has also been a big name in German-language pop music for many years. Hansi Hinterseer is a pop singer whose first album went gold in Austria in just six months. Like other Austropop artists, he sings simple, romantic, cheerful songs. Other popular Austropop singers are Georg Danzer, Wolfgang Ambros, Rainhard Fendrich and Stefanie Werger.

Jazz

Jazz is a big favourite and Austrians such as Joe Zawinul, Karl Ratzer, Hans Koller and Friedrich Gulda have made significant contributions to the international jazz scene. It shouldn't be difficult to find jazz performances in your area. In Vienna, Jazzland in the 1st district is the best known club and Porgy and Bess is another popular club. Several other places alternate live jazz with other kinds of music. In May, the Konzerthaus presents the International Spring Jazz Music Festival, and in June and July, Jazzfest Wien is held in clubs and open-air venues, as well as at the Staatsoper and concert halls.

Street Performers

Kärntner Strasse and Graben, the two main pedestrian zones in Vienna's old city centre, are full of street performers. Anything goes, from breakdancing to comedy acts and mimes, from untalented singers to highly enjoyable quartets. There is an international flavour also, with Italian opera singers and South American folk groups joining the fray. Winter or summer, these performers are out there putting on an entertaining show for spare change.

Nightlife

The young and hip crowd prefer to spend their free nights hitting the clubs. In general, most bars and clubs are tucked away and may take a while to discover. In Vienna, one of the more obvious places is known as the Bermuda Triangle: it is in the 1st district, bordered by Rabensteig, Ruprechtsplatz and Seitenstettengasse, and is jam-packed with bars, clubs and people. Bäckerstrasse, north of Stephansplatz, is also lined with bars. In the summer, head to the Volksgarten near the Hofburg, where music (from techno to classical) is broadcast into the park. Many people also head out to the Donauinsel, the island in the middle of the Danube River. The shore is lined with restaurants and bars. If heavy smoking bothers you, these open-air events are good options. If you want to party in Salzburg, check out http://www.salzburg-night.at. In Innsbruck, discos and night clubs are listed on http://www. innsbruck-tourismus.com. For a listing of discos and clubs in Graz, including Irish and British bars, investigate http://www. vrgraz.at under local-guide.

Enjoying Classical Music Today

If you love classical music, you probably could not be in a better place. Even if you are not a great enthusiast, the quality of the performances staged in Austria might just turn you into one. Vienna and Salzburg are regarded as top musical cities, but cities like Linz and Innsbruck also have much to offer. We begin with Vienna.

Musikverein

The Musikverein, the concert hall where the Viennese Philharmonic Orchestra and other internationally renowned orchestras, conductors and soloists perform, is a pure delight. It was built in the late 1860s and is most famous for the annual New Year's Day concert, broadcast live around the world. If you can't attend that concert (you have to book more than a year in advance), you have hundreds of others to choose from. You must attend a concert in the lavishly decorated Grosser Saal (Main Hall). The acoustics are impeccable, which means that even the seats behind the orchestra are well worth the price. Depending upon the programme, tickets may be difficult to obtain. You might want to consider becoming a member or purchasing a subscription. For those of you on a tight budget, *Stehplätze* provide an opportunity to hear the greatest symphonies in the world for very little money.

Remember that Austrians dress up quite elegantly when they attend the theatre, opera or a concert. Even if you purchase a cheap ticket for a *Stehplatz*, you are expected to look nice. This means absolutely no sneakers or jeans.

These cheap tickets are sold shortly before the performance, but you should arrive early because a long line can form. Then you will be allowed entry into a standing room area at the back of the hall. Once the show begins and you become lost in the music, you won't even notice that you are standing as the hours slip by.

Dinner For You?

After enjoying a wonderful performance, there is no better way to end the evening than to enjoy a quick dinner at a restaurant or coffeehouse. You will notice many other patrons flocking to nearby establishments and you should go immediately if you want to secure a table. Although it is quite normal, Susan remembers doing a double-take the first time she saw a woman in a long evening gown and fur coat eating a *Frankfurter* with her husband. If you're not that hungry, then go to enjoy a coffee and a scrumptious pastry.

Konzerthaus

The Konzerthaus is another beautiful place to enjoy first-class musical performances. This is home to the Vienna Symphony Orchestra, but other world-class artists, not necessarily classical ones, also take the stage. The building houses three concert halls: the Grosser Saal, the Mozartsaal and the Schubertsaal.

Staatsoper

The Staatsoper (State Opera House), just a few blocks from the Musikverein, is another jewel. Located along the Ringstrasse at the end of Kärntner Strasse, it was the first of the great buildings on the Ring. It was completed in 1869 and opened with Mozart's *Don Giovanni*. It was nearly destroyed in 1945 after being bombed during World War II, but was rebuilt and reopened in 1955 after the occupying forces had left. The Staatsoper's programme changes daily and offers an incredible variety of operas and ballets over the course of the year (September through June). Tickets go on sale exactly one month before the performance, and again a subscription would ensure you a ticket. The Staatsoper also has *Stehplätze*, some of which have excellent locations. The

Tickets for classical music concerts geared to visitors can be purchased at fair prices from street vendors in most tourist areas in Vienna.

view from the main floor is spectacular for the price of the ticket. You must queue early, but once inside you can mark your space by tying a scarf around the rail in front of you. You can also purchase a standing room season pass, which allows you to buy one standing room ticket per performance through normal ticket sales.

Volksoper

The Volksoper (People's Opera) is located along the Gürtel (a wide street that encircles the city, the name means 'belt') in the 9th district and offers primarily operettas, although you can also see ballets, operas and musicals. Most of the performances are in German, although some may be in their original language with electronic German subtitles. The Volksoper also provides about 100 *Stehplätze*.

Vienna Boys' Choir and Church Music

Perhaps Vienna's best-known symbol is the Vienna Boys' Choir. Founded by Emperor Maximilian I in 1498, it has continued to this day with only a small break between 1918 and 1924. Choir members perform mass at the Burgkapelle in the Hofburg every Sunday from mid-September to June. They are a pure joy to hear, but if you'd rather not be surrounded by tourists, there are a number of other churches where you can attend mass and hear beautiful music.

The Augustinerkirche (part of the Hofburg), the Universitätskirche, Saint Michael's and Stephansdom, all in the old centre, feature a mass on Sundays and holy days with either an orchestra, quartet and/or choir. The first three churches may also be crowded at the height of the tourist season, but many Viennese do attend these masses, giving a sense of normalcy. The Stephansdom, however, tends to be overrun by tourists, even though attempts are made at keeping pure sightseers in the back. Susan once attended Sunday mass here and was shocked to witness a woman near her being photographed receiving communion. Churches are not well heated in winter so be sure to dress warmly.

Classical Music for the Novice

Programmes designed for tourists delight audiences with well-known classical pieces by performers in period costume. They are light-hearted and entertaining, while they maintain the high quality found in the somewhat more serious regular season performances. If you want an easy introduction to classical music, these performances are for you. Keep in mind, however, that some of these shows are held only during the height of the tourist season.

Mozart's best-loved works are magically presented at the Musikverein about three times weekly during the summer. Works of Mozart and Strauss are performed at the Orangerie at Schönbrunn Palace, complete with professional dancers.

Schönborn Palace on Renngasse in the 1st district offers a similar programme by the Wiener Residenzorchester, while the Wiener Konzertquintett performs the works of Beethoven, Bach, Vivaldi, Haydn and Mozart. The Hofburg and the Liechtenstein Palace (1st district) are also venues for classical music.

Marionette Theatres

For something different, you might want to attend one of the marionette theatres where operas, ballets and other stories are performed by marionettes. In Vienna, you can see such a show at Schönbrunn Palace, which was quite famous during Maria Theresa's reign. Salzburg also has its own very popular Marionette Theatre.

Music Festivals and Regional Venus
Viennese Festivals

Ever proud of their rich classical music history, many Austrian cities host at least one full-scale music festival, often in honour of a specific composer. The Viennese celebrate the Wiener Festwochen in May and June with special musical and theatrical performances and art exhibitions. This is considered the main festival in Vienna, yet there are numerous other festivals held in the capital throughout the year. The Vienna Spring Festival in March and April features works from the Baroque period to the 20th century. The OsterKlang Festival is celebrated at Easter and highlights the Viennese Philharmonic Orchestra and other world-renowned orchestras. The Festival of Early Music, or Resonanzen Festival, in January at the Konzerthaus celebrates religious and secular music from the 14th to 17th centuries.

At the other end of the spectrum is the Wien Modern Festival, which highlights contemporary music. Concerts are held at different venues throughout Vienna in October and November. KlangBogenWien is held in July and August to offset the absence of the Viennese Philharmonic and the opera companies from the music scene. This festival highlights modern music theatre, operetta and concerts.

Salzburg

Salzburg is well known for its summer Salzburger Festspiele. The festival was established in 1920 and features works by Mozart, the city's most famous son. It started with the original production of *Jedermann* (*Everyman*) by Hugo von Hofmannsthal. The festival opens every year with a performance of this play in the Cathedral plaza, but it has grown to include several different plays and operas, and many concerts.

Although Mozart is the main focus, there are new works by young composers. At first only the Viennese Philharmonic performed at the festival, but since 1931, highly distinguished international orchestras and conductors have played in Salzburg. Performances take place throughout the city at the Mozarteum (the musical academy), the Grosses Festspielhaus (Large Festival Hall), the Landestheater and Mirabell Palace. Tickets can be pricey and may be difficult to obtain (in general well over 200,000 people attend). If you can't make it, the city has other less crowded festivals for you to enjoy. The

Haus für Mozart, formerly the Small Festival Hall, is another musical venue.

Mozart Week is celebrated every January. The Easter Festival has added to this beautiful holiday since 1967. In June, the Pfingsten (Whitsun) Festival is devoted to Baroque music and focuses on the works of Händel and Bach. Musical events take place throughout the summer at Hellbrunn Palace and Hohensalzburg Fortress and in several of the city's gardens and courtyards. Salzburg's Cultural Days have offered ballet, music and opera since 1972. During Advent (the four weeks before Christmas), singing performances get you into the Christmas spirit. Many flock to the small town of Oberndorf, north of Salzburg, to hear *Silent Night* where it was written and first performed. Finally, the Marionette Theatre is a wonderful way to interest children in opera. Bad Ischl in the Salzkammergut, not far from Salzburg, hosts the Operetta Festival every July and August.

Linz

Linz, just two hours west of Vienna, was home to Anton Bruckner. He was organist at the Linz Cathedral for 14 years and his presence can still be felt in the city. A modern concert hall built on the banks of the Danube was named Brucknerhaus in his honour. Every fall, Linz celebrates Brucknerfest, which highlights many of Bruckner's hymnal symphonies, as well as those of other great composers. Performances throughout the regular season range from classical to folk, jazz and world music, and there is also a programme for children. The Bruckner Orchestra plays at the Landestheater.

More on Linz

Linz is also the site of the Klangwolke Festival, a mixture of art and technology, and the Pflasterspektakel, a street artists' festival in the pedestrian zone.

Lower Austria

Franz Schubert spent the summers from 1820 to 1828 in the town of Atzenbrugg (halfway between Tulln and Saint

Pölten). So every May and June, the town celebrates the Schubertiade Music Festival.

Grafenegg Castle near Krems presents concerts from May through October. Every other year, it hosts Romantic Music Week. Christmas season brings 'Grafenegg Advent' in early December. In the summer, you can see operetta at the Open-air Theatre in Baden, and plays at Perchtoldsdorf and Neulengbach. Saint Pölten and Krems are the main venues for the Danube Festival. The town of Melk, best known for its majestic abbey, is home to the Summer Theatre Festival.

Burgenland

Burgenland honours Haydn, the chief conductor of the Esterházy dynasty's private orchestra from 1761 until 1790. The Haydnsaal at the Esterházy palace in Eisenstadt offers concerts and matinee chamber music from September until July. It's definitely worth a visit, especially since Haydn himself conducted many of his own works there. A highlight of the musical season is Haydn Days, a festival that features his works as well as those of other composers.

The Mörbisch Lake Festival is held outdoors in the small town of Mörbisch on the large Neusiedler Lake. Operettas are performed here in the summer warmth. Nearby, the Opera Festival Saint Margarethen is held in July and August in the town of the same name, in a quarry with the stage set deep between the rocks. Lockenhaus Castle, near the Hungarian border, hosts a chamber music festival every summer.

Bregenz

Bregenz, the capital of Vorarlberg, is world-famous for its annual festival. The city lies on the shores of the Bodensee (Lake Constance), and every July and August, an elaborate floating stage is built. The audience, safe on dry land, enjoys lavish productions of operas and operettas, musicals and ballets.

Innsbruck

Innsbruck hosts an Early Music Festival in August that highlights Baroque music. Performances are primarily held at Ambras Palace. Year-round musical events are performed at the Kongresshaus (Convention Centre), Stadtsäale and Konservatorium (music school). The Tiroler Symphony Orchestra performs at the Tiroler Landestheater.

Styria and Carinthia

Every June since 1985, Graz, Styria's beautiful capital, has celebrated Styriarte, a festival highlighting classical music. The Styrian Autumn Festival, Austria's largest avant-garde festival, is celebrated in Graz and the surrounding towns. But you don't have to wait for a festival. You can attend one of the many performances at the beautiful Graz Opera House or the Schauspielhaus.

The Carinthian Summer Festival has been held in Ossiach and Villach since 1969. Mostly religious pieces are performed.

Choices and More Choices!

Instead of having nothing to do, in Austria you may be overwhelmed by your choices of entertainment. Performances and art exhibitions are well advertised. You'll notice fliers posted on large round pillars and on any available surface. In Vienna, people are even hired to dress up in period dress to entice tourists to buy tickets. In general, venues are closed during July and August, when the official symphonies and ballet, opera and theatre companies are on vacation. Special festivals abound to make up for their absence.

Balls (Bälle)

In January, Vienna celebrates the New Year with lavish balls. This time of the year is called Fasching. In essence, the name refers to Fat Tuesday, the eve of Ash Wednesday (Aschermittwoch), but it is also a general term describing the period beginning on the 11th hour of the 11th day of the 11th month, and ending with Ash Wednesday.

Balls abound, hosted by various organisations. There are balls held for members of certain professions, for example: *Rot Kreuz Ball* (Red Cross Ball), *Ball der Pfarre*

Floridsdorf (Clergymen's Ball), *Installateurball* (Plumbers' Ball), *Technikerball* (Technicians' Ball), *Ärzteball* (Doctors' Ball), *Ball der Zollwache* (Customs Guards' Ball), *Zuckerbäcker Ball* (Confectioners' Ball) and *Kanalwerkmeister Ball* (Sewer Managers' Ball). Some ethnic groups put on lively cultural dances at their balls, examples being *Ball der burgenländischen Kroaten* (Burgenland's Croatian Ball), *Russische Ballnacht* (Russian Ball Night) and *Ball der Griechen* (Greeks' Ball). A ball with a twist is the *Rudolfina Redoute Ball*. Here, single women enter wearing masks, which they take off at midnight to reveal their identities to their dancing partners. Another noteworthy event is the Life Ball, which raises money for AIDS research. This is an offbeat ball for those who like to make wild and crazy fashion statements for a good cause. High schools and dance schools also organise balls.

The Opera Ball is the highlight of the Viennese ball circuit. On the eve of Lent or Fasching, the opera house is magically transformed into a sumptuous dance hall. Rows upon rows of chairs are removed from the audience section, and in their place a dance floor emerges. Those who can afford a ticket dress in their best: a long evening gown for the women and black suits with tails for the men. The attendees wait

with bated breath to see which famous star the self-made millionaire Richard Lugner will bring with him to the ball. Outside the opera house, as in decades gone by, people peacefully protest the extravagance of the event.

Debutantes in white gowns and their young tuxedoed escorts open each ball with a dance. They walk onstage in an orderly fashion, showing off their outfits, and then dance a waltz. When they go offstage, everyone else may begin to dance. If you are at a popular ball, it may be difficult even to dance because the dance floor is that crowded.

Anyone with a ticket can go to the balls. Prices differ based on whether you want to sit at a table, have a meal (if served), or just dance all night, but you can expect to pay around € 50 per ticket. Most balls are advertised with ticketing information included. A ball pamphlet, available at information centres, lists all the balls lined up for the year. As you buy your ticket, be sure to ask about the dress code. Not all balls require long gowns and suits with tails. Julie has been to several where women wore short dresses and men wore off-black or gray suits.

Theatre

You'll need a good command of German to enjoy one of the most celebrated German-language theatres, the Burgtheater. Located on the Ring, this theatre is visually spectacular and boasts some of the best German plays and actors in the world. It is said that a German-speaking actor has not 'made it' until he or she has performed at the Burgtheater.

The Akademietheater, located at the Konzerthaus, is operated in conjunction with the Burgtheater and is also highly respected. The Volkstheater and Theater in der Josefstadt have a rich and long history performing great works in German.

A musical is easier to enjoy if your knowledge of German is limited. The Theater an der Wien has a very impressive history. Beethoven's *Fidelio* premiered here in 1805. Johann Strauss's *die Fledermaus* and Franz Lehár's *The Merry Widow* also premiered here, as did many of Johann Nestroy's pieces. Today, however, the theatre is dedicated to staging musicals.

More musicals can be seen at the Raimundtheater, also located in the 6th district. The Ronacher presents musicals and more abstract shows.

Cabaret

Not only must your German be good, but your Viennese dialect as well, if you want to enjoy Vienna's cabarets. These shows, which comprise satirical sketches relating to a theme or a current political situation, offset by the occasional song-and-dance number, are popular among Viennese. Politicians are often the butt of the jokes, but they can be seen in the audience laughing with the rest.

English-language Theatre

If you enjoy plays but lack the German facility to attend one of these theatres, there are three English-language theatres in Vienna. The English Theatre in the 8th district stages plays with professional American and British actors. Two smaller theatres in the 9th district, the International Theatre and Fundus, also give performances in English.

Being Involved

If you prefer to be up on the stage instead of in the audience, the VIC Players (a United Nations theatre group) invites all English speakers who are interested to take part in the group's productions. Contact the United Nations office in Vienna for details.

Cinema

Austria has produced some good film-makers. Perhaps the most well known is Otto Preminger, who became big in Hollywood. A new generation of directors is making some interesting films. One of the best known is Michael Haneke, whose film *The Piano Teacher* won the Grand Prix at the Cannes Film Festival in 2001.

Every October brings the Viennale Film Festival, which showcases some fine international films. In November, children can enjoy the International Children's Film

Festival. Films from across the world are shown in their original language with German translation available on a headset. During the summer, a huge screen is erected in the Rathausplatz, where concerts, operas and ballets are all shown free of charge. To make the evening even more enjoyable, a number of stalls are set up selling food from many different countries. There are also open-air cinemas set up in the Augarten and the Prater.

Architecture

Perhaps the most famous artist and architect of the late 20th century was Friedensreich Hundertwasser. He brought whimsy into Austria's rather austere, neutral buildings. Combining bold colours and wobbly geometric shapes using natural products such as tile, wood and ceramics, he invented a radically new way of living—floors full of soft bumps, for example, because in nature, the ground is not flat. The Hundertwasserhaus on Kegelgasse in the 3rd district is definitely worth a look. At first glance, you may not realise that this unconventional, colourful and creative building is a public housing block. It was completed in 1985 and people currently live there so entry is prohibited, but you can visit the

Friedensreich Hundertwasser applied his whimsical style to many different projects, such as this rest stop on the A2 Autobahn.

small shopping mall across the street, which he also designed. If you'd like to see more of his work, visit the KunstHausWien, just a few blocks away on Weissgerberstrasse. This museum houses the permanent collection of Hundertwasser's paintings and also hosts temporary exhibits. The garden café is a fun place to relax. He also designed the Fernwärme power plant, a church in Styria, a rest stop along the A2 Autobahn and a fantasy-like spa, among other works.

Literature

Following World War II, some authors continued writing in a traditional vein, while others, like those in the 'Vienna Group', were more avant-garde. One of the best known contemporary authors is Peter Handke. The late Thomas Bernhard is another popular author who wrote from the 1960s until his death in

1989. Elfriede Jelinek won the Nobel Prize for Literature in 2004. These authors have been joined by Johannes Mario Simmel, Ingeborg Bachmann, Gerhard Roth, Peter Turrini and Michael Köhlmeyer.

MUSEUMS

What should you do on Sunday with all stores and most restaurants closed? Spend all day at one of the many museums throughout the country! Entrance fees are not cheap, so choose your museum carefully. Often, children, students, teachers and senior citizens pay a reduced fee. Many cities offer some type of card that provides access to museums over a specific period. In Vienna, you have the option of purchasing an annual museum pass that lets you into many museums. If you have guests and plan on seeing a number of museums within 72 hours, purchase the Vienna Card which provides unlimited access to public transportation and reduced rates at certain museums, shops and restaurants.

Visiting a Museum

National museums are free twice a year: National Museum Day on 18 May and Austria National Day on 26 October. Within Vienna, certain municipal museums are free on Friday before noon, excluding public holidays. Virtually all museums are closed on Monday. Tuesday through Sunday, they tend to be open from 10:00 am to 6:00 pm, although the hours may vary.

Vienna

Vienna has so many museums that once you have taken in every permanent collection, the temporary exhibits will still keep you occupied. Vienna's most famous museums are the Kunsthistorisches (Art History) Museum and Naturhistorisches (Natural History) Museum. The former has one of the best collections of 16th and 17th century art by masters such as Brueghel, Rubens, Velázquez, Titian, Dürer, Rembrandt, Van Dyck and Cranach. It also has an Egyptian and Near Eastern Collection, Greek and Roman Antiquities, and Sculpture and

The Kunsthistorisches Museum and Naturhistorisches Museum are Vienna's most famous museums and are wonderful places to visit.

Decorative Arts. Do not try to see the entire museum in one day, but rather pick a section and stroll through it at a leisurely pace, then enjoy a coffee afterwards at the famous Museum Café.

The Naturhistorisches Museum, which faces the Kunsthistorisches Museum across the Maria Theresa Plaza, is best known for the Venus of Willendorf, a small statue of a woman representing fertility dating from 20,000–30,000 BC found in the Wachau region of Austria.

Across from these two museums is the new Museum Quartier, which houses many different museums, including a children's hands-on museum, the 'Zoom Museum'. This great museum has an arts and crafts room, a permanent ocean area and a rotating exhibit. A second museum, the Leopold Museum, has impressionist art on display. The third museum is the Modern Art Museum (MUMOK). The complex also includes a large theatre that stages all kinds of performances: modern ballet, musicals, international revues, theatre, etc. There is also a smaller children's theatre. Of course, it wouldn't be complete without the lovely restaurants. In the summer, activities head outdoors, such as children's and musical programmes.

Among the more interesting museums in Vienna is the Albertina in the Hofburg. Founded in 1768 and well known for its extensive collection of graphic arts, it boasts a large number of pieces by the master Albrecht Dürer. The Schatzkammer (Treasury), also located in the Hofburg, houses priceless religious and secular objects. Here you can view the orb and scepter, and the imperial crown of the Holy Roman Emperor of the German Nation, dating from the 10th century.

The Akademie der bildenden Künste (Academy of Fine Arts), established in 1692, has a small picture gallery, its most famous piece being *The Last Judgement* triptych by Hieronymus Bosch. The Museum des 20. Jahrhunderts (Museum of the 20th Century) houses more contemporary pieces of art and hosts temporary exhibitions as well. The Liechtenstein Museum houses the masterpieces from the Princely Collections in Vaduz.

The Museum für angewandte Kunst (Museum for Applied Arts), or the MAK, has a collection of beautifully designed objects used in everyday life. Kunstforum Bank Austria showcases important 19th and 20th century art. The Kunsthalle Wien in the 4th district presents temporary exhibitions of contemporary and modern art. It also has a great restaurant and café that looks out onto the museum.

The Künstlerhaus, which today displays contemporary art, was the official exhibition hall for artists studying at the Academy at the turn of the 20th century. In 1897, a group of 19 artists who deemed the academy too conservative broke away to form the Secession. The Secession building was used as a headquarters to exhibit their Jugendstil art. Completed in 1898, the building is beautiful and quite distinctive. It contains Gustav Klimt's *Beethovenfrieze* and hosts temporary exhibits of modern art.

You can feel a part of history at the Sigmund Freud Museum on Berggasse 19. This is where the psychoanalyst lived and worked from 1891 to 1938, although not many of his original possessions remain. You can also visit the Jewish Museum of the City of Vienna, the Historical Museum of the City of Vienna and the Austrian Museum of Folklore.

For a more macabre look at Vienna, visit the Funeral Museum, or learn the history of torture in the Museum of Medieval Legal History.

The Museum of Military History traces the many years of Austrian military might and displays the car in which Franz Ferdinand was riding when he was shot. There are three resting places for royalty. The Habsburgs lie in the Imperial Crypt at the Kapuzinerkirche on Neuer Markt, while their hearts are in the Augustinerkirche and their organs in the crypt at Stephansdom. If you happen to enter the Stephansdom subway station, look for the lovely Romanesque Virgilkapelle (Chapel of Saint Virgil) that was unearthed when work started on the subway line.

If you prefer museums with a light-hearted theme, Vienna has an eclectic array: the Teddy Bear Museum, Circus and Clown Museum, Doll and Toy Museum, Clock Museum and Globe Museum. You can also visit the Fiaker Museum (*Fiaker* are horse-drawn carriages that make their way slowly through the old city) or Prater Museum (the local amusement park). If those aren't enough, try the Tram Museum, Soccer Museum, or even Schnaps Museum.

Remembering the Composers

Many former residences of the great composers have been turned into museums. While some may not have many original artifacts, you can see how they lived, and in many cases, enjoy their music as well. Entry to these museums is generally not expensive, and if you particularly like the composer, you can spend your visit listening to recordings of his works.

Mozart, Austria's favourite son, was born in Salzburg, and the house of his birth is a popular tourist attraction in the centre of the old city on Getreidegasse. Mozart lived in a number of places in Vienna, but the most famous is the Figaro House behind the Stephansdom on Domgasse, where he composed *The Marriage of Figaro*.

Beethoven, adopted by the Austrians as one of their own, was a somewhat unruly and loud tenant and changed residences often. In Vienna, you can visit the Pasqualatihaus, Heiligenstädter Testamenthaus and Eroica Haus, all former

Beethoven homes. His apartment in Baden is also open to the public.

Johann Strauss's home is a museum, as are Schubert's birthplace and the house in which he died. Haydn fans should visit Eisenstadt to see Haydn's house and the Esterházy palace. The Haydn Museum in Vienna was his home later in life. In this house, there is a room dedicated to Brahms, who also lived in Vienna for a while. Brahms composed his fourth symphony in Mürzzuschlag, a small town in Styria about two hours from Vienna. This summerhouse has been turned into a delightful award-winning museum covering the many aspects of his life and work.

Paying Your Respects

If you wish to pay your respects, visit the Zentralfriedhof (Central Cemetery) where Beethoven, Schubert, the entire Strauss family, Brahms, Schoenberg and Gluck are buried. Though Mozart is buried in an unmarked grave in Saint Marxer Friedhof, there is a large memorial to the composer in the Ehrengräber (Tombs of Honour) section of the Zentralfriedhof. Gustav Mahler, who converted to Catholicism because of anti-Semitism, was buried in Grinzinger Friedhof in 1911. His tombstone was designed by Jugendstil architect and Wiener Werkstätte co-founder, Josef Hoffman. Another option is to take a stroll through the Stadtpark in Vienna, which is dotted with busts and statues of the great composers, as well as authors and painters.

Salzburg

In addition to Mozart's birthplace, you can visit the Rupertinum Museum of Modern and Contemporary Art and Carolino Augusteum Museum. The Natural History Museum has aquariums, a reptile zoo, insect gallery and dinosaur exhibit. You can also experience first-hand the salt mines that produced much of the region's wealth. Stiegl's Brauwelt shows how beer is made, and the museum provides historical information on the beverage. In Salzburg, you can also see the tombs of the prince-archbishops in the crypt of the cathedral.

Innsbruck

The Museum of Tyrolean Folk Art has wonderful displays of Tyrolean costumes, living quarters, furniture and tools—a great introduction to Tyrol. The Tyrolean Provincial Museum Ferdinandeum houses the largest collection of Gothic art in Austria. You can also find the old masters here as well as Baroque art. The Maximilianeum has original art pieces, weapons and gold and coins from the treasury. The Tyrolean Regional Museum, located in Maximilian I's arsenal, offers a varied collection related to the history of Tyrol—cartography, music, hunting, avalanches and the fire brigade. The Alpine Museum has Alpine art from two centuries, maps, antique mountain climbing equipment and models of mountain refuges.

The Tyrolean Imperial Militia Museum has displays on regiments from World War I and the legendary regiments that guarded the old mountain borders of Tyrol. The Kaiserjägermuseum Bergisel (Military Museum) and Andreas Hofer Gallery pay homage to the heroes of the 1809 Battle of Bergisel against Napoleon's troops.

Visiting the Hofkirche

The Hofkirche (Court Church) contains the memorial tomb of Maximilian I (he is actually buried in Wiener Neustadt, south of Vienna). The marble sides of the sarcophagus are carved with scenes highlighting his reign. Surrounding the tomb are 28 larger-than-life figures (26 of them cast in bronze, the rest in copper) representing his ancestors and relatives by bloodline or marriage, and admired heroes. One of the best statues is of King Arthur by Albrecht Dürer. The church also contains the tomb and memorial of the Tyrolean hero Andreas Hofer (1767–1810).

The world-famous Swarovski crystal company is headquartered in nearby Wattens. Crystal Worlds, built to celebrate the firm's 100th anniversary, has some unique displays—a crystal dome, a wall made of 12 tons of crystal and a simulated crystal rain shower. While in Innsbruck, you can also visit the Bell Museum. The Grassmayr family has been making bells for 14 generations. At the museum, you can see bells of all sizes being modelled and cast, and finally, rung.

Linz

In Linz, visit the Nordico City Museum, Francisco Carolinum Provincial Museum, 'Linz-Genesis' Museum in the Old City Hall building, Adalbert Stifter House and Linz New Gallery, an art hall opened in 1947. Every autumn, the Ars Electronica Centre, a museum of the future, stages a festival of art and technology.

Graz

The Zeughaus (Arsenal) in this jewel of a city holds more than 29,000 weapons, armour and even a horse. The Ancient Art Gallery's collection of medieval art includes altars, crucifixes and stained glass. The Styrian Folklore Museum displays reconstructions of Styrian living quarters. About 16 km outside of Graz, the Austrian Open Air Museum begins. Houses from the different provinces of Austria have been built over 100 acres to show how rural Austrians live.

Other Cities

Vorarlberg Museum in Bregenz has beautiful religious art from churches in the province. Also of note is the Jewish Museum Hohenems.

In Klagenfurt, you can visit the Landesmuseum, which has exhibits on the nature, history and culture of Carinthia. The nearby Freilichtmuseum Maria Saal is an open-air museum displaying typical buildings. Minimundis is an open-air museum of internationally famous buildings.

The Jewish Museum and the Jewish Quarter in Eisenstadt, capital of Burgenland and once home to many Jews, are also worth seeing.

PALACES AND CASTLES

Austria boasts an incredible number of spectacular palaces and impressive fortified castles. No longer homes for nobility nor defense against a feared enemy, many of these palaces and castles can now be enjoyed by everyone. Some have been turned into fascinating museums, others welcome you with pleasant restaurants and hotels, and still others are the magical settings for summer concerts and operettas. Except for those in Vienna, most palaces and castles are closed from November until April.

Vienna
Schönbrunn

Schönbrunn Palace was the summer residence of the Habsburgs. Built on the grounds of a former hunting lodge, its gardens are as well worth visiting as its Rococo and Baroque apartments. Construction on the current building began after the Turkish siege of 1683 under the guidance of architect Johann Bernhard Fischer von Erlach, but it wasn't until the reign of Maria Theresa (1740–80) that the building was expanded to its present state. The gardens were also extensively developed at this time.

Two tours are available, the Imperial Tour and the Grand Tour. The former entitles you to see only half of the rooms open to the public. Invest in the second tour, and you will see some of the best rooms, which are excluded from the first tour. The Blue Chinese Salon, Porcelain Room and Miniatures Room are among the finest on display, but the Millions Room is by far the best. Miniature 17th century Persian watercolours are set into the walls, although their simple beauty is overwhelmed by the accompanying decor. There is a great deal of information on Princess Elizabeth (Sissi), given Austrians' love for her, but it is somewhat ironic as she did not spend much time at Schönbrunn.

The gardens include the Gloriette, Neptune Fountain, Palm House, Zoo (the oldest continuously working zoo in the world), Roman Ruins (replicas built for the gardens), Butterfly House, Obelisk and innumerable paths that wind through floral gardens, trees and hedges. You may easily while away a beautiful sunny afternoon. Bring a picnic!

Hofburg

The Hofburg contains the Imperial Apartments, Treasury, Church of the Augustines, Court Chapel (where the Vienna

Boys' Choir sings), several museums (including the Albertina), Spanish Riding School, Esperanto Museum, Austrian National Library and government offices. Some 20 rooms in the Imperial Apartments, the city residence of Emperor Franz Josef and Empress Sissi, are open to the public.

Spanish Riding School

Located within part of the Hofburg is another of Vienna's trademarks, the Spanische Reitschule (Spanish Riding School), where tourists flock to see the performance of the legendary white Lippizaner horses. Commercialism aside, it is still enjoyable to watch these beautiful horses as they execute graceful, ballet-like movements. The horses received their name from the town of Lipizza in present-day Slovenia, where the line began during the time of Maximilian II by crossbreeding horses from Spain with horses from Italy and Arabia. Karl VI created the Winter Riding School, providing a home for the horses in a new annex to the Hofburg, built in 1735. It is difficult to obtain tickets and they are away on tour quite often, so plan this visit well in advance. It is easier to attend the training sessions which offer an entertaining show just the same.

In the wake of Slovenia's independence from Yugoslavia, the Slovenian government filed a claim against Austria's use of the name 'Lippizaner' before the European court, arguing that they hold the right to the name, since Lippiza is a town in Slovenia.

Belvedere

The Belvedere was built by architect Johann Lukas von Hildebrandt for Eugene of Savoy, a French prince who helped Austria repel the Turks in 1683. The palace was completed in 1723. Following his death, it became the property of the emperor. It was the home of Archduke Franz Ferdinand before he was assassinated in 1914. Its most important moment in history was on 15 May 1955, when the Austrian State Treaty was signed by the United States, France, Britain and the Soviet Union, granting Austria independence and sovereignty. Austrian Foreign Minister Leopold Figl waved the treaty from a balcony, declaring "Austria is free!" to the crowd below.

The Belvedere (*belvedere* is Italian for 'beautiful view') is actually two palaces, Upper Belvedere and Lower Belvedere, separated by beautifully laid out gardens. The admission fee allows entry into both. The Upper Belvedere houses Austrian works from the 19th and 20th centuries, including many pieces by the late 19th century artist Hans Makart. The museum is famous for its collection by Jugendstil artists, notably *The Kiss* by Gustav Klimt. See it to appreciate Klimt's unique style. Also on display are *Judith I*, other portraits and some of his wonderful landscapes. Two rooms are devoted to Egon Schiele, a controversial artist whose works have been described as obscene. Two others devoted to Oscar Kokoschka show mainly works he completed while living in Vienna in the early 1900s.

The Lower Belvedere contains Baroque art, but the rooms are interesting in and of themselves. By far the most intriguing is the Goldkabinett, a small room decorated entirely with gold walls, mirrors and Oriental vases. Adjacent to the building is the Orangery and its Museum of Medieval Art. This museum has an impressive display of 12th to 16th century art.

Burgenland

Burgenland was of great strategic value to Austria, and especially to Vienna. The Turks had to pass across these lands en route to the capital. Thus, many fortified castles were built high atop hills to stop the advancing armies. Hence the name 'Burgenland'—land of the castles. One of the best castles to visit is Forchtenstein, 22 km south-east of Wiener Neustadt. Built in the 14th century by the Counts of Mattersdorf, the castle was enlarged when it passed into the possession of the Esterházy family around 1635. It houses a very large collection of arms and armour (close to 20,000 items on exhibition in 32 rooms) used in the defense of Austria, as well as some Turkish items seized during the invasions of 1529 and 1683. It is the largest private collection in central Europe open to the public.

Salzburg

The first thing you see upon entering the city of Salzburg is the Hohensalzburg, a huge fortress atop the hill that overlooks and protects the city. Work on the castle began in 1077, and archbishops lived there until the end of the 15th century.

A cog railway takes you to the top, where you can explore the castle, its chapel, the fortress and puppet and regiment museums, then enjoy the view from the café.

The most photographed view is of the fortress from the Mirabell Palace and the Mirabell gardens. Archbishop Wolf Dietrich von Raitenau, who in spite of being a man of the church, married Salome Alt in the late 16th century, had this palace built for her and their many children. Even if you do not enter the palace, no trip to Salzburg would be complete without a walk through the beautiful gardens.

Construction of the Residenz in the town centre also began under Archbishop Wolf Dietrich in 1595. A young Mozart conducted many concerts in its Conference Hall. It now houses the Residenzgalerie (primarily 17th and 18th century art), the Modern Gallery and Rupertinum Collection of contemporary art, as well as hosting art shows and musical events. Tours of its state apartments are available.

Although not in the town centre, Hellbrunn Palace is definitely worth a visit. This was the summer residence of Archbishop Marcus Sitticus. The gardens are full of the water tricks and games that he played upon his guests. The highlight of the gardens is a theatre with 113 tiny mechanical figures, all powered by water. Go with a good sense of humour, and protect your camera.

Venture into the Salzkammergut and visit the Imperial Villa in nearby Bad Ischl. This is the small town where Emperor Franz Josef spent all of his summers. Franz Lehár also lived and composed a number of his works here and his former home is now a museum.

Innsbruck

Innsbruck's Hofburg was built during the reign of Maria Theresa and completed in 1777. The Rococo State Rooms can be viewed and the gardens are a treat. The most impressive room is the Giant's Hall, which contains a ceiling fresco that glorifies the House of Habsburg.

The Goldenes Dachl (little golden roof) is the signature attraction. Contrary to the legend that it was built by 'Friedrich the Penniless' to prove his wealth, it was commissioned by Maximilian I. Dating from 1500, this small balcony on the

The Hohensalzburg Fortress is a spectacular castle well worth a visit and it offers visitors a stunning view of the city of Salzburg and its surroundings.

former Ducal Palace is topped with 2,657 gilded shingles. It was built to commemorate Maximilian's second marriage, to Bianca Maria Sforza of Milan, in 1494.

On the edge of the city lies Ambras Castle, built in 1564 by Archduke Ferdinand II for his wife Philippine, a commoner who was never accepted by the royal family. It has some beautiful interiors—specifically the Spanish Hall—and lovely gardens. It became Austria's first museum in 1580 after Philippine's death. Today, you can see some glorious treasures inside the Chamber of Wonders.

Lower Austria

The Danube River runs through this province. An important waterway, it was the centre of life for many. As you meander along the river, you will notice the many castles and fortresses that have stood here for centuries. The wonderful medieval town of Dürnstein is the highlight of the valley. Leaving your car outside town in one of the special parking lots, stroll though the old walled city and, if you have the energy, climb to the ruined fortress high on the hill. This is where Richard the Lionheart was held captive in the 12th century. He was arrested for offending the Babenberg ruler Leopold V on his way back from the Crusades. Legend says that King Richard's minstrel Blondel wandered throughout the region singing until the king heard him and told him of his fate. This, however, is just another of the legends that Austrians hold dear. England did in fact have to pay a hefty ransom for the return of her king and it was used to develop Vienna. Farther upstream are the Aggstein ruins. Climbing through the remains of this large castle is fun for both kids and adults, and the views are worth the effort.

Styria

Strolling through the quaint streets of Graz takes you along the Mur River to the base of the Schlossberg. As the name suggests, the ruins of a 15th century fortress sit atop this large hill. The castle, originally built to protect the city from the Turks, is the source of the city's name, Graz, which is derived from the Slovenian *gradec*, meaning small castle.

Schlossstrasse

A pleasant way to pass a weekend is to meander from one castle to the next, following the Schlossstrasse (a route that will allow you to see fine examples of historic castles). The 'Castle Road' passes through Burgenland into Styria. Some of the highlights along the road are Lockenhaus, Bernstein, Stadtschlaining and Güssing. You can stop to tour the castles and small museums between April and November. Many castles offer lodging, and you can spend a quiet evening strolling around the grounds or nearby town and enjoy a meal with a glass of the local wine.

MONASTERIES AND CHURCHES

Driving along the Autobahn from Salzburg and Linz to Vienna, you can't miss the immense yellow Benedictine Abbey at Melk. Founded in 1089, it has an interesting library and an awe-inspiring Baroque church. Umberto Eco's *The Name of the Rose* takes place here.

The Göttweig Benedictine Monastery perched on a hill is also a day trip from Vienna. After viewing the crypt and gatehouse dating from the Middle Ages and the Imperial Wing built later, eat in the restaurant and enjoy the view of Krems and the Danube.

Much closer to Vienna is the Augustine Monastery Klosterneuburg, on the other side of the Kahlenberg bordering Vienna to the north. It was founded in the 12th century and contains the famous enamelled Verdun altar and Gothic stained glass. Entrance to the museum allows you into the Baroque imperial apartments, still in their original state, and to a medieval art collection.

In Tyrol, you can stroll around the beautiful Stams Cistercian Monastery, founded in 1273. In Upper Austria, you can see the observatory at the Benedictine Monastery in Kremsmünster and tour its science-related collection. The Benedictine Monastery in Admont, south-west of Linz, boasts the largest monastic library in the world. In Carinthia, the Benedictine Monastery of Saint Paul is home to the largest monastic art collection north of the Alps.

Quietly sitting in the mountains in northern Styria is the lovely town of Mariazell and its awe-inspiring pilgrimage church. A monk founded the church in 1157. Not long after, it was reported that its small Virgin Mary with Child statue could perform miracles. Soon people started visiting the church to ask for favours or to give a prayer of thanks, making it the most important place of pilgrimage in Austria. Prayers are directed at the Virgin and Child, who are now dressed in an elaborate gown and encircled by a finely detailed silver lattice.

FESTIVALS AND CUSTOMS

The succession of festivals is a central part of Austrian life. Many customs have their roots in pagan rituals, which were guided by the cycle of seasons and the movement of celestial bodies. It was believed that both friendly and evil powers influenced the earth and its growth and fertility, powers so strong that they also affected people. The rituals served as a means of protection from things that people could not understand. When the Catholic Church came to gain converts, missionaries embellished these traditions with Christian themes. Angels and devils and the concept of good and evil took on a central role.

Epiphany

Epiphany on 6 January is a time to remember the manifestation of Christ's birth to the Magi. Catholic boys dress up in Oriental dress to represent the three wise men, Caspar, Melchior and Balthazar. Led by a star bearer, they go from house to house seeking donations, singing traditional carols and swinging their incense carrier. On each house, they chalk three crosses to banish evil spirits. The money raised is used to fund church projects around the world.

The Glöckler of Ebensee in Upper Austria is celebrated on the evening of 6 January, after evening prayers. In a tradition that dates to the 16th century, a group of 20 men from various villages of Ebensee runs to farms or homes within a certain radius. They are dressed in white shirts and trousers, and wear belts hung with cowbells. On their heads, they wear gigantic *Lichtkappen* (lighted caps) of various shapes decorated with ornaments and symbols. The caps weigh up to 15 kg and are illuminated from within. The purpose of the custom is to drive away the evil spirits of Ebensee.

The Glöckler of Ebensee, wearing exquisite lighted caps, get ready to dance in front of various homes on the eve of 6 January.

In the Rauris valley in Salzburg province, the legendary beaked Perchten of Rauris are out on the eve of 6 January, warding off mischief from house and farmstead and ensuring that everything is clean. The half-bird, half-witch costume is worn chiefly by men. Their beaks are about 60 cm long, and their clothing includes overalls, headscarves, baskets worn on the back, wooden scissors and brooms. If a home is found to be unclean, they threaten to open the stomach of the housewife. The stomach is considered a symbolic receptacle for the filth swept up by the Perchtens' broom. However, when they are entertained with food, wine and gifts, they forget to look too closely in all the corners and instead frolic and have fun with the owners of the households.

Easter Holidays

Shrove Tuesday (Fat Tuesday, Fasching or Carnivale) is the day before Lent. More importantly, it refers to a period of time when many festivals are celebrated throughout Austria up to and including the last day for drinking alcohol and feasting on certain foods before the abstinence of Lent begins.

A popular alpine festival is the Schemenlaufen of Nassereith in Tyrol, held once every three years on the last Sunday before Lent. The *Scheller* symbolises the male element, or winter, while the *Roller* is the female component, or spring. Three sweepers, beautifully dressed in carved wooden masks and wearing crowns made with feathers (a fertility symbol), finery, ribbons and mirrors are assigned to the *Roller*, to sweep away the snow, or winter. Also included in the procession are *Kübellmajen*, or witches; *Engelspritzer*, the Moors who splash water according to the ritual of an ancient fertility cult; *Ruassler*, who instill respect in the crowd; *Sackner*, who keep order; and *Schnöller*, who drive away winter with long-handled whips. The highlight is the fight between the bear and the *Scheller*. The bear symbolises fertility (spring) and must always win the fight against the evil *Scheller* (winter).

Bonfire Sunday in Vorarlberg celebrates a heathen ritual very likely started by the Celts. The bonfires can reach as high as 15 metres, and are lit several days before the first Sunday in Lent. Schoolchildren go around begging for wood and straw, and a bonfire master supervises the making of the bonfire.

Easter (Ostern), the day of Christ's resurrection, is heralded with more carnivals, processions, concerts and costumes. It is a day of joy following the lean and pensive 40 days of Lent. Most towns and cities have Easter markets where Easter baskets, special breads, decorated eggs and ornaments are sold.

Children in Austria love this holiday not only because it means two weeks off from school, but also because it is a time to look for coloured eggs, eat a glut of chocolate bunnies and chocolate eggs, and receive gifts from family members. Many Austrians attend church on this day to have their Easter basket lunches blessed.

You can easily buy beautifully painted eggs at any of the Easter markets throughout Austria.

The first Sunday after Easter, Catholic children in their second year of primary school receive Holy Communion for the first time. Girls wear white dresses and floral wreaths on their heads and boys wear suits. In some areas of Austria, the costume is a bit different. In Höchst in Vorarlberg, for example, the boys wear crowns of ivy leaves called the *Chappel*, showing that they are children of God or a king, while the girls wear garlands and veils.

Pentecost/Whitsun (Pfingsten) is held 50 days after Easter. Whitsun, or the festival marking the descent of the Holy Spirit, is celebrated in Arbesthal, near Bruck an der Leitha in Burgenland. An old custom there was recently revived: a young man and a schoolboy cloaked entirely in a framework of hazelnut branches and greenery both become the Whitsun kings. On Whit Monday, the Whitsun kings and the folk dance group walk through the town, stopping at various locations where the townsfolk recite a special verse and sing the Whitsun king song. The procession ends behind the main church.

Every year, the farming community of Tressdorf in the Mölltal in Carinthia put on the Mölltal passion. This wordless play depicts Christ's last days on earth. There are only roles for men (Mary Magdalene and Mary do not appear); during both world wars, the women carried on with the play in the absence of their menfolk, as it was thought to be unlucky if the play was skipped.

The second Thursday after Whitsunday is the feast of Corpus Christi (the Body of Christ, or Blessed Sacrament). There are festive processions and magnificent pageantry throughout the land. In Deutschlandsberg in western Styria, the processional route and four gospel altars are decorated with artistic and incredibly detailed carpets of flowers.

The town of Hallstatt in the Salzkammergut in Upper Austria has celebrated a Corpus Christi procession since 1623. After mass, the crowd boards boats elaborately decorated with garlands and flowers. The priest boards a special boat, and the procession makes its way to various stops along the route. The most important stop is the Salzberg (salt-giving mountain), Hallstatt's livelihood, which the priest blesses. For the last three centuries, Hallstatt has been a key area for mining salt, which was highly valued in the past, much as gold is today.

The Sunday after Corpus Christi, a strong boy is elected to swing a large flag beautifully decorated with the coats of arms of both the house of Esterházy and the Holy Roman Empire in Neckenmarkt, Burgenland. The tradition hails back to 1620, at the beginning of the Thirty Years War, when the men from Neckenmarkt helped Count Nicholas Esterházy defeat Bethen Garbor, a Hungarian rebel king. A grateful Count Esterházy reduced their rent and allowed them to dress in full regalia during special festivals. The flag is a historical artifact that has been restored several times.

Maypoles and Labour Day

In May, it is common to see the Maypole in many parts of Austria; this is a pine tree put at the top of a pole up to 20 metres tall and decorated with ribbons. The Maypole is a symbol of fertility, happiness and prosperity. It used to be erected for newly married couples so that they would be blessed with many children. Today, young men erect the Maypole on 30 April, then guard it as it is customary for boys from other villages to try to steal it. Losing the Maypole embarrasses the owners, who must then search for it. In a part of Deutschkreutz in Burgenland, it is still the custom to place small Maypoles by wayside shrines and statues of saints the night before 1 May.

Unfortunately, Maypoles today are often used for political purposes. They are usually decorated in a political party's colours as an advertisement and also to create a rallying point.

Labour Day (Tag der Arbeit) is on 1 May, a day off for all working people. It is also a favourite day of politicians, who make never-ending speeches at political rallies. Parades abound in all the major cities, so park your car and walk around to enjoy the festivities.

Summer Festivals

Bonfires all over Austria mark the Summer Solstice. Fire, as tradition has it, symbolised great power, warding off peril and pestilence in midsummer. Today, bonfires mark the sun's

Maypoles, which symbolise fertility, are centres of festivals in small villages.

reaching its zenith, on the first Saturday or Sunday after 21 June. There are also bonfires marking saints' days: Saint Vitus fires on 15 June, John the Baptist fires on 24 June, and fires for Saint Peter and Saint Paul on 29 June.

In two neighbouring villages in the Lungau region in Salzburg, there are beautiful processions celebrating Saint John (24 June) and Saint Paul (29 June). Each procession is heralded with beautifully-decorated poles called *Prangstangen*, 6–8 m tall, weighing 45–80 kg, and covered with garlands of

40,000 flowers. Only single, eligible men may carry the poles. They wear a traditional costume with a heavy white scarf tied around one shoulder, which the pole is then fitted into. After the procession, the poles are brought into the church and remain there until 15 August, Assumption Day.

The poles are made lovingly by farming families. A week before each procession, wildflowers such as daisies, arnica, pinks, gentians and lady's mantle are collected. The women make up the garlands and the men tie them around the poles. The origins of the tradition are not known. Some believe that several centuries ago, a plague of locusts and beetles destroyed the harvest and ate the trees. A vow was made soon thereafter to protect trees and crops forevermore from a plague of that nature; decorating the poles symbolised disguising the crops and trees from their destroyers.

15 August is Assumption Day (Maria Himmelfahrt), when the Virgin Mary ascended to heaven. In parts of western Austria, it is also when the church blesses a variety of herbs. Different herbs are collected depending upon the region. In Lofer in Salzburg province, the bunch should consist of 72 different herbs. Small bunches are more common, but they should contain at least the following herbs: arnica, goldenrod, camomile, brown gentian, mint, yarrow, woodruff and horsetail—all sun-dried in the garden. Some are added to cattle fodder to make the animals more resistant to disease, and some burned at Christmas and New Year to bring good luck and prosperity.

Samson the Giant

In the Lungau region in Salzburg and around Murau in Styria, several villages have a giant they call Samson. This giant is a symbol of strength. One man carries Samson, a figure usually 6 metres tall made from wood and papier-mâché, wearing a cuirassier's helmet and a cloak over his striped tunic and carrying a halberd. There are usually four helpers standing by in case Samson's bearer wavers and falls. Samson is usually seen after church festivals or processions, when he is taken from house to house to perform a dance before guests of honour.

There are different versions of how this figure originated. Some say Capuchin monks brought him in from Bavaria. Others, that Samson is a relic of Baroque-style processions. Yet others think the Celts used large figures for special celebrations. Lungau people believe, however, that he was built to frighten the raiding Turks.

Herds and Harvests

The ritual driving down of herds of cattle happens on 15 September in the Schwarzenberg of the Bregenzerwald, a mountainous area outside Bregenz, the capital of Vorarlberg. The weather starts turning cold at about this time, and the cattle are driven down from the Alps into the warm valley. Tradition holds that to prevent demons and ghouls from noticing the long trek up and down, the cattle have to be 'veiled'.

Today the cattle are decorated only on the way down with beautiful headdresses of pine, fir twigs, ribbons and flowers, to show joyful and thankful celebration for the safe summer on the mountain. The townspeople give the cattle and cowherd a warm welcome in the middle of the square, and cowbells are then removed.

Harvest Thanksgiving, held between the end of September and the end of October, is the anniversary of the dedication of the local church. Although no actual harvest takes place, traces of days of yore are represented in the procession to the church. The women are usually in their local costume, the children carry sheaves or a basket of fruit to be blessed by the priest, and there is also the traditional harvest crown and harvest garland. The festivities, which are similar throughout Austria, include a street party with food, beer and wine stalls, rides for children, farmers selling cheese and meat and toys and clothes for sale.

National Day

26 October sees much patriotic flag-waving throughout Austria as the people commemorate the day in 1955 when the last of the World War II troops (English, American, Russian and French) left. It is also known as 'fitness day', and many people

go out for long walks. Entrance to the parliament building and all national museums is free of charge on this day.

Saint Martin's Day (Martinmas)

In the east of Austria and Burgenland where Saint Martin is the patron saint, 11 November is a time to eat goose (*gans*) and drink wine. This meal is a feast that brings family and friends together. Legend has it that there was once a Roman soldier named Martin who cut his coat in half with his sword to share it with a shivering beggar. This soldier was to become bishop of Tours. The eating of goose comes about because he took refuge among a gaggle of geese to avoid being consecrated as a bishop, but the noise they made gave his hiding place away. Kindergarteners remember Saint Martin by making lanterns of different styles and materials. At dusk, the lanterns provide light as these children and their parents go for a walk through their neighbourhood.

Christmas Markets (Chriskindlmärkte)

The end of November is when Christmas markets, or *Christkindlmärkte*, spring up throughout Austria, offering wonderful warm punches and wines, sweets that will tickle your fancy, beautiful ornaments, wooden toys, crafts and much more. The most popular ones are found around the *Rathaus* of most cities, although there are unique and intimate markets tucked away in villages or castles. Chat with your neighbours or watch out for posters about the markets. Wonderful activities for children abound near the Christmas markets, such as the making of wooden toys, glass and silk painting, candlemaking, cookie baking and more.

Saint Nicholas Day

6 December marks the beginning of the Christmas season, when children look forward to a visit from Saint Nicholas (representing goodness) and dread meeting his evil companion, Krampus (representing the devil). On the eve of 6 December, children sometimes leave their boots outside their room, in the hope of receiving nuts and fruit from Saint Nicholas if they have been good, instead of lumps of coal

Krampus, who represent evil, wrecks havoc at a Christmas market in Innsbruck on Saint Nicholas Day.

from Krampus if they have been bad. Today, coal is never received, except as a joke, and instead of fruit and nuts, children are given presents and specially-decorated bags of sweets and chocolates. Saint Nicholas dresses in a red robe with gold trim, a red and gold bishop's hat, a long white beard and white gloves, and carries a staff. Krampus, who accompanies him, is also dressed in red, but wears a red mask, horns and tail, and has one foot made up as a hoof. He carries a bag of coal and a large, long chain to gather and hold children who have been bad. Strictly speaking, Krampus Day is 5 December, but because of all the festivities normally going on at that time, Krampus Day is celebrated together with Saint Nicholas Day.

In East Tyrol, the Klaubaufgehn is celebrated. It is a time to celebrate Saint Nicholas, but, especially in the town of Matrei, it is also an excuse to work off aggression, settle feuds and have a good brawl or two. The proceedings begin at 6:00 pm for three days beginning 4 December. The *Klaubäufe* (somewhat like the Krampus) start by ringing bells attached to their waist. They are dressed in a costume made from corn leaves and wear masks with grotesque grimaces. Saint Nicholas arrives with his retinue: two angels, one carrying a bell and a lantern, and the other a basket of cookies and fruit; a *Lotter*, the accordionist; and the *Litterin*, who begs for alms from spectators. They walk from house to house and will only cross the threshold of a house if they are welcome. Saint Nicholas asks about the children's behaviour over the past year and distributes his gifts. In the meantime, the *Lotter* plays a tune while the *Litterin* collects alms. Outside, the *Klaubäufe* make a terrible commotion as they also want to visit. Saint Nicholas decides whether or not to let them in. In days gone by, the *Klaubäufe* would take the main table and bring it outside to dance on; if the table was damaged, it was a bad omen for the owner. Saint Nicholas is supposed to have the ability to prevent bad things from happening and to stop whatever raucousness may ensue.

Crib visiting in Tyrol is a tradition that became popular in 1223, when Saint Francis of Assisi had a crib set up in a cave in Greccio forest to illustrate Christ's incarnation. The crèche (the tableau of Christ in his crib, with Mary, Joseph, the three wise men and farm animals looking on) then became the symbol of Christmas, rather than the Christmas tree as we have come to know it.

Sculpted crèches became extremely popular during the 17th century Counter-Reformation in Tyrol. Some of the most exquisite and ornate ones date from that period. Today, famous sculptors create crèches that can be as large as a farmhouse room. Sculptured crèches can be found in the villages of Zirl, Rum, Götzens, and, above all, Thaus near Innsbruck.

Crèches can be viewed in Tyrol from 26 December until 15 January. Friends, acquaintances and strangers are welcome to go through homes and view the crèches. A sign reading *Weihnachtskrippe* welcomes them into the home.

Christmas Eve (Weihnachten) is traditionally the evening when families get together, have a good meal, sing Christmas carols and open presents around the Christmas tree. Many Austrian children don't believe in Santa Claus but in the Baby Jesus. Children write letters to him at the beginning of Advent (four weeks earlier), asking him for things they would like. The letters are left on the windowsill.

Christkindl in Lower Austria is an actual town made famous by its name. Children also send their Christmas wish lists there, and many people go to this town especially to have their Christmas letters postmarked with its name.

Silvester (New Year's Eve)

Silvester is a huge celebration in the provincial capitals. Many Austrians prefer to stay home and celebrate the night in a more relaxed way. They have their own fireworks display, eat decorated sandwiches (always open-faced) and drink *Sekt* (sparkling wine). They also pass good luck to each other through the exchange of marzipan, ceramic and cloth pigs, chimneysweeps and four-leaf clovers. To foresee what luck the year will bring, many buy lead pieces especially made for New Year's. A piece of lead is put on a spoon, melted over a candle, then quickly plunged into cool water. Whatever form the lead takes reveals the character of the coming year.

Vienna's 1st district turns into a stage on New Year's Eve, with many different bands performing live outdoors. As the night progresses and becomes more rowdy, people start setting off fireworks amidst the crowds. The highlight is when the bells of Saint Stephen ring in the New Year. Beware, however, after the last bell has tolled: many crazy people throw their bottles of *Sekt* up in the air!

Public Holidays
- New Year's Day (1 January)
- Epiphany (6 January)
- Easter Monday
- Labour Day (1 May)
- Ascension Thursday
- Whitmonday
- Corpus Christi
- Assumption (15 August)
- National Day (26 October)
- All Saint's Day (1 November)
- Immaculate Conception (8 December)
- Christmas (25 December)
- Saint Stephen's Day (26 December)

OUTDOOR ACTIVITIES AND SPORTS

Prater

Especially if you have children, don't miss the Prater in Vienna. This large green area and amusement park was hunting grounds for the aristocracy until Emperor Josef II opened it to the public. When the waltz was at the height of its popularity, the cafés here were crowded with people who came to dance. The relatively small amusement park has rides for thrill seekers of all ages. The park is famous for the over 65-metre tall *Riesenrad* (Ferris wheel), which has become a symbol of Vienna. Although there are no high-tech rollercoasters, the smaller, older ones still provide an exciting ride. There are brand new slingshot and bungee-type rides for the more daring. Some attractions open year-round, but most close between November and March. The rides operate from morning until midnight. The Hauptallee is a pedestrian-only street full of people walking, rollerblading and cycling. The large park is great for picnicking or sports.

River Cruises

An exciting way to see Vienna, Lower Austria and some of the neighbouring countries is to take a cruise along the Danube.

The Prater in Vienna, formerly imperial hunting grounds, has an amusement park, restaurants and plenty of green areas for sports.

The Vienna cruise is short and not particularly captivating. A longer, more delightful journey takes you through the Wachau valley. A river trip allows you to see the castles that line the Danube the way they were meant to be seen. You can travel from Vienna to Tulln, Dürnstein, or all the way to Melk and back. Alternatively, drive to Krems (where the Wachau begins) and travel by boat between Krems and Melk. You can even take your bicycle and explore the area that way. If you feel adventurous, take a *Schnellboot* (fast boat) to Bratislava or Budapest—Bratislava for the day, Budapest for the weekend. The trips take 1½ hours and 5½ to 6½ hours respectively. None of these journeys can be made during the winter.

Winter Sports
Skiing

Austrians revel in the approach of winter because they know how to take full advantage of the season with skiing, snowboarding, ice skating, sledding and Alpine style curling. So don't hide out in your heated home, but bundle up and venture out for some fun in the snow.

Skiing is second nature to Austrians, who grow up skiing and are among the best in the sport—not surprisingly, as Alpine skiing was first developed in Tyrol. On winter weekends, cities empty as everyone flocks to nearby resorts. If you ski, you'll be anxious to hit the slopes too, but keep in mind that some consider the runs here more challenging than those in the United States. Runs are categorised by colour according to difficulty: beginners blue, intermediates red and advanced black. Ski lessons are available for first timers and those who wish to brush up on their skills.

The Viennese frequent Semmering, Annaberg, Josefsberg and Wechsel, all about one hour away in Lower Austria. On holidays and during winter vacation, they travel much farther to even better resorts, although they prefer to stay within Austria and rarely ski in the Swiss, French or Italian Alps. Families tend to return to the same resort year after year. In Tyrol, Seefeld (near Innsbruck) and Ischgl are among the favourites, while Kitzbühel and Saint Anton are popular with the wealthier set. In Vorarlberg, Lech and Zürs are by far the best known. They are expensive, but offer high quality infrastructure, such as helicopters. In Salzburg, Austrians head to Badgastein, Saalbach-Hinterglemm, Zell am See and Obertauern. The World Cup race has been held in Schladming in Styria, another popular resort. Nassfeld in Carinthia is also a great place to ski.

Skiing Gear

Clothing and equipment play an important role in skiing. Everything the Austrians use is of high quality. This appears to be the one time that Austrians wear brightly-coloured, non-conservative clothing.

Make reservations well in advance and be aware that every province has its own 'ski week'. As part of the school year, students take a week-long ski trip. Each province is assigned its own week so that the runs do not become overcrowded and every school in the province will go skiing that specific week. All Austrians learn to ski very young, so don't be discouraged by the kids' abilities.

Snowboarding is becoming increasingly popular, especially among the young. It is considered 'cooler' than skiing. Snowboarding is permitted at all resorts, and some problems have arisen as snowboarders and skiers must share runs. Some resorts hope to establish separate runs, but that is not expected to happen anytime soon.

Skiing is a social activity, and after a day on the slopes, Austrians enjoy a big meal and drink *Glühwein* and *Schnaps*. On the downside, they often light up cigarettes as soon as the skis are off. Heavy smoke may be the only disadvantage to passing the evenings in ski lodges.

Summer skiing is possible in a few places in Tyrol, Salzburg and Styria. The best-known location for the sport is 40 minutes outside of Innsbruck, at the Stubai Glacier. Other areas in Tyrol are the Upper Tux valley and above Mayrhofen on the Gefrorne Wand glacier.

Cross-country skiing, although less popular than downhill skiing, is another great way to enjoy winter. If you live in Vienna, you needn't go far to indulge in the sport. Besides a 4-km trail in the Vienna Woods between Cobenzl and Kreuzeiche, there is also good cross-country skiing near Mariazell. Seefeld near Innsbruck has 200 km of cross-

There are many beautiful places for skiing in Austria, and the sport has won the hearts of Austrians and visitors alike.

country trails. Many other resorts, like Kitzbühel, are well equipped for cross-country skiing.

Ice-skating

Ice-skating is another way to enjoy being outdoors during the winter months. In Vienna, there are public ice-skating rinks at the Rathaus and the Stadtpark. They charge an entrance fee and for skate rental. The Rathaus has two large rinks and some amazing paths where you can skate quickly and in a zig-zag pattern around the garden. At night, the ambience changes with live bands and DJs playing dance and hip-hop music. During carnival season, the Rathaus rink offers shows complete with ice princesses and princes.

There is plenty of skating and ice sailing on the Neusiedlersee in Burgenland. Every other major city and all ski resorts have ice-skating rinks, but the best is in Innsbruck, where you can skate at the Olympic rink.

If skating is not for you, you can try your hand at curling at the Rathaus rink. A cold-weather event would not be complete without something to keep you warm. Stalls surround the Rathaus rink selling food, coffee, and, of course, *Glühwein*.

Yet, in the winter, all you need is a snow-covered hill to have fun, and this makes tobogganing the easiest sport to practice. It doesn't require lessons and kids love it. If you are searching for a somewhat substantial hill, there is a toboggan run near Cobenzl in the Vienna Woods.

Summer Sports
Hiking

Wandern, a favourite pastime in Austria, combines hiking, strolling and observing. With all the rural and scenic areas in Austria, a perfect setting can always be found. Thanks to the efforts of the Viennese in 1870, who launched a campaign to stop the sale and subsequent razing of the Vienna Woods, today's generation can enjoy the forest and all it has to offer. The Vienna Woods comprise about 80,000 acres of beech trees and conifers, with oak, elm, maple, poplar and aspen commonly seen. They stretch from the foothills of the Alps to the Vienna city limits. Innumerable paths crisscross through the trees, the most famous passing through the Helenental near Baden. If you plan on doing a lot of hiking, get vaccinated for encephalitis, which is carried by ticks. Most Austrians have been vaccinated because bites are not uncommon. The woods provide ample opportunity for horseback riding, swimming, fishing and simply relaxing. Many lovely *Gasthäuser* (inns) and *Heurigen* are located in the Vienna Woods.

The Lainzer Tiergarten on the edge of the 13th district is a large section of the Vienna Woods. It was once a royal hunting reserve and is currently home to native wildlife. One of the numerous trails through the park leads to the Hermesvilla built by Franz Josef for his Sissi. It hosts exhibitions and has one of the park's many restaurants. There are two entrances to the park: the Nikolaitor on Himmelhofgasse and the Lainzer Tor on Hermesstrasse. If you want to see wild animals like elephants and lions, you must visit the safari park in Gänserndorf, half an hour north-east of Vienna. It also has a petting zoo and playground.

Bicycling

As you walk through the cities, you'll notice designated bicycle lanes everywhere. If you are driving or walking, do take care because there are a significant number of bikes on the road, particularly in summer. Maps of bike routes for major cities like Linz, Graz, Innsbruck, Salzburg and Saint Pölten are found in local tourist information offices. The city of Vienna alone has over 500 km of cycling paths, 40 km of which can be found on the Donauinsel (Danube Island). The Prater is another good place for cycling.

The Donau Radweg (Danube Bike Path) covers 305 km and stretches from Passau in Germany to Hainburg near the Austrian border with Slovakia. The Wachau section is particularly pleasant. You can even cycle around Neusiedler Lake. It takes more than a day, camping is possible, and you need your passport because the southern tip lies in Hungary. If you are up to it, you can participate with 13,000 other riders in the 355-km Tour de Mur that takes place every June in Styria. Of course, there are many bicycling paths throughout Austria, including some challenging ones in Alpine areas.

Rules and Rental

In Vienna, bikes are allowed on the subway and trains, but with some restrictions: not during rush hours, with a half-price ticket for the bike and confined to areas with a blue-and-white bicycle sign. If you don't own a bicycle, rent one at the following train stations: Westbahnhof, Südbahnhof and Bahnhof Wien Nord. You can also rent bicycles on the Donauinsel and at the Prater amusement park.

Donauinsel

Not only can you ride your bike on Donauinsel, but there are also walking paths, large greens for picnicking or playing soccer and a trampoline-like play area for children that floats on the river. You can rent bikes and rollerblades near the Reichsbrücke. The Viennese head to the island to sunbathe and swim in the river. After a day of sports, you can relax with a drink or a meal in one of the many clubs or restaurants. The Donauinsel is easily reached by taking the U1 subway, or you can park nearby and cross over to the island.

Water Sports

In the summer, Austrians take to the water to swim, sail, windsurf or canoe. Hundreds of lakes dot the country amid beautiful surroundings. Closest to Vienna is the Neusiedlersee in Burgenland, the only steppe lake in Europe. It averages 2 metres in depth, making it very warm in the summer, but is an incredible 30 km long. If you go, plan a full day because you have to pay to enter the lake area.

The lakes of the Salzkammergut are colder but have a more romantic setting. Carinthia is another wonderful area with almost 200 lakes; the most popular is Wörthersee. The shores are lined with hotels and more affordable pensions. Less well known are the lakes of Tyrol. Achensee is the largest in the region and provides good facilities. Many resort areas also provide swimming pools.

For those who are stuck in Vienna, follow the locals and swim in the Danube. The Strandbad Alte Donau has beaches and swimming pools. You can also rent rowboats and sailboats. The Donauinsel has beaches, a regular pool and a wave pool. If you're walking along the river, don't be surprised to find little piles of clothes here and there. People tend to swim in their underwear, especially when they are trying to catch some sun on their lunch hour. At the far end of the island is a nudist beach.

If walking and water sports are too tame for you, try rock climbing and hang-gliding. Hohewand, just south of Vienna, is a sheer cliff wall that is perfect for such activities. Rock climbing is possible in many Alpine resorts.

If you don't want to swim in the river, there are many indoor and outdoor swimming pools to enjoy. Brochures listing all the pools are available from the City Information Office at City Hall. Their quality is good and all have lifeguards on duty. Many pools offer classes for children and adults. The Stadionbad in the Prater has six pools and waterslides in addition to the big pool. The Krapfenwaldbad in Grinzing is set amidst vineyards and overlooks Vienna. The Schafbergbad sits high up in the hills of the 18th district. The Hallenbad Döbling has a fantastic children's pool, and for those living in the 13th district, there is the Hallenbad Hietzing.

Dancing

Ballroom dancing will come in handy if you plan on attending a ball. There are many *Tanzschule* (dance schools), and some have private lessons in English. In Vienna, check out Ellmayer (Bräunerstrasse 13, 1st district), Immervoll (Hietzinger Hauptstrasse 6, 13th district) and Wiater (Martinstrasse 96, 18th district). For dance schools throughout the country, check out the website http://www.tanz.or.at.

Spectator Sports

Austrians are especially proud of their world champion professional skiers, including Hermann Maier, Toni Sailer, Franz Klammer, Karl Schranz, Annemarie Moser-Pröll and Renate Götschl. Austrian skiers consistently rank among the best in international competitions. Austria has played host to many world and European championships in a variety of disciplines, among them Alpine Skiing World Championships,

Nordic Skiing World Championships, Ice Hockey World Championships and ski jumping competitions. If you want to fit in, keep abreast of professional ski events; they are likely to come up in conversation.

Austrians also enjoy watching *Fussball* (soccer) matches, and their national team made it to the 1998 World Cup. Many Austrians are interested in motor and motorcycle racing. There is a Formula 1 track near Graz. Austria's most famous driver is Niki Lauda, who won the Formula 1 World Championship title in 1975, 1977 and 1984. Jochen Rindt, Franz Wurz, his son Alexander Wurz and Gerhard Berger are other well-known names. Austrians also enjoy betting on the horses races. Races take place at the Freudenau Track at the Prater on specific days. If you're only interested in betting, there are a number of places to do so, often located in train stations.

Spas

Austria has a number of spa resorts that treat a variety of ailments and offer curative waters, curative mud treatments, kneipp cures, dietetic treatments and acupuncture. Thermal baths are found all over the country, in Alpine resorts and in eastern Austria. Sulfur springs are said to be good for joints, muscles, the nervous system and certain skin problems. Baden, near Vienna, is famous for its sulfur springs, as is Bad Goisern in the Salzkammergut. Iodised springs, such as Bad Hall in Upper Austria, are helpful in curing metabolic and circulation disorders and vision and glandular problems. Salt springs are said to be good for gynecological and respiratory problems and can be found in Bad Ischl in Upper Austria and Salzerbad in Lower Austria. Bicarbonate-bearing waters, such as those at Bad Gleichenberg in Styria, are ingested to treat stomach, intestinal and kidney ailments. The waters at Badgastein are special because of their radon content, which is believed to help relieve rheumatic pain. Radon cannot be retained by the body and is eliminated within 2–4 hours. Many spas also use mud treatments to help those suffering from inflammation of the joints and certain skin problems. You can undergo such treatments at Grosspertholz and Bad

Harbach in Lower Austria. As you might have guessed, *Bad* is German for baths, and any town with *Bad* in its name will have thermal baths. At Bad Vöslau, a special grape cure is offered during the grape harvest. Schärding, in Upper Austria, is known for its Kneipp hydrotherapy cures.

Travelling

In order to fully enjoy many of these activities, you'll need to travel throughout Austria. The roads are excellent and no destination is ever more than a day's drive away. The major cities offer a wide array of accommodations, from charming hotels to affordable pensions. If you are looking for a quiet weekend in a small town or rural community, there are many options. A good choice is a *Bauernhof*, or family farm. The lodgings are comfortable and you are always made to feel welcome. The homemade meals are another draw. Your hosts are especially nice if you have children, because many are working farms and the kids can help out. A weekend at one of these farms is extremely affordable.

Another possibility for those with children is *Kinder Hotels* (Children's Hotels). They offer babysitting services and even full-scale play centres where you can leave your children for the day. Everything is geared toward the children, from activities to meals. It takes the pressure off you so you can enjoy the vacation as well.

CHAPTER 8

THE GERMAN LANGUAGE

UNABHÄNGIGKE KLÄRUNGEN

'I prefer German opera even though it means
more trouble for me. Every nation has its own opera...
Is not German as singable as French and English?
Is it not more so than Russian? Very well then!
I am now writing a German opera for myself.'
—Wolfgang Amadeus Mozart, composer,
in a letter to his father in 1783

THE GERMAN LANGUAGE CAN BE MIND-BOGGLING. German, surprisingly enough, is a relative of English. In fact, German, English and Dutch are known as West German languages. High German, which is used today, comes from a Saxon dialect. Other German speakers often regard the version spoken in Austria as singsongy. Once you have taken a few German lessons and your ear has become used to the language, things get easier.

Within Austria itself, there are regional differences. For example, the German spoken in Vorarlberg is much closer to the German they speak in neighbouring Switzerland than in other parts of Austria. Accordingly, the Tyrolian dialect is distinct and can be quite difficult to understand. Don't worry about learning all these dialects, however, because all Austrians will communicate with you in High German.

For those living in the capital, if you think, 'Fine, I'll be living in Vienna, the cosmopolitan capital city of Austria where they only speak the formal German (Hoch Deutsch)', then you'd better think again. Vienna probably has more dialects within its districts than any other Austrian city, as it has always been home to a variety of ethnic groups,

Susan remembers staying on a farm in Upper Austria near Schärding and being very proud of the fact that she could hold a conversation with the owner. Thinking that the local dialect was not all that complicated, she was crestfallen when the woman took a phone call and began speaking in a dialect that was utterly unintelligible. At that point, she decided just to focus on High German.

Learning German will help make day to day errands much easier.

primarily from neighbouring countries. The language is a cache of terms from Czech, Hungarian, Italian, Yiddish and even medieval Teutonic. For example, the word *Beisel*, which refers to a bar, is derived from the Hebrew *bayith*, meaning house. In fact, Viennese theatre and literature are where the Viennese dialect shines through. Many operettas by Viennese composers such as Strauss and Lehár also make use of the dialect spoken by the common man. It takes a special ear and frame of mind to understand what is being said.

Here is an example of a *Wiener Deutsch* (Viennese German) sentence, broken up into phrases. The proper German equivalents are given in the next column and the English translation follows. See if you can make it out:

Viennese German
Kuaz und Guad von Herbert Pirker
Denkmoeschuz-wikl
Min schenbrunna bod
Haums wos beinaund
De aan woens oreissn
De aundan woens eahoetn
Brenna wü kana
S denkmoeaumd
Benimmd si

Wia wauns des soezaumd waa
Und wauns so weidaged
Kennan
Wuaschd ob des bod
Offn is oda zua
Olle midaund
Bodn ge

Proper German
Kurz und Gut von Herbert Pirker
DenkmalSchutz-Wickel
Mit Schönbrunner Bad
Haben's etwas bei einander
Die einen wollen es abreisen
Die anderen wollen es erhalten
Brennen will keiner
Das Denkmalamt
Bennimt sich
Wie wenn es das Salzamt wäre
Und wenn es so weiter geht
Können
Wurst ob das bad
Offen ist oder zu
Alle mit einander
baden gehen

English Translation
'Short and Good' from Herbert Pirker
Monument Trouble
There is statue protection trouble at the Schönbrunner pool.
They have a difficult situation. One wants to tear it down, the
other wants to keep it up. No one wants to pay. The Statue
office behaves itself as the Salt office would. And if it goes
too far, then it doesn't matter if the pool is open or closed,
as we will all be in trouble.

THE INFORMAL AND FORMAL 'YOU'

German is very formal. While the English language does
not distinguish between a formal and an informal 'you',

Wäu kana brend gean z'vü!

If you thought German was difficult, wait until you hear the Viennese dialect. This sign translates as '*Weil keine brennt gerne zu viel*', or 'Because no one likes to get too burnt'.

in German, such formality is very much in use. *Du* is the informal 'you', and *Sie* the formal 'you'. If, for example, you were talking to an adult whom you had just met, you would use the *Sie* form of 'you'. For example:

Wo wohnen Sie? (Where do you live?)

If I knew the person well and they asked me to please use *per Du*, then I would say the following instead:

Wo wohnst Du? (Where do you live?)

If you are speaking to a child or to someone you have become friendly with, use the *Du* form. Some of the older folk always expect the courtesy of *Sie*, even from a long-time acquaintance. The formal *Sie* would also be used with shopkeepers, your boss and the stranger on the street.

SENTENCE CONSTRUCTION

Sentence construction is one of the most difficult aspects of learning German. The reason that it is hard to master is that in German, the verb often ends a sentence, whereas in the English translation it would come in the centre. For example:

Ich muss in die Schule gehen. (I must go to school.)
Ich hole dich um 4 Uhr ab. (I will pick you up at 4:00.)

Thus, one is forced to listen intently to what is said in order to understand the meaning of a long drawn-out sentence. On the other hand, it is a good means of teaching children to listen. The problem for the student of the German language is that when speaking, one cannot translate from one's own language, but instead must think in a whole different way. It is an experience similar in many ways to playing the piano for the first time.

THE MANY DIFFERENT CASES

The declension of the cases of the German language is the cause of many mistakes. The English language does not change with the case being used, but German does. There are four cases: nominative, accusative, genitive and dative. In each case, the pronoun, adjective and noun change. For example:

Nominative	*Mein guter Freund*	My good friend
Accusative	*Meinen guten Freund*	My good friend
Genitive	*Meines Guten Freundes*	Of my good friend
Dative	*Meinem guten Freund*	To my good friend

CAPITALISING NOUNS

One simple and seemingly easy rule is that all nouns are capitalised. This would make any elementary student very happy indeed. However, confusion sometimes arises when you are not sure whether the noun is actually a person or a thing. For example:

Die Rose ist eine Blume. (The rose is a flower.)

GENDER

Nouns can be feminine, as in *Die Zeitung* (the newspaper); masculine, as in *Der Mann* (the man); or neutral, as in *Das Restaurant* (the restaurant). There is no rhyme or reason for which noun gets which gender, but there are patterns. Take this as a challenge for the memory.

COMPOUND WORDS

Compound words are mesmerising. Several words are 'scrunched' into one. Some examples are:

Kinderbewahrungsanstalten	Childcare
Donaudampfschifffahrts gesellschaftskapitän	Captain of the Danube Steamship Company
Unabhängigkeitserklärungen	Declaration of Independence
Wiederherstellungsbestrebungen	Endeavor to reconstruct

GERMAN IS PHONETIC

The loveliest part of the German language is that it is phonetic. All vowels and consonants are pronounced, and the tricky ones lie only with a few sounds:

*rei**ch*** (rich)	Like Lo**ch** in Lo**ch** Ness but pronounced very softly
*Sch**üssel* (bowl)	Has the 'sh' sound, as in **sh**ame
***z**ahlen* (to pay)	Pronounced 'ts'
*M**u**tter* (mother)	Same vowel sound as in b**oo**k
***V**ogel* (bird)	Pronounced with a hard 'f', as in **f**ood
*s**t**ehen* (stand)	Pronounced as if there was a 'ch' between **s** and **t**
*sto**ß*** (push, knock)	Ends with a sharp 's'. The German language is slowly evolving to replace the **ß** with a double s, or 'ss'.

Quelle (source)	Pronounced '**kv**'
Julia (proper name)	Pronounced '**y**' as in **y**ule
wandern (to hike)	Pronounced '**v**' as in **v**an

Pay special attention to *umlaute*, fondly known as the 'rascalion upper double dots'. If pronounced badly, the word is not understood. *Süd* (south) is like the French 'u' as in 'sur'; *Männer* (men) uses the same vowel sound as in 'fair'; and *schön* (pretty) is like the 'o' in 'some'. If you are typing a letter and do not have *umlaute* on your keyboard, type an 'e' after the vowel; for example, instead of *schön*, write *schoen*. Remember, the secret is to soften those vowel sounds.

ANIMAL NAMES AND THEIR CALL

One of the most interesting aspects of the language is that animals are named according to the sound they make: *Kuckkuck* is cuckoo bird, *Pfau* is peacock, *Uhu* is owl, *Kuh* is cow, *Bär* is bear and *Krähen* or *KraKra* is crow.

NUMBERS

Reading or writing numbers can be an extremely trying endeavor. Either way, one must think backwards after the

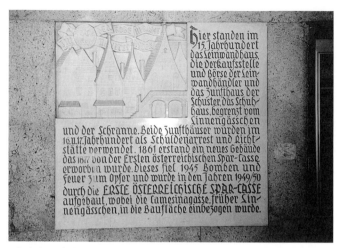

A little knowledge of German will help you find your way around a number of cultural venues where no translations are offered.

number 20. For example, 21 is read as 'one and twenty' or *einundzwanzig*. When writing a number, it is always good practice to leave plenty of space and start writing the number backwards as it is read off.

The next challenge is to tell the time. If it is 8:30, the time is read as *halb neun* and sometimes written as ½ 9. If it is 8:15, it will be read as *viertel neun* and sometimes written as ¼ 9. Take note that Austrians may also write or say the time using the 24-hour clock.

A COMMENT FROM MARK TWAIN

Mark Twain, the famous American writer and satirist, felt very strongly about the German language. This is what he wrote:

'Surely there is not another language that is so slipshod and systemless, and so slippery and elusive to the grasp. One is washed about in it, hither and thither, in the most helpless way; and when at last he thinks he has captured a rule which offers firm ground to take a rest on amid the general rage and turmoil of the ten parts of speech, he turns over the page and reads, 'Let the pupil make careful note of the following exceptions.' ... There are ten parts of speech, and they are all troublesome. An average sentence, in a German newspaper, is a sublime and impressive curiosity; it occupies a quarter of a column; it contains all the ten parts of speech—not in regular order, but mixed; it is built mainly of compound words constructed by the writer on the spot, and not to be found in any dictionary—six or seven words compacted into one, without joint or seam—that is, without hyphens; it treats of fourteen or fifteen different subjects, each enclosed in a parenthesis of its own, with here and there extra parentheses, making pens with pens; finally, all the parentheses and reparentheses are massed together between a couple of king-parentheses, one of which is placed in the first line of the majestic sentence and the other in the middle of the last line of it—after which comes the VERB, and you find out for the first time what the man has been talking about; and after the verb—merely by way of ornament, as far as I can make out—the writer shovels in 'haben sind gewesen gehabt haben geworden sein,' or words to that effect, and the monument is finished. I suppose that this closing hurrah is in the nature of the flourish to a man's signature—not necessary, but pretty. German books are easy enough to read when you hold them before the looking-glass or stand on your head—so as to reverse the construction—but I think that to learn to read and understand a German newspaper is a thing which must always remain an impossibility to a foreigner.

'My philological studies have satisfied me that a gifted person ought to learn English (barring spelling and pro-nouncing) in thirty hours, French in thirty days, and German in thirty years. It seems manifest, then, that the latter tongue ought to be trimmed down and repaired. If it is to remain as it is, it ought to be gently and reverently set aside among the dead languages, for only the dead have time to learn it.'

—Mark Twain, 'The Awful German Language' from *A Tramp Abroad*, 1880.

DOING BUSINESS IN AUSTRIA

CHAPTER 9

'*Morgenstund' hat Gold im Mund.*'
'The early bird catches the worm.'
—Proverb often heard in Austria

THE ECONOMY

Austria's economy was in shambles following World War II. The Marshall Plan pumped much-needed money into the country, and eventually the economy took off. In 1995, Austria joined the European Union and its economy became integrated with the other markets of the region. In 2002, the common currency of the EU, the Euro (€), replaced the Austrian Schilling.

Schillings to Euros

The official exchange rate was 13.67 Schillings to € 1. Following the conversion, many items seemed more expensive than before. Some suspect that instead of doing the proper math, people merely dropped a zero from the price in Schillings. For example, a worker who before might have received a tip of 50 Schillings, now gets € 5 instead of a more accurate € 4.

Historically, Austria has had a strong public sector, characterised by a large number of publicly-owned companies and heavy regulation of the economy. Many industries, like banking, manufacturing, electricity, telecommunications and transportation, were nationalised following World War II. In an effort to reduce its budget deficit to comply with the stability programme for the Euro, Austria began a series of privatisations. The telecommunications sector allowed

Traditionally, monopolies and oligopolies ran the economy. Various associations and chambers made decisions instead of letting them fall to the 'free hand' of the market. For example, The Association of Pharmacists decide when and where a new pharmacy is needed.

private competition and prices have fallen. Portions of other publicly-owned firms such as banks, Austria Tabak and the Vienna Airport have been sold. Not all have gone smoothly and there has been some resistance, but the programme is moving forward.

Austria's economy is considered to be among the top economies within the EU. Key economic indicators like unemployment and inflation are better than those found in the rest of Europe. The country has been enjoying steady growth, around 1 to 2 per cent. Export-oriented industries and construction drive economic growth.

ECONOMIC SECTORS
Industry
Industry and mining together account for about 35 per cent of GDP. The main industries in Austria are foodstuffs, beverages, tobacco, mechanical and steel engineering, electronic products, chemicals and plastics, transportation equipment, construction and textiles. In general, most manufacturing outfits are small. The few exceptions include iron and steel plants in Linz and Styria, which produce enough material for

The Schwechat refinery meets almost all of Austria's oil and gas needs.

the entire country, and an aluminum plant near the border with Germany that is one of the largest in Europe.

Austria is famous for crystal (Swarovski), porcelain, leather and ski equipment. Not only does the country produce top of the line skis, it is also a major manufacturer of ski lifts.

Mining

Important minerals have been mined in this region since prehistoric times. The key minerals found in Austria are iron ore, lignite, gypsum, salt, limestone and magnesite. Aluminum, lead and copper are also produced here.

Energy Resources

Austria lacks major energy sources and must import more than 80 per cent of its oil and natural gas. Most of the latter is piped in from Russia. While small reserves of oil can be found north of the Alps, it is mainly imported from the Middle East. Near the airport on the outskirts of Vienna is the Schwechat refinery, one of the largest in Europe.

Most of the power produced within Austria comes from hydroelectric power stations located in mountain areas, the Alpine foothills and on the Danube River. In fact, Austria is the number one producer of hydroelectric power in the EU. Nuclear power is not generated in the country.

Austria is interested in developing alternative sources of energy, such as wind power.

Cultural centres like Salzburg draw large numbers of foreign visitors. Tourism is a very important sector of the Austrian economy.

Service Sector

The entire service sector accounts for the largest percentage of GDP, ringing in at about 62 per cent. Financial services represent a key sector of the economy. Yet, it is the tourist industry that dominates the sector, bringing in substantial revenue. Tyrol leads the provinces, welcoming the highest number of both international and domestic tourists. In the winter months, ski resorts across the country are packed. Germans make up the largest group of foreign visitors by far, and an overwhelming majority of tourists are European.

Agriculture

Agricultural production is an important part of the Austrian identity. A drive through low-lying areas reveals farms, orchards, vineyards, grazing and pastureland. In fact, roughly 18 per cent of the country is farmland. Practically all farms are family operated, and over half are small-scale enterprises. In spite of EU subsidies, only about a third of farmers earn enough from farming to cover living expenses; the rest must seek additional sources of income.

About two-thirds of agricultural products are derived from animals, with an emphasis on dairy yield. The main crops cultivated are corn, barley, wheat, rye, potatoes and sugar beets. In the east, there are a significant number of vineyards and orchards where apples, plums, apricots, peaches and pears are grown. Austria is nearly self-sufficient in food production. Together with forestry, agriculture accounts for about 3 per cent of GDP.

Forestry

Almost half of Austria's surface is covered with forests and woods, and about 12 per cent of its exports are timber, timber products and paper products. After years of exploitation, reforestation efforts are being made, and new techniques such as controlled thinning have been introduced.

International Trade

Austria's main trading partners are its fellow countries in the EU. Over 60 per cent of exports are to EU members, with Germany receiving the lion's share and Italy coming in second. Important non-EU trading partners are Switzerland and eastern European countries, with Hungary topping the list. Outside of Europe, a significant amount of trade is conducted with the United States and Japan. Almost half of all exports consist of machines and transport equipment; manufactured goods make up another quarter; and consumer goods, chemicals, foodstuffs, tobacco, raw materials and energy make up the rest. Environmental technologies are also an important aspect of international trade.

Austrian businesses are taking part in the globalisation process, although staying primarily within Europe. Austrian direct foreign investment is focused mainly in Germany and in the new EU member states of central and eastern Europe and, increasingly, in south-eastern Europe. In the first few years following the collapse of communism, about 40 per cent of direct foreign investment in eastern European countries came from Austria. That percentage has since declined as other countries (mainly from the EU) have headed into these markets. Once heavily invested in countries like Hungary and the Czech Republic, Austrian firms are now also looking toward Ukraine, Serbia, Montenegro, Bosnia and Herzegovina, Bulgaria and even Albania.

Austria itself experienced a surge in investment when foreign firms picked Austria (most notably Vienna) as a base for their forays into these same markets. A significant number of important multinational corporations, headquartered in the United States and in EU countries, initially set up offices in Vienna to oversee their expansion into the former eastern bloc. In addition to the obvious benefits of living in Vienna, foreign executives knew they could rely on a valuable labour force that has close links, both cultural and linguistic, with these markets. Lately, the surge in this type of investment has tapered off.

BUSINESS CUSTOMS

The average office is formal in the way employees interact with one another and with clients. There is an emphasis on doing the 'right thing'. Of course, to some non-Austrians, this can mean an atmosphere that is rather uptight. The greatest difference for many foreigners, however, is that what you know doesn't count as much as who you know.

Etiquette

Etiquette is standard in a business setting. Shaking a client's or a colleague's hand is customary and a good way to begin a relationship or maintain one. Punctuality is central to the process of any business meeting and is a principle adhered to by employees. Appointments should be made well in advance and it is considered rude to cancel a meeting at the last minute. Meetings are formal and follow a certain protocol. It is best to get to the point at hand after only a bit of small talk. Stick to your agenda and schedule, the meeting should end at the prearranged time. Do not be offended if the Austrians seem blunt; they merely want to discuss the topic at hand and will expect detailed information. Meetings are followed by significant amounts of written communication.

Business Cards

Exchanging business cards is customary although it is not done with any type of fanfare. Because of their interest in titles, it would be a good idea to put any advanced degrees or honours you have received on your card. It is also a nice gesture to have one side of your business card written in German.

Dress

At work, the average businessman or businesswoman wears a classic, dark-coloured suit to work, civil servants dress down and blue-collar workers wear uniforms. For instance, garbage collectors wear orange and construction workers wear blue.

How to Conduct Business

- Be punctual.
- Dress conservatively.
- Shake hands.
- Use the formal 'you' (*Sie*) and last names.
- Stick to the agenda and schedule.
- Follow up with written correspondence.
- Offices are formal and colleagues don't normally socialise after hours.

Titles

There is a predisposition for the use of titles, handed down from the Habsburgs. Although the law has banned the use of noble titles, the list of professional titles is endless. Titles serve the dual purpose of advancing your status and of flattering people who will, hopefully, make a difference in your professional life.

The strict use of titles affects how Austrians perceive and relate to one another.

Sie

In addressing one another, one's boss is either Mr (*Herr*) or Ms (*Frau*), followed by the family name. The boss is always addressed with the formal 'you' (*per Sie*). If someone were your elder, the same formality would be applicable. For your colleagues, begin with the formal 'you' (*per Sie*) and then, after a while, you should be able to use the informal 'you' (*per Du*).

In academia, *Herr Professor* or *Frau Professor* is used to address a teacher. *Frau Professor* could also be the wife of a professor, but the same would not apply to a man married to a *Frau Professor*. The title *Doktor* is held by a PhD, a master's degree begets you a *Herr* or a *Frau Magister*, and for an engineer (who, like *Herr Magister*, also has had six years of university training), a *Diplom-Ingenieur*.

Colleagues

Most expatriates who work in managerial positions do get along well with their Austrian subordinates. There are differences in work ethics, but the boss is treated with respect. For an expatriate with an Austrian employer, the offices are comfortable to work in. The formality, however, can be stifling. There isn't much laughing or joking around. The people you work with are all referred to as colleagues (*Kollege/Kollegin*), meaning people you will only relate to in a business or formal setting. Most often, you will refer to each other by last name only. It is understood that colleagues are not people you mix with on a social basis. There is a tendency to keep work and social time separate and the company doesn't put pressure on its employees to get together for social events.

The flip side of the stuffiness is that it serves to protect one's private sphere and keeps working relationships uncomplicated and free of silliness, wounding gossip and ugly bickering. The time it takes to get to know other Austrians is valuable, as it allows a slow, peaceful and respectful development of the relationship. A friend of Julie's who is now a professor at the Music School in Vienna appreciated the transition between using the formal *per Sie* with professors of hers while she was studying, to the informal *per Du* with the same teachers after she herself was accepted as an equal doing the same work.

Human Factors in the Working Environment

A lot of thought is put into trying to make employees happy in their working environment. There is an awareness of human factors such as natural lighting, spacious room (no cubicles) and plenty of ventilation. Bathrooms in offices are enclosed and provide much-needed privacy.

ATTITUDE TOWARDS BUSINESS

Austrians are not known to pursue their career aggressively. However, they are very aggressive against equal or lower ranks. They want to maintain and protect their job and salary (which they never speak about to one another) from younger, aspiring colleagues. It could be equated to a cat-and-mouse game.

Wheeling and Dealing

Austrians are thought of as businesspeople who don't like to have things in black and white, but who rather enjoy the idea of bargaining and trying different ways to get what they want. There is a saying, '*In Wien beginnt der Balkan* …', literally 'the Balkans begin in Vienna'. In a sense, the old-fashioned marketplace is still at work.

The Private Businessperson

The average businessperson is content to get the job done. It is very rarely that one puts in overtime or works on the weekend to do more than expected. In general, management doesn't create enough incentive to encourage a faster pace of work, or to bring out the full creative potential of its workforce.

Social Security

Every Austrian is covered by a comprehensive social security system that ranks among the best in the world. In addition to welfare benefits, a pension plan and health, unemployment and disability insurance, the system provides well for families by way of family allowances and extended maternity leave.

Changing Jobs

There is not much desire to move from job to job. Most Austrians stay with the same company because they get comfortable and become used to the status quo. Perhaps this attitude has to do with their way of handling problems: many will ignore it or complain about it and go on. Surprisingly enough, it would be easy for most Austrians to gain new employment, as Austria's social security system is so comprehensive that changing jobs would not have any effect on vacation pay or retirement. The system does, however, hit those who start their own business or go freelance. Salaried earners are worshiped by the system, and anyone daring to leave the social system is punished.

Starting Your Own Business

Leaving the social system requires strength of character, a great business IQ and quite a bit of capital. The business that you begin cannot be a gamble. There is little help for those who fail. If loans are taken out to help your business survive and you still do not succeed, your life will never be the same. The result is that Austria is last on the entrepreneurial totem pole in Europe.

Success is a Bad Word

You could be one of the most hardworking people in your office, or you could have created something new and different, but the sceptical Austrian will just shake his head and wonder who helped you out, or tell you in no uncertain terms that there are dozens of people just like you. Lack of opportunity, few jobs at the top and a highly educated population breed cynicism in the majority.

This attitude gives rise to contempt for new inventions too. It is called *österreichisches Erfinderschicksal*, or the Austrian's fate for being ignored when he comes up with anything new. The bureaucracy will find various reasons to degrade the invention: we have never done that before; we have always done it another way; or, if we accept yours, anyone could come along and try and convince us of their ideas. Thus, modernisation takes a backseat to tradition. Titles and status take on more meaning than they should, and creative, hardworking people, even perhaps a few geniuses here and there, are squelched before they even begin.

The Civil Servant on the Job

Jokes are made about the clerk or official (*Beamten*). It is said that in government offices, the traffic of clerks arriving late and leaving early can be as bad as a car jam on a busy highway. Lunchtime can be, well, any time. Sick leave seems to be every other day, although after one day you need a doctor's note (still, there is no restriction on the amount of sick leave you can have). Then there are the holidays and vacations. The holidays correspond generally to the Catholic holidays, and vacation time depends on your status (up to eight weeks a year).

The bureaucracy is so great that it requires an astronomical workforce (25 per cent of Austria's workforce) to keep it

running. Employment as a clerk doesn't require much education, and many clerks are hired for social reasons, which propagates the abuse of privileges. Many clerks aspire to become tenured or to join the permanent (*pragmatisiert*) staff, which brings job security.

Working Hours

One issue on which Austrian labour unions remain immovable is the duration of the workweek. Austria has some of the most limited business hours in all of Europe. Many big businesses would like longer hours, in order to be able to operate on evenings and Sundays. Opponents argue that extended business hours would reduce employees' flexibility and time with family, and would hurt small family-owned businesses. Even though most Austrians say they would probably shop on Sundays if possible, three-quarters of those polled do not think business hours should be extended.

Women in the Workforce

Women in Austria are at work. Their education is as good as men's, enabling them to land professional positions. About 44 per cent of the labour force is female. While 60 per cent of female employees work full-time, 40 per cent hold part-time positions in retail, health, social services and the service industries. Many women say they would like to work full-time, but are unable to either because they cannot find full-time employment or because of their childrearing duties. Childcare shortages are reported in certain parts of Austria, primarily in rural areas. This translates into lower wages for women. The gender pay gap is about 33 per cent, near the average for the European Union. In the political arena, 34 per cent of seats in parliament in 2004 were held by women.

The hardest time for an office is when a female employee has a baby. Besides granting maternity leave of 24 months (or up to 30 month depending on the circumstances), the firm must pay an allowance of roughly € 500 per month and guarantee the employee's job when she returns.

Service? Was ist das?

Service is still a foreign word to many government offices, stores, restaurants and coffee shops. In many government offices, the clerk decides when to come to your aid. If you push, the clerk will pull back.

In stores, and especially in boutiques, you are often judged by your outward appearance: hair, clothing and shoes. Of course, it helps to have shopped there before or to know someone with a title who has sent you to 'this special boutique'. In larger stores, the outlook is different, but the customer is still rarely king. Try to take something back and the store employee might come up with the line that 'if you can't handle the product, it's your own fault'. Of course, service in upscale or tourist-oriented restaurants, shops and hotels is much better.

FAST FACTS

CHAPTER 10

'The straight line is ungodly.'
—Friedensreich Hundertwasser, architect and artist

Official Name
Republic of Austria

Flag
Three equal horizontal bands of red (top), white (middle) and red (bottom)

National Anthem
Land der Berge, Land am Strome

National Flower
Edelweiss, a small white flower. It is actually very rare and grows at higher elevations.

Time
Standard time zone: GMT + 1
Daylight saving time: GMT + 2

Country Code
43

Climate
Temperate; continental, cloudy; cold winters with frequent rain and some snow in lowlands and snow in mountains; moderate summers with occasional showers

Föhn: These are warm, dry winds that come from the Alps. They are strongest in Tyrol but can be felt all the way in Vienna. These winds are said to cause people to feel out of sorts and cranky. They are believed to be responsible for an increased number of suicides.

Avalanches: The greatest natural threat to Austria is an avalanche. Although those most at risk are thrill seekers who ski at very high altitudes on unstable powder, deadly avalanches occasionally hit more populated areas.

Location
Central Europe, bordered by Germany, the Czech Republic, Slovakia, Hungary, Slovenia, Italy, Switzerland and Liechtenstein

Land Area
Total: 83,870 sq km (32,382.4 sq miles)
Land: 82,444 sq km (31,831.8 sq miles)
Water: 1,426 sq km (550.6 sq miles)

Highest Point
Grossglockner: 3,798 m (12,460.6 ft)

Lowest Point
Neusiedlersee: 115 m (377.3 ft)

Natural Resources
Oil, coal, lignite, timber, iron ore, copper, zinc, antimony, magnesite, tungsten, graphite, salt, hydropower

Population
8,192,880 (July 2006 est.)

Ethnic Groups
German-speaking 98 per cent. Six officially recognised ethnic groups live primarily in the eastern and southern parts of the country. They are Croats, Hungarians, Slovenes, Czechs,

Slovaks and Romany. (In order to be an officially-recognised ethnic group, its members need to have lived in Austria for at least three generations and be Austrian citizens.) Other significant groups include Turks and Bosnians.

Religion
Roman Catholic 73.6 per cent, Protestant 4.7 per cent, Muslim 4.2 per cent, other faiths 3.5 per cent, agnostic 12 per cent and the remaining 2 per cent provided no information.

Official Language
German

Government
Federal republic

Capital
Vienna

Administrative Divisions
Nine federal provinces: Burgenland, Kärnten (Carinthia), Niederösterreich (Lower Austria), Oberösterreich (Upper Austria), Salzburg, Steiermark (Styria), Tyrol, Vorarlberg, Wien (Vienna)

Currency
Euro (€)

Gross Domestic Product (GDP)
$309.3 billion

Agriculture Products
Grains, potatoes, sugar beets, wine, fruit, dairy products, cattle, pigs, poultry, lumber

Industries
Construction, machinery, vehicles and parts, food, metals, chemicals, lumber and wood processing, paper and paperboard, communications equipment, tourism

Exports
Machinery and equipment, motor vehicles and parts, paper and paperboard, metal goods, chemicals, iron and steel, textiles, foodstuffs

Imports
Machinery and equipment, motor vehicles, chemicals, metal goods, oil and oil products, fuels, foodstuffs

Airports
55 (25 with paved runways)

FAMOUS PEOPLE
Franz Josef
Last great emperor of Austria, ruled from 1848 until his death in 1916. The city of Vienna flourished during this time, but the Austro-Hungarian Empire began to break apart under his reign.

Sissi
Empress Elisabeth of Austria. Beautiful wife of Franz Josef who is still loved by the Austrians. Murdered in Switzerland by an Italian anarchist.

Maria Theresa (1717–1780)
First female to rule the Austria-Hungarian Empire. She was a respected and powerful leader.

Bruno Kreisky
Affectionately known as Emperor Bruno, Kreisky and his Socialist Party ruled Austria from 1970 until 1983. He instituted a number of liberal domestic reforms and increased Austria's role in international affairs.

Kurt Waldheim
Secretary General of the United Nations from 1972–1981 and President of Austria from 1986–1992. Questions regarding his participation in Nazi-era crimes caused controversy within Austria and internationally.

Jörg Haider

Governor of Carinthia and former head of the FPÖ right-wing party, which he later left to create a new party, The Alliance for Austria's Freedom. He has caused much controversy with his anti-immigration and populist comments.

Franz Joseph Haydn (1732–1809)

Classical music composer who spent 29 years in the commission of the royal Esterházy family at their palaces in Eisenstadt, Burgenland and Esterhaza, Hungary.

Wolfgang Amadeus Mozart (1756–1791)

One of the greatest composers of all time. Born in Salzburg, he produced a vast and highly-respected collection of musical pieces, including symphonies and operas. He is Austria's most beloved son.

Ludwig van Beethoven (1770–1827)

Although born in Germany, Austrians love to claim him as one of their own. He lived many years in Vienna, where he produced magnificent concertos and symphonies.

Franz Peter Schubert (1797–1828)

Composer of 600 *Lieder* (songs) and numerous symphonies, masses, quartets and sonatas.

Johann Strauss Jr. (1825–1899)

Composer of the famous *Blue Danube Waltz*, among many other waltzes, polkas and operettas. Affectionately known as the 'Waltz King'.

Johannes Brahms (1833–1897)

Traditional classical music composer of the Romantic Period.

Gustav Mahler (1860–1911)

Composer of post-Romantic classical music, including nine symphonies. Conductor of the Vienna Opera House for ten years before moving to New York City as the conductor of the New York Philharmonic Orchestra.

Anton Bruckner (1824–1896)
Often called 'God's musician', this classical music composer is known for his symphonies and masses.

Arnold Schoenberg (1874–1951)
Introduced atonality and the 12-tone technique to music composition in the early 20th century.

Gustav Klimt (1862–1918)
Fin de siècle artist and president of the Secession, whose most famous piece *The Kiss* is often reproduced.

Egon Schiele (1890–1918)
Early 20th century artist who is most noted for his semi-pornographic drawings and paintings.

Oscar Kokoschka (1886–1980)
Early expressionist artist.

Otto Wagner (1841–1918)
Father of modern Viennese architecture and member of the Secession. Designed the *Stadtbahn* (the Vienna railway network), which dates from 1898.

Friedensreich Hundertwasser (1928–2000)
Artist and architect who combined bright colours, wobbly geometric shapes and natural materials in his building used for everyday life.

Ferdinand Raimund (1790–1836)
Dramatist who used humour and farce in his plays.

Johann Nestroy (1801–1862)
Playwright who employed Viennese dialect and word play in his comedies.

Adalbert Stifter (1805–1868)
Writer and poet of the Biedermeier period. *Der Condor* is among his more famous works.

Franz Grillparzer (1791–1872)
Highly-respected poet and playwright.

Arthur Schnitzler (1862–1931)
Popular *fin de siècle* playwright and author, whose works are known for tackling anti-Semitism.

Robert Musil (1880–1942)
Author whose most famous work is the novel *The Man Without Qualities*.

Josef Roth (1894–1939)
Novelist who often wrote about imperial Austria. His best known work is, perhaps, *The Radetzky March*.

Peter Altenberg (1859–1919)
Viennese poet who lived the Bohemian life, spending his time in coffeehouses, most notably the Café Central.

Georg Trakl (1887–1914)
Expressionist poet born in Salzburg. His poems reflect the carnage he witnessed in World War I.

Sigmund Freud (1856–1939)
Founder of psychoanalysis.

Simon Wiesenthal
Jewish Holocaust survivor and Nazi hunter. Born in Ukraine, but after World War II lived in Vienna until his death in 2005. He founded the Jewish Documentation Centre in Vienna.

Thomas Bernhard (1931–1989)
Well-known author and playwright whose works and comments tended to cause controversy.

Wolf Haas (born 1960)
Best-selling author, primarily of crime novels. A number of his works have been turned into successful movies.

Elfriede Jelinek (born 1946)
Contemporary and controversial author who was awarded the Nobel Prize in Literature in 2004. Her most famous book is *The Piano Teacher*.

Peter Handke (born 1942)
Famous and controversial author.

Hedy Lamarr (1913–2000)
Austrian-born Hollywood actress.

Romy Schneider (1938–1982)
Film actress, noted for portraying Empress Sissi.

Hansi Hinterseer (born 1954)
Former skier who is now a popular folk singer.

Joe Zawinul (born 1932)
Very successful jazz musician who has collaborated with many artists, including Miles Davis.

Falco (1957–1998)
Internationally-recognised pop musician. His hits included 'Amadeus', 'Der Kommissar' and 'Vienna Calling'.

Anton 'Toni' Sailer (born 1935)
Considered to be one of the best all time Apline skiers. He won three gold medals at the 1956 Olympics (downhill, slalom and giant slalom).

Franz Klammer (born 1953)
Alpine skier who won a gold medal at the 1976 Winter Olympics in Innsbruck.

Hermann Maier (born 1972)
Very successful Alpine skier who has won four World Cup titles, two Olympic gold medals and three World Championship titles.

Renate Götschl (born 1975)
Alpine skier who has won two Olympic medals.

Benjamin Raich (born 1978)
Alpine skier who won two gold medals at the 2006 Winter Olympics.

Niki Lauda (born 1949)
Formula One driver who won World Championship titles in 1975, 1977 and 1984.

ABBREVIATIONS

AUA	Austrian Airlines
ÖBB (Österreichische Bundesbahn)	Austrian Federal Railway
EN	EuroNight (International and Domestic Train)
ÖAMTC (Österreichischer Automobil-, Motorrad- und Touring Club)	Emergency Road Service and Towing
ÖMV (Österreichischer Mineralölverwertung)	Austrian Oil Company
ORF (Österreichischer Rundfunk)	Austrian Radio and Television Network
TA (Telekom Austria)	Austrian Telecom
EU	European Union
ÖVP	People's Party
SPÖ	Social Democrats
FPÖ	Freedom Party

PLACES OF INTEREST
Vorarlberg
- Bregenz: This city sits on the shore of Bodensee (Lake Constance). Performances during the city's summer festival take place on a floating stage.
- Lech and Zurs: Top of the line but pricey ski resorts.

Tyrol

- Innsbruck:
  - Goldenes Dachl (little golden roof): This small balcony, dating from 1500, on the former Ducal Palace is topped with 2,657 gilded shingles. It was commissioned by Maximilian I to commemorate his second marriage to Bianca Sforza of Milan.
  - Hofkirche: Contains the memorial tomb of Maximilian I, which is surrounded by 28 large figures representing his ancestors, relatives and heroes. The best statue is of King Arthur by Albrecht Dürer.
  - Ambras Castle: On the outskirts of Innsbruck, this 16th century castle houses collections of armour, art, books and exotic objects.
- Stams Monastery: A Cistercian Abbey with over 180 rooms dating from the 13th century. Its carved altar, designed in the shape of a tree, is worth the trip.
- Kitzbuhel, Saint Anton, Ischgl and Seefeld: Internationally-acclaimed ski resorts.
- Tux Valley: Offers skiing in the summer months.

Salzburg

- City of Salzburg:
  - Hohensalzburg Fortress
  - Mirabell Palace and Gardens
  - Birthplace of Mozart
  - Residenz
  - Getreidegasse
  - Hellbrun Palace
  - Sound of Music Tours
- Eisriesenwelt (World of the Ice Giants): Underground caves with massive ice formations.
- Untersberg: Mountaintop near the town of Saint Leonhard accessible by cable car with spectacular views of the ice-covered mountains and the lakes of the Salzkammergut region.
- Krimml Falls: Largest waterfalls in Europe.
- Bad Hofgastein and Badgastein: Popular ski resorts.
- Zell am See: Picturesque lakeside town, close to glaciers that allow year-round skiing.

Carinthia

- Klagenfurt: Capital city, known for the dragon fountain in the main square erected in 1593 to commemorate the city's founding.
- Hochosterwitz: To get to the castle on the top of the hill, you have to pass through the 14 gates that once protected it.
- Wörthersee: A popular summer destination, this lake is great for swimming, boating, windsurfing and sailing.
- Maria Wörth: Town sitting on a tiny peninsula that juts out into the Wörthersee.
- Hohe Tauern National Park: Site of the Grossglockner, the tallest mountain in Austria.
- Magdalensberg: Archeological excavations of Celtic and Roman ruins.
- Maria Saal Cathedral: 14th century pilgrimage church located on a hilltop just north of Klagenfurt.
- Nassfeld: Ski resort.

Styria

- Graz: Capital city, the historic city centre has been declared a United Nations Cultural Heritage Site. Visit the top of the Schlossberg and see the Uhrturm (bell tower). Other sites include the Landhaus, the Opera House and Cathedral. Childhood home of Arnold Schwarzenegger.
- Mariazell: The church, founded in 1157, is now the most important pilgrimage site in Austria. A small statue of the Virgin Mary and Child is reported to be able to perform miracles. People visit to ask for favours or give thanks.
- Benedictine Abbey of Admont: One of Austria's most famous monasteries, it is home to the largest monastic library in the world.
- The Erzberg mountain and the Iron Route: See where much of Austria's iron is mined and enjoy some outdoor activities like hiking, along the way.
- Saint Barbara in Bärnbach: Church that was remodelled by Hundertwasser.

Upper Austria

- Linz: Pöstlingberg hill; Landhaus, formerly Linz College, where the astronomer Johannes Kepler taught.
- St. Florian Abbey: Pilgrimage site for over a thousand years. The composer Anton Bruckner often played the organ here and is buried in the church's crypt.
- Salzkammergut region (although this region lies in three provinces, the heart of the Salzkammergut is located in Upper Austria.): Some of the largest and most beautiful lakes are Attersee, Traunsee, Mondsee and Hallstattersee.
  - The town of Hallstatt has been called the most beautiful lakeside village in the world and is a UNESCO World and Nature Cultural Heritage Site.
  - The church in the town of Mondsee is where the wedding scene in the movie *The Sound of Music* was filmed. Other towns of interest are Saint Wolfgang and Saint Gilgen. Gmunden is noted for its colourful pottery. Franz Josef spent his summers in Bad Ischl, thus drawing the aristocracy and other important people of the 19th century here as well.
- Braunau, Obernberg and Schärding: Three towns along the Inn River close to the border with Germany. Schärding has a lovely Baroque town centre and is also known as a health resort that uses the hydrotherapy cure invented by Sebastian Kneipp.
- Steyr: One of the best-preserved main squares in all of Austria. Make sure you see the gothic Bummerlhaus.

Lower Austria

- Wachau valley: Beautiful valley along the Danube River dotted with apricot orchards and vineyards.
- Dürnstein: Popular medieval town in the Wachau. You must park your car outside of town before strolling through the narrow streets of this walled city. You can climb to the fortress ruins that overlook the town. This is where Richard the Lionheart was held captive in the 12th century.
- Aggstein: Climb through the ruins of this ancient castle high up over the Danube.

- Krems, Und, Stein: Medieval towns at the end of the Wachau valley. Krems has been restored and is a lovely tourist destination.
- Melk Abbey: Tour the Emperor's Gallery, the Marble Hall, the library and the church decorated lavishly in gold.
- Baden: Lovely town known for its curative baths. An easy drive or train ride from Vienna, it's a perfect place to spend the day. Stroll through the town or head to the spa, the casino or the Kurpark. Sixty kilometres of trails that pass through the Vienna Woods begin here in the Kurpark.
- Klosterneuberg: Just north of Vienna, this monastery houses the Verdun Altar.
- Vienna Woods: The forests surrounding Vienna are a great place to hike or merely wander.

Vienna

- Stephansdom: Vienna's main cathedral, located in the geographical centre of the city. This Romanesque and Gothic church has been an important part of the city since the 13th century.
- Staatsoper: Opera House.
- Volksoper: People's Opera House, mainly operettas performed in German.
- Musikverein: Home to the Vienna Philharmonic Orchestra.
- Vienna Boys' Choir: Internationally-recognised boys choir that was originally founded in 1498. They perform on Sundays (except in summer) at the Burgkapelle in the Hofburg.
- Spanish Riding School: Where the graceful Lippizaner horses perform.
- Belvedere: Palace originally built for Eugene of Savoy, now a museum most noted for its collection of Jugendstil artists, especially Klimt, Schiele and Kokoschka.
- Schönbrunn Palace: Summer residence of the Habsburgs. Tour the palace and then spend the afternoon out in the gardens or at the zoo.
- Kunsthistorischesmuseum: Fine arts museum, noted for its 16th and 17th century art.

- Museum Quartier: A complex that houses a number of museums, such as the Museum of Modern Art and a children's museum, performance centres and restaurants.
- Hundertwasserhaus and KunstHausWien: The first is the colourful public housing complex designed by architect Friedensreich Hundertwasser. You can admire it from the outside, since entry is not allowed to the public, but you can view Hundertwasser's art and other exhibits at the KunstHausWien a couple of streets away.
- Prater: Amusement park in the centre of Vienna famous for the *Riesenrad* (large ferris wheel).
- Gasometer: Huge gasholders from the Simmering Gasworks that date from 1896 have been renovated and now house stores, restaurants, apartments and a movie theatre.

Burgenland
Eisenstadt
- Esterházy Palace: Home to the royal Esterházy family and where Josef Haydn lived and worked for many years. You can tour the palace, or hear hear Haydn's music performed in the Haydnsaal concert hall.
- Austrian Jewish Museum and Jewish quarter of Unterberg: Throughout history, Eisenstadt was home to many Jews.
- Forchtenstein castle: Its museum houses a huge collection of arms and armour (close to 20,000 items on exhibition).
- Schlossstrasse (Castle Road): Burgenland means land of castles, built to protect Vienna from the Turks. Some of the highlights on this route, which continues into Styria, include Lockenhaus, Bernstein, Stadtschlaining and Güssing.
- Neusiedlersee: Huge steppe lake, about 30 kilometres long but averages only 2 metres deep. Popular in summer for water sports, especially wind surfing.
- Rust: Small town noted for the storks that nest atop the chimneys.

CULTURE QUIZ

SITUATION 1

You've been invited to a small dinner party by some new Austrian friends. Eager to make a good impression, you:

Ⓐ Arrive about 15 to 20 minutes later in order to give the hosts enough time to get everything ready.

Ⓑ Quickly proceed to the living-room area where the other guests are after saying hello to the hosts, and begin introducing yourself to everyone.

Ⓒ Arrive exactly at the hour specified, greet your hosts, hand the hostess a beautiful bouquet of flowers, and wait to be introduced to the other guests.

Ⓓ If you are a man and want to be truly European, greet each woman by taking her hand and raising it almost to your lips and say *"Küss die Hand"*.

Comments

Ⓐ Never appropriate if the hosts are Austrians. Guests are expected to be on time and arriving late is considered rude. Susan was once reprimanded for arriving 5 minutes late. If you've run into some unforeseen problems or heavy traffic, you should call and notify your hosts.

Ⓑ If you are attending a small dinner party, you should wait to be introduced to each of the guests. This actually makes it much easier on you if you don't know anyone there. If it is a large party, the hosts probably won't introduce you to everyone, perhaps just a couple of people so that you can join in a conversation. You can then meet other people on your own.

Ⓒ Yes, this is the best way to impress your new friends. By arriving on time, you show your hosts that the invitation is important to you. By giving the hostess flowers or a bottle of wine, you are thanking her for all the effort she has put into the evening. It would also be a good idea to send a thank you note by mail the following day.

O The *Küss die Hand* greeting is practised only in certain circles and a foreigner can look especially stupid trying it out. Our advice is to leave it to the experts and just shake hands as most Austrians do. Only once you have established a close relationship can you greet each other by kissing on both cheeks, starting with the right one. This, of course, does not apply for greetings between men. You may never attain this level, however, and to avoid any embarrassment, you should wait for the Austrian to make the transition from a handshake. Don't assume that the time is right.

SITUATION 2

You have just started working for an Austrian company. Your German is good but you are not aware of the formalities on the job. You greet your co-worker by her first name. She, in turn, greets you by your last name and asks you how you are doing by using the formal 'you' or *per Sie*. What do you do?

A Tell her that where you come from, you are immediately on a first-name basis with colleagues.

B Tell her not to be so stuffy, to hang loose.

C Correct yourself and ask her a question by using her last name and use *per Sie* until further notice.

D Look for another job.

Comments

A You may appear rather ethnocentric. On the other hand, your co-worker might understand that things are different around the world. However, in Austria, one greets another in a more formal manner.

B Choosing **B** might make her react very negatively. As in **A**, formality is often a way for relationships to develop slowly and to be sure you know the person you are dealing with before revealing yourself.

C The only way to go is with **C** if you want to keep in good stead with your co-worker. This behaviour will win you points with every Austrian you meet.

❶ This is the loser's way out. Every job you have will end the same way unless you work with your own kind at an embassy or consulate.

SITUATION 3

After a long, tiring day on the ski slopes, you decide to unwind in a hot steamy sauna. Knowing it to be mixed, you put on your one-piece bathing suit to hide any little imperfections and head off. When you open the door, you gasp: everyone is stark naked. Do you:

❶ Alert the management and tell them to call the police because there's an orgy taking place.

❷ Sit down in the far corner, subject to puzzled stares.

❸ Make a mad dash to the privacy of your room where you can enjoy a nice hot bath alone.

❹ Strip off your suit, sit down and join the conversation.

Comments

❶ This is obviously not the correct answer. Austrians are comfortable being naked in the sauna or at a nudist beach and there is nothing sexual about the experience.

❷ You could do this if you really want to be in the sauna but just can't take off your suit. The Austrians would think it very odd though, and wouldn't be able to figure out just why you are wearing your bathing suit.

❸ This is a good option if being in the sauna makes you uncomfortable, but you have to settle for a bath instead of a sauna.

❹ If you can, go ahead and join in. Nudity is not out of the ordinary for Austrians so they won't stare or pay any more attention to you than to anyone else. While they don't use their towels to cover up, you could drape yours strategically for your own comfort.

SITUATION 4

Your cupboards and fridge are bare and you need to go to a grocery store. You buy everything in sight, then load it all onto the conveyor belt. The cashier rapidly checks your items through but then you realise that your groceries are merely piling up next to the cashier's elbow as there is no rear conveyor belt. She is fuming and the people behind you are hemming and hawing. What to do?

ⓐ Quickly, like a madperson, start piling purchased groceries back into your cart.

ⓑ Stare at her with a look of amazement.

ⓒ Ask her in your broken German for an explanation for the lack of rear conveyor belts and baggers.

ⓓ Take your time; either put everything back in the cart or have some plastic bags ready and pack then and there.

Comments

ⓐ This is the best answer, and what most people do to keep up with the cashier. Most Austrians shop several times a week to avoid making large purchases or go once a week to larger grocery stores where rear conveyor belts are found.

ⓑ This would make matters worse and most likely end with the cashier swearing and people behind you adding odd comments.

ⓒ Like **ⓑ**, this would confuse the cashier as most people never question the system. And the cashier most likely would not even know that rear conveyor belts exist.

ⓓ Risky, but if you can handle the pressure, go for it! Julie used to bag groceries, so for her, there would be no other option but to do it right there and then!

SITUATION 5

You're celebrating a special birthday and have invited a few of your new friends to a Saturday night party. You have food, wine and music and the party has been a great success, but by no means a big bash. Just after 10:00 pm, the doorbell rings. It's the police telling you that a neighbour has called to complain about the noise at such a late hour. Surprised, because the party is not especially loud, you:

ⓐ Tell the police what they want to hear, close the door and resume festivities.

Ⓑ Phone the neighbour you believe made the complaint, call her an 'old cow' and tell her to get a life.

Ⓒ Offer the police a bribe so that you can continue partying.

Ⓓ Make sure to invite all of your neighbours to your next party so that they'll be at your place having fun instead of at home suffering.

Ⓔ Apologise to the police, turn off the music and try to talk softly, or else end the party prematurely.

Comments

Ⓐ This is what many foreigners might choose to do, but it's really not a solution. The neighbours will continue to complain, the police will return, and the party might end on a sour note.

Ⓑ This childish response certainly won't help smooth relations with your neighbours.

Ⓒ Bribing the police could land you in big trouble.

Ⓓ Inviting your neighbours might work the next time, but then again it might not. Your neighbours may leave earlier than your other guests, and once home could turn around and call the police because they are now ready to sleep.

Ⓔ Unfortunately, this is the only option. You are living in a country where not only is loud noise late at night prohibited, but even reasonable noise levels (for a large group) can elicit calls to the police. Hopefully, you can still have fun with the noise level down. However, if a conversation between six people has brought the police, you might have to call it a night. Another option might be to have an afternoon barbeque that starts and ends earlier.

SITUATION 6

You haven't yet registered with the police and you desperately need your *Meldezettel* to get your driver's licence. It's 9:00 am and by the time you get to the proper room, there are already 50 people waiting in line. You sit, waiting your turn. After 30 minutes, you realise that only people with numbers are being called in. You finally see the number machine and, feeling stupid, take your number after many other people have strolled in behind you. You try and tell the people behind closed doors of your dilemma but are only barked at and told to wait your turn, with the remark, "Can't you read the sign that says 'don't come in unless your number is called?'" What do you do?

Ⓐ Demand proper attention.
Ⓑ Wait patiently for your number to be called.
Ⓒ Try and talk to someone with a number that is soon to be called to see if you can go first.
Ⓓ Go home and cry.

Comments

Ⓐ Choosing **Ⓐ** will only make the civil servants scream louder. No one is special, and if you goofed, you must pay and learn from your mistake.

Ⓑ This is the wisest choice. You might have to wait a long time but you will eventually get what you need in order to get other important paperwork accomplished. In many cases, the *Meldezettel* acts like an identification card.

Ⓒ This will give someone a reason to laugh his or her head off but at least you will find out that Austrians have a sense of humour.

Ⓓ This will not get you what you need and you will only have to return another day. Better to conform and stay calm.

SITUATION 7

You decide to go out for a nice dinner. The hostess takes you to your table where you sit down, order a glass of wine and begin to relax. As you glance at the table next to you, you notice a huge dog laying on the floor underneath the table. Dumbfounded, you:

Ⓐ Go over to the table and tell the dog owners that if they quickly get the dog out of there, you won't tell the management.

Ⓑ Call over the waitress and tell her in no uncertain terms that you want that dog out of the restaurant and that you can't believe this animal has been allowed in.

Ⓒ Comment to your dinner partner on the hairy guest at the next table and enjoy your dinner.

Comments

Ⓐ, Ⓑ Both responses are inappropriate because many owners take their dogs with them to eat. If you complain about their presence, you might be the one who is the object of everyone's ire.

Ⓒ This is the correct response. You will see dogs welcomed in many restaurants. In fact, the waitstaff often provide them with their own bowl of water. Soon you won't even notice your canine neighbours because they are so well behaved.

DO'S AND DON'TS

DO'S

- Get a *Meldezettel* (registration form) within three days of arrival in Austria.
- Apply for a drivers licence within six months of arrival if you plan on being in Austria for a longer period of time.
- Arrive exactly on time for social events or business meetings.
- Bring a small gift for the hostess, for example flowers, chocolates or wine.
- Greet people you have just been introduced to by shaking hands. Kissing people on the cheek is reserved for very close friends.
- Greet people when entering a public space, like a store, with *Grüss Gott*. Say it loudly, even if you don't immediately see anyone.
- Use the formal 'you', *Sie*, with people you have just met, especially with those who are older than you or if you meet someone in a formal setting.
- Be aware of people's professional and academic titles.
- Round up your bill at a restaurant, adding up to but not necessarily a 10 per cent tip.
- Dress conservatively and elegantly. Always dress up if you are going to the Opera House, the Musikverein or any other theatre. Most balls require tuxedos and long evening gowns.
- Offer to remove your shoes upon entering someone's home. Sometimes slippers will be provided for you.
- Bring your own bags to the supermarket. Reload your groceries into the cart after they have been scanned and bag them yourself at the bagging counter.
- Be at home to let in the chimney sweep when he is scheduled to be in your neighbourhood.
- Travel to the different regions of Austria because they are all so unique.

DON'TS

- Participate in loud or rowdy behaviour in public, whether on the streets, in restaurants or on public transportation.

- Make a lot of noise after 10:00 pm or at any time on Sundays. This applies to parties or household chores such as mowing the lawn.
- Block trams or drive down the tram tracks, unless specifically allowed.
- Eat with your fingers. Always use a knife and fork.
- Be alarmed or offended to see bathers who are topless, in their underwear or sometimes even naked. Nudity is not a big issue to the Austrians.
- Throw away your recyclables. Bins for paper, glass, plastic, metal and compost are conveniently located in every neighbourhood.
- Use your boss's first name. Many relationships remain on a formal level and require you to use only the person's last name.
- Be surprised to see dogs everywhere, including at the table next to you in a nice restaurant. Just watch where you walk!
- Try to get away with not paying for public transportation which runs on the honour system. If you are caught riding *Schwarz*, you will be highly embarrassed and forced to pay a steep fine.
- Offer a police officer a bribe under any circumstances.
- Plan on doing your shopping for the week on Sundays. This day is meant to be a day of rest, to be spent with your family. It is not a day to run errands or do chores.

GLOSSARY

Essentials

Hello	*Grüss Gott* / *Servus* / *Guten Tag*
Goodbye	*Auf Wiedersehen* / **Wiederschauen** / **Wiederhören** / **Tschüss** / **Baba**
Thank you	*Dankeschön* / **Dankesehr**
Please, welcome	*Bitte* / *Bitteschön* / **Bittesehr**
Excuse me, pardon me	*Enschuldigen Sie* / *Pardon*
Where is...?	*Wo ist...?*
Where is the toilet or restroom?	*Wo sind die Toiletten?*
Where is the underground?	*Wo ist die U-Bahn?*
What is your name?	*Wie heissen Sie?*
What time is it?	*Wie spät ist es?*

* Words in bold are used more often in Austria.

In a Restaurant

Do you accept credit cards?	*Nehmen Sie Kreditkarten?*
I'd like to make a reservation.	*Ich möchte einen Tisch reservieren.*
The menu, please.	*Die Speisekarte, bitte.*
I would like ... (when ordering in restaurants, for example)	*Ich hätte gern...*
Something to drink?	*Zu trinken?*
The check, please.	*Zahlen, bitte.*
(Paying) together? or separately?	*(Zahlen Sie) Zusammen oder Getrennt?*

In a Restaurant	
(You give exact amount plus tip.)	*Das stimmt schon or danke.*
To eat in or to go?	*Zum hier-essen oder zum mitnehmen?*
A doggie bag, please? (Austrians don't normally do this)	*Können Sie mir das einpacken, bitte?*

Signs	
Exit	*Ausgang*
Entrance	*Eingang*
One way street	*Einbahnstrasse*
Platform	*Gleis*
Underground	*U-bahn*
Push	*Drucken*
Pull	*Ziehen*
Don't walk on the grass	*Rasen betreten verboten*
Toilet	*Die Toiletten*
Water closet (toilet)	*WC*
Water (from the tap)	*Leitungswasser*
Automatic teller	*Bankomat*
Cashier	*Kassa*
Pharmacy	*Apotheke*
Bakery	*Bäckerei*
Drugstore	*Drogerie*
Delicatessen	*Feinkost, Delikatessen*
Fish shop	*Fischhandlung*
Pastry shop	*Konditorei*
Grocery store	*Lebensmittelladen*
Stationery store	*Papiergeschäft*
Health food store	*Reformhaus*
Wine shop	*Weinhandel*

Titles	
Master's degree	*Mag. (Magister)*
PhD	*Dr. (Doktor)*
Mrs	*Frau*
Miss	*Fräulein*
Mr	*Herr*
Engineering degree (five-year study in high school with two-year hands-on job)	*Ing. (Ingenieur)*
Master's in Engineering	*Dipl. Ing. (Diplom Ingenieur)*

Gas Station	
Full tank, please.	*Super volltanken, bitte.*
Gas	*Benzin*
Diesel	*Diesel*

Geography	
Austria	Österreich
Provinces:	*Bundesländer:*
Carinthia	Kärnten
Lower Austria	Niederösterreich
Upper Austria	Oberösterreich
Styria	Steiermark
Tyrol	Tirol
Vienna	Wien
Mountain	*Berg*
Castle	*Burg*
Small road or street	*Gasse*
House	*Haus*
Palace	*Schloss*
Lake	*See*
Street	*Strasse*

Geography	
Valley	*Tal*
Woods, forest	*Wald*
Wine quarter	*Weinviertel*

Riding a Bus or Train	
Where do I buy a ticket for the bus (or train)?	*Wo kann ich einen Fahrschein kaufen?*
What time does the bus (or train) leave?	*Wann fährt der Autobus (der Zug) ab?*
Have you seen the conductor (train)?	*Haben Sie den Schaffner gesehen?*
Your ticket, please (train).	*Die Fahrscheine bitte.*
Is this seat reserved (train)?	*Ist dieser Sitz reserviert?*
May I sit next to the aisle (window)?	*Darf ich beim Gang (Fenster) sitzen?*
Where is the dining wagon?	*Wo ist der Speisewagen?*
Is this a smoking (non-smoking) cabin?	*Ist das ein Raucherabteil?*
Where is this train (bus) going to?	*Wo fährt dieser Zug (Autobus) hin?*
Is this my stop?	*Muss ich hier aussteigen?*
Do I get on here?	*Muss ich hier einsteigen?*
Can you show me on the map?	*Können Sie mir es auf der Karte zeigen?*
First Class	*Erste Klasse*
Second Class	*Zweite Klasse*

Shopping	
Can you help me?	*Können Sie mir bitte helfen?*
I am just looking.	*Ich schaue nur.*
How much does it cost?	*Was kostet es?*
How much does that cost?	*Wieviel kostet es?*

Shopping

Anything else?	*Ausserdem? Noch einen Wunsch?*

Grocery Shopping

Where are the fruits and vegetables?	*Wo finde ich das Obst und Gemüse?*
Do I need to weigh the fruits and vegetables?	*Muss ich das Obst und Gemüse abwiegen?*
Aisle 1	*Gang eins*
May I have a bag?	*Ein Sackerl, bitte?*
Could you open up a new counter?	*Kassa, bitte?*
Bottle receipt	*Flaschenzettel*
Shopping cart	*Einkaufswagerl*
Do you have change?	*Haben Sie Kleingeld?*

Clothing Store

Clothing	*Bekleidung*
Women's clothing	*Damenmoden*
Men's clothing	*Herrenmoden*
Boutiques	*Boutiquen*
Department stores	*Kaufhäuser*
Do you have a smaller (bigger) size?	*Haben Sie eine kleinere (grössere)?*
Can I try this on?	*Darf ich das anprobieren?*
How much does it cost?	*Wieviel kostet das?*

Accommodation

I'd like a single (double) room.	*Ich möchte ein Einzelzimmer (Doppelzimmer).*
How much is it per night/ per person?	*Wieviel kostet es pro Nacht/ pro Person?*

Accommodation

Is breakfast included?	*Ist Frühstück inbegriffen?*
Where is the bath/shower?	*Wo ist das Bad/die Dusche?*

Idiomatic Expressions

I want to get to the bottom of this.	*Der Sache will ich auf den Grund gehen.*
I'll attend to that personally.	*Das werde ich selbst in die Hand nehmen.*
I'm on duty.	*Ich habe Dienst.*
Off duty/not working.	*Außer Dienst/Betrieb.*
I came to Vienna specially to see you.	*Ich kam eigens nach Wien, um dich zu sehen.*
Kindly give me your attention for a moment.	*Schenke mir bitte kurz deine Aufmerksamkeit.*
For what reason?	*Aus welchem Grund?*
Not without reason.	*Nicht ohne Grund.*
To fight tooth and nail.	*Sich mit Händen und Füßen wehren.*
You scratch my back, I'll scratch yours.	*Eine Hand wäscht die andere.*
The actual crux of the matter.	*Der eigentliche Kern der Sache.*
You have done me a favour.	*Du hast mir einen guten Dienst erwiesen.*
Could you do me a big favour?	*Könntest Du mir einen großen Dienst erweisen?*
One good turn deserves another.	*Ein Dienst ist des anderen Wert.*
Can I avail myself of your services?	*Kann ich deine Dienste in Anspruch nehmen?*
I'm at your service.	*Ich stehe dir zu Diensten.*
I wouldn't be seen dead in that coat.	*Den Mantel möchte ich nicht einmal geschenkt bekommen.*

Idiomatic Expressions

Shall we skip going to the museum?	*Wollen wir uns den Besuch des Museums schenken?*
To make fun of something.	*Etwas lächerlich machen.*
To make someone laugh.	*Jemandem zum Lachen bringen.*

RESOURCE GUIDE

All phone numbers are listed as long distance calls within Austria. For international calls into Austria, dial the country code (43) + number, but drop the first 0. Drop the area code when you are making a call in the same area. When a number includes a hyphen or slash, this indicates a direct dial extension. –0 will connect you with the main switchboard or operator, who can then direct your call.

In this section, the postal code is preceded by an A-. This should be used when sending mail to one of the following addresses from outside of Austria (A denotes Austria). If you are sending mail within Austria, drop the A. For example, Zentrales Fundamt, Wasagasse 22, 1090 Wien.

Within Vienna, the district can be ascertained from the two middle digits of the postal code. For example, 1090 indicates the 9th district. Addresses may also be given (although not when sending a letter) in the following manner: 9, Wasagasse 22, i.e., 9th district, street name (Wasagasse), and street number (22).

EMERGENCIES
- Police: 133
- Fire: 122
- Ambulance: 144

LOST AND FOUND
- Zentrales Fundamt
  A-1090 Vienna
  Tel: (01) 313-449-211

POST OFFICE (MAIN BRANCH)
- Fleischmarkt 19
  A-1010 Vienna
  Tel: (01) 577-677-1010

MEASURES
The metric system is used: 220 volt electrical appliances only.

TELEPHONE INFORMATION
Area Codes
- Vienna: 01
- Bregenz: 05574
- Graz: 0316
- Innsbruck: 0512
- Klagenfurt: 0463
- Linz: 0732
- Salzburg: 0662
- St. Pölten: 02742
- Eisenstadt: 02682

Directory Assistance
- For Austria and Germany: 118-11
- For other foreign countries: 118-12
- Technical service: 111-20 (if you have problems with your phone line)
- Telekom AustriaPostfach: 1001-1011
  WienHotline: 0800-100-100; Fax: 0800-100-109
  International Hotline: (43) 59059-1-59100
  Website: http://www.telekom.at

Long Distance Telephone Companies
Some of these companies offer plans, others require you to simply dial a specific number before placing your call and others offer prepaid cards. Some bundle services, offering long distance, Internet and mobile phone.
- **1031 Telekom**
  Website: http://www.1031telekom.at
- **1036 Hallo**
  Website: http://www.1036hallo.at
- **3U TELECOM GmbH**
  Website: http://www.3utelecom.at
- **ACN Communications Service GmbH**
  Website: http://www.acneuro.com
- **AmiGA Telecom GmbH**
  Website: http://www.amiga.at
- **BilligNet**
  Website: http://www.billignet.at

- **Indigo Networks GmbH (Sipgate)**
  Website: http://www.sipgate.at
- **iT Symbiose GmbH**
  Website: http://www.its.at
- **IT Technology GmbH**
  Website: http://www.talk2u.at/
- **AustriaPhone**
  Website: http://www.austriaphone.at
- **LIWEST Kabelmedien GmbH**
  Website: http://www.liwest.at
- **MITACS Telekomservice GmbH**
  Website: http://www.mitacs.com
- **RedTelecom Ag**
  Website: http://www.redtelecom.com
- **Streams Telekommunikations GesmbH**
  Website: http://www.easycall.at
- **TCN BetriebsgesmbH**
  Website: http://www.tcn.at
- **TeleDiscount**
  Website: http://www.telediscount.at
- **Vocalis Austria GmbH**
  Website: http://www.vocalis.at

Mobile Phone Companies

- **A1 (Mobilkom)**
  Website: http://www.a1.net
- **T-Mobile**
  Website: http://www.tmobile.at
- **One**
  Website: http://www.one.at
- **Drei (H3G)**
  Website: http://www.drei.at
- **Telering**
  Website: http://www.telering.at
- **Tele2**
  Website: http://www.tele2.at
- **Bob**
  Website: http://www.bob.at

- **Yesss**
  Website: http://www.yesss.at
- **eety**
  Website: http://www.eety.eu

INTERNET PROVIDERS
- **Chello**
  Website: http://www.chello.at
    - Vienna
      Tel: (01) 9606-0600
    - Wiener Neustadt
      Tel: (02622) 992-99
    - Graz
      Tel: (0316) 915-15
    - Klagenfurt
      Tel: (0463) 915-15
    - Tirol
      Tel: (0512) 931-0930
- **Telekom Austria**
  Tel: 0800-100-130
  Website: http://www.aon.at
- **Tele2 (UTA)**
  Tel: 0800-240-020
  Website: http://www.tele2uta.at
- **eTel Austria AG**
  Tel: 0800-008-000
  Website: http://www.etel.at
- **inode**
  Tel: 059-999-3500
  Website: http://www6.inode.at

TRANSPORTATION
Train Stations
- **Franz Josef Bahnhof**
  9, Althanstrasse 10
- **Südbahnhof**
  10, Wiedner Gürtel 1B
- **Westbahnhof**
  15, Europaplatz (on the Gürtel)

Train Information
- Tel: (01) 1717

Taxis
In Vienna, call any of these numbers:
- 313-00
- 401-00
- 601-60
- 814-00
- 910-91

Airport Taxis
For taxis and buses from the Salzburg airport, see http://www.salzburg-airport.com (arrival and parking section). For taxis serving Innsbruck's airport and many other towns and cities, see http://www.taxi-obergurgl.com.
- **Airport Service Wien**
  Tel: (01) 676-351-6420
  Website: http://www.airportservice.at
- **C & K Airport Taxi**
  Tel: (01) 17-31 or 44-444
- **Airport Transfer Service**
  Tel: (01) 7007-359-10
  Website: http://www.ats-vie.com

NEWSPAPERS
See Chapter Five.
Online newspaper website: http://www.austriatoday.at

TELEVISION AND RADIO
See Chapter Five.

EDUCATION
German Language Classes
- **ActiLingua Academy**
  Wattmanngasse 15
  A-1130 Vienna
  Tel: (01) 877-6701
  Website: http://www.actilingua.com

- **Berlitz School of Languages**
  Tel: 0820 / 820-082
  Website: http://www.berlitz.at
- **Alpha Sprachinstitut Austria**
  Schwarzenbergplatz 16
  A- 1010 Vienna
  Tel: (01) 503-6969
  Website: http://www.alpha.at
- **International Language Services (ILS)**
  Getreidemarkt 17/5
  A-1060 Vienna
  Tel: (01) 585-5347
  Website: http://www.dolphin.at
- **Internationales Kulturinstitut (IKI)**
  Opernring 7
  A-1010 Vienna
  Tel: (01) 586-7321
  Website: http://www.ikivienna.at
- **University of Vienna (Universität Wien)**
  Wiener Internationale Hochschulkurse
  Alser Strasse 4 Hof 1.16
  A-1090 Vienna
  Tel: (01) 4277-24101
  Website: http://www.univie.ac.at/WIHOK
- **University of Klagenfurt**
  Universitätsstrasse 90
  Tel: (0463) 241-80
  Website: http://dia.uni-klu.ac.at
- **Inlingua Salzburg**
  Universitätsplatz 17
  Tel: (0662) 871-101
  Website: http://www.inlingua-salzburg.at
- **DIG (Deutsch in Graz)**
  Kalchberggasse 10
  A-8010 Graz
  Tel: (0316) 833-900
  Website: http://www.dig.co.at
- **Innsbrucker Hochschulkurse Deutsch (IHD)**
  Innrain 52

A-6020 Innsbruck
Tel: (0512) 587-233
Website: http://www.uibk.ac.at/ihd/
- **Deutsch-Institut Tirol**
Am Sandhügl
A-6370 Kitzbühel
Tel: (5356) 712-74
Website: http://www.deutschinstitut.com
For a list of more German institutes, see http://www.campus-austria.at

Preschools
- **Internationaler Montessori Kindergarten—The Children's House**
Julius-Payer-Gasse 9
A-1220 Vienna
Tel: (01) 263-1056
Website: http://www.montessori-vienna.at
- **The International Montessori Preschool**
Marc-Aurel-Strasse 5/16
A-1010 Vienna
Tel: (01) 533-2024
Email: dekleva.montessori@chello.at
- **United Children Internationaler Kindergarten**
Stumpergasse 49-51
A-1060 Vienna
Tel: (01) 597-0006
and at:
Praterstrasse 24/5
A-1020 Vienna
Tel: (01) 276-4470
Website: http://www.unitedchildren.at
- **Vienna English Preschool**
Leonard Bernstein Strasse 4/6/4/1
A-1220 Vienna
Tel: (01) 282-5906
Website: http://www.viennaenglishpreschool.com
- **International Private Children House**
Mariahilferstrasse 62/20

A-1070 Vienna
Tel: (01) 522-5666
Website: http://www.privat-kindergarten.com
- **Arche Noah Wien International Privatkindergarten**
  Quellenstrasse 102/ (entrance) Van der Nüll-Gasse 29
  A-1100 Vienna
  Tel: (01) 641-9495
  Website: http://www.archenoah.vienna.at

Schools
(Some also offer preschool classes.)
- **Vienna Elementary School**
  (Kindergarten–Fourth Grade)
  Lacknergasse 75
  A-1180 Vienna
  Tel: (01) 470-4600
  Website: http://www.vienna-elementary-school.at
- **American International School**
  Salmannsdorfer Strasse 47
  A-1190 Vienna
  Tel: (01) 401-320
  Website: http://www.ais.at
- **Danube International School**
  Josef Gall-Gasse 2
  A-1020 Vienna, Austria
  Tel: (01) 720-3110
  Website: http://www.danubeschool.at
- **Vienna International School**
  Strasse-der-Menschenrechte 1
  A-1220 Vienna
  Tel: (01) 203-5595
  Website: http://www.vis.ac.at
- **Vienna Christian School**
  Wagramerstrasse 175
  A-1220 Vienna
  Tel.: (01) 2512-2501
  Website: http://www.viennachristianschool.org
- **Japanese School in Vienna**
  Prandaugasse 2

A-1220 Vienna
Tel: (01) 204-2201
Website: http://www.japaneseschool.at

- **Lycée Francais de Vienna**
  Liechtensteinstrasse 37a
  A-1090 Vienna
  Tel: (01) 317-2241
  Website: http://www.lyceefrancais.at
- **Lauder Chabad Campus (Jewish)**
  Rabbi-Schneerson-Platz 1
  1020 Wien
  Tel: (01) 3341-8180
  Website: http://www.lauderchabad.at
- **Islamic Schools**
  See http://www.derislam.at for a list of Islamic schools
- **Salzburg International Preparatory School**
  (Boarding school for grades 9–12, American style education)
  Moosstrasse 106
  A-5020 Salzburg
  Tel: (0662) 824-617
  Website: http://www.ais-salzburg.at
- **St. Gilgen International School**
  (Day or boarding school for children ages 11–18)
  Ischlerstrasse 13
  A-5340 St. Gilgen
  Tel: (06227) 20-259
  Website: http://www.stgilgen-internation-school.at
- **Graz International Bilingual School**
  Marschallgasse 19-21
  A-8020 Graz
  Tel: (0316) 771-050
  Website: http://www.gibs.at

INTERNATIONAL, CULTURAL, SOCIAL AND VOLUNTEER ORGANISATIONS

- **American Women's Association of Vienna (AWA)**
  Singerstrasse 4/11
  A-1010 Vienna

Tel: (01) 966-2925
Website: http://www.awavienna.com

- **Women's Career Network, Vienna**
  Website: http://www.wcnvienna.hypermart.net
- **Australian Women's Association**
  Australian Embassy
  Mattiellistrasse 2-4
  A-1040 Vienna
  Tel: (01) 512-8580
- **Austro-American Institute of Education (Amerika-Institut)**
  Opernring 4
  A-1010 Vienna
  Tel: (01) 512-7720
  Website: http://www.amerika-institut.at
- **Austro-American Society**
  Stallburggasse 2
  A-1010 Vienna
  Tel: (01) 512-3982
  Website: http://www.members.aon.at/auamsoc
- **OAG (Austro-American Society for Graz)**
  Grand Hotel-Wiesler
  Grieskai 4-8
  A-8020 Graz
  Tel: (664) 333-1728
  Website: http://www.oag.at
- **ÖAG Kärnten (Austro-American Society for Carinthia)**
  Tel: 0463/ 281-807
  Website: http://www.oeag-ktn.at.tt
- **Befrienders** (English speaking crisis hotline)
  Tel: (01) 713-3374
- **British Community Association**
  British Embassy
  Jaurèsgasse 12
  A-1030 Vienna
  Tel: (01) 716-1300
  Website: http://home.pages.at/bca-vienna/
- **British Council**
  Siebensterngasse 21

A-1070 Vienna
Tel: (01) 533-2616
Website: http://www.britishcouncil.org/de/austria
- **Contact**
(This group welcomes new people to Austria.)
Tel: (01) 714-6720
- **United Nations**
Wagramer Strasse 5
A-1400 Vienna
Tel: (01) 26060
Fax: (01) 263-3389
Website: http://www.unvienna.org
- **United Nations Women's Guild**
Vienna International Center
Wagramer Strasse 5
Room F0919
A-1400 Vienna
Tel: (01) 260-024-276 or (01) 260-264-284
Website: http://www.iaea.org/unwg
- **International Women's Association of Graz**
Strasserhofweg 47
A-8045 Graz
Website: http://www.iwagraz.org

EMBASSIES AND CONSULATES
- **Australian Embassy**
Mattiellistrasse 2-4
A-1040 Vienna
Tel: (01) 506-740
Website: http://www.australian-embassy.at
- **British Embassy**
Jaurèsgasse 12
A-1030 Vienna
Tel: (01) 716-130
Website: http://www.britishembassy.at
- **British Consulate**
Jaurèsgasse 10
A-1030 Vienna
Tel: (01) 716-135-151

- **Canadian Embassy**
  Laurenzerberg 2
  A-1010 Vienna
  Tel: (01) 5313-83000
  Website: http://www.kanada.at
- **Indian Embassy**
  Kärntner Ring 2
  A-1010 Vienna
  Tel: (01) 505-8666
  Website: http://www.indianembassy.at
- **Irish Embassy**
  Rotenturmstrasse 16-18, 5th floor
  A-1010 Vienna
  Tel: (01) 715-4246
  Website: http://www.foreignaffairs.irlgov.ie
- **Japanese Embassy**
  Hessgasse 6
  A-1010 Vienna
  Tel: (01) 531-920
  Website: http://www.at.emb-japan.go.jp
- **South African Embassy**
  Sandgasse 33
  A-1190 Vienna
  Tel: (01) 320-6493
  Website: http://www.saembvie.at
- **U.S. Consulate**
  Parkring 12a
  1010 Vienna
  Tel: (01) 3133-97535
  Website: http://www.usembassy.at
- **U.S. Embassy**
  Boltzmanngasse 16
  A-1090 Vienna
  Tel: (01) 313-390
  Website: http://www.usembassy.at

BUSINESS ORGANISATIONS

- **American Chamber of Commerce**
  Porzellangasse 35

A-1090 Vienna
Tel: (01) 319-5751
Website: http://www.amcham.at
- **British Trade Council in Austria**
Laurenzerberg 2
A-1010 Vienna
Tel: (01) 533-1594
- **Austrian Foreign Trade Promotion Organization**
Website: http://www.austriantrade.org
- **Austrian Business Agency**
ABA-Invest in Austria
Opernring 3
A-1010 Vienna
Tel: (01) 588-58-0
Website: http://www.aba.gv.at
- **Austrian Institute of Economic Research**
1103 Vienna
P.O. Box 91
Tel: (01) 798-2601-0
Website: http://www.wifo.at

AUSTRIAN GOVERNMENT

- **The Austrian Press and Information Service**
3524 International Ct. NW
Washington, D.C. 20008 (USA)
Tel: (1-202) 895-670
Fax: (1-202) 895-6750
Website: http://www.austria.org or http://www.austrianinformation.org
- **Federal Chancellery of Austria**
Website: http://www.austria.gv.at
- **HELP**
Website: http://www.help.gv.at
Mostly in German but it tells you everything you need to know to help you glide through the bureaucracy.
- **Austrian Foreign Ministry**
Website: http://www.bmaa.gv.at

HOSPITALS AND CLINICS
Vienna

- **Allgemeines Krankenhaus (AKH)**
  Währinger Gürtel 18-20
  A-1090 Vienna
  Tel: (01) 404-000
- **Doctors-on-call Service (Ärztefunkdienst)**
  Tel: (01) 1771 (Mon–Fri, 7:00 am–7:00 pm)
  Tel: (01) 141 (Mon–Fri, 7:00 pm–7:00 am, Sat, Sun and holidays)
  You may use the service line 1771 to find a doctor in your vicinity.
- **On Duty Pharmacy Service** (Apothekenbereitschafsdienst)
  Tel: (01) 1550 (If you need to locate a pharmacy after hours)
- **Sozialmedizinisches Zentrum Ost (SMZ)**
  Langobardenstrasse 122
  A-1220 Vienna
  Tel: (01) 288-020
- **Rudolfinerhaus**
  Billrothstrasse 78
  A-1190 Vienna
  Tel: (01) 36036-0
  Website: http://www.rudolfinerhaus.at
- **St. Annakinderspital (Children's Hospital)**
  (If an emergency, take the child to the AKH)
  Kinderspitalgasse 6
  A-1090 Vienna
  Tel: (01) 401-70
  Website: http://www.stanna.at
- **Lainz Krankenhaus**
  Wolkersbergenstrasse 1
  A-1130 Vienna
  Tel: (01) 801-100
- **Krankenhaus Rudolfsstiftung**
  Juchgasse 25
  A-1030 Vienna
  Tel: (01) 711-650

- **Goldenes Kreuz**
  Lazarettgasse 16-18
  A-1090 Vienna
  Tel: (01) 401-110

Eisenstadt
- **Krankenhaus der Barmherzigen Brüder**
  Esterhazystrasse 26
  A-7000 Eisenstadt
  Tel: (02682) 601–0

Graz
- **Krankenhaus der Barmherzigen Brüder**
  Marschallgasse 12
  A-8020 Graz
  Tel: (0316) 7067–0
- **Landeskrankenhaus Graz**
  Auenbruggerplatz 1
  A-8036 Graz
  Tel: (0316) 385-0
- **Krankenhaus der Stadt Graz**
  Albert Schweitzer Gasse 22
  A-8010 Graz
  Tel: (0316) 912-410

Innsbruck
- **Allgemeines öffentliches Landeskrankenhaus Innsbruck**
  Anichstrasse 35
  A-6020 Innsbruck
  Tel: (0512) 504–0
- **Privatklinik Triumphpforte Innsbruck**
  Leopoldstrasse 1
  A-6020 Innsbruck
  Tel: (0512) 5909–0

Klagenfurt
- **Krankenhaus der Elisabethinen**
  Völkermarkter Strasse 15–19

A-9020 Klagenfurt
Tel: (0463) 5830–0

Linz

- **Krankenhaus der Barmherzigen Brüder**
  Seilerstätte 2
  A-4020 Linz
  Tel: (0732) 7897–0
- **Krankenhaus der Stadt Linz**
  Krankenhausstrasse 9
  A-4020 Linz
  Tel: (0732) 7806–0

Salzburg

- **Allgemeiner öffentlicher Landeskrankenanstalten**
  Müllner Hauptstrasse 48
  A-5020 Salzburg
  Tel: (0662) 4482–0
- **Krankenhaus der Barmherzigen Brüder**
  Kajetanerplatz 1
  A-5020 Salzburg
  Tel: (0662) 8088

DOCTORS AND DENTISTS

For a list of English-speaking doctors and dentists please see the
US embassy website at Website: http://www.usembassy.at.

INSURANCE

- **Allianz**
  Hietzinger Kai 101-105
  A-1130 Vienna
  Tel: (01) 05-9009
  Website: http://www.allianz.at
- **Generali Versicherung**
  Landskrongasse 1-3
  A-1010 Vienna
  Tel: (01) 515-900
  Website: http://www.generali.at

- **Wiener Städtische**
  Main Office (there are branches in most districts)
  Ringturm, Schottenring 30
  A-1010 Vienna
  Tel: (01) 50-350-20000
  Website: http://www.wienerstaedtische.at

BANKS

- **Bank Austria Creditanstalt**
  Am Hof 2
  A-1010 Vienna
  Tel: (01) 505-050
  Website: http://www.ba-ca.com
- **Erste Bank**
  Graben 21
  A-1010 Vienna
  Tel: (01) 501-002-0111
  Website: http://www.erstebank.at
- **BAWAG (Bank für Arbeit und Wirtschaft AG)**
  Seitzergasse 2-4
  A-1010 Vienna
  Tel: (01) 534-530
  Website: http://www.bawag.com

SHOPPING
Vienna

- **1st district: Kärntner Strasse, Graben, & Kohlmarkt**
  These two streets are filled with exclusive clothing boutiques, china and silver shops, lingerie shops, and wonderful stationery and bookstores. The Dorotheum, also in the first district, is an upscale auction house/pawnshop that specializes in quality antiques. It's fun to browse even if you can't afford to buy anything.
- **6th and 7th districts: Mariahilfer Strasse**
  Along this extremely long street between the outer Ring and the Westbahnhof are funkier clothing stores, large department and home furnishing stores, large book and music stores (often combined with coffee shops), discount clothing stores, toy stores, etc.

- **11th district: Simmeringer Haide**
  This complex has a large Media Markt (electronics), Metro (bulk food warehouse where membership or diplomatic card is required), and other stores.
- **Gasometer:**
  Huge 19th century gas holders were renovated and now house shops and restaurants and apartments.
- **12th district: Meidlinger Hauptstrasse**
  Long street that runs between the U4 and U6 underground lines. Full of large and small stores.
- **19th district: Döblinger Gürtel**
  Brand new, modern and trendy mall.
- **20th district: Millennium Mall**
  Department stores and boutiques are found on the lower levels of a skyscraper alongside the Danube on Handelskai.
- **21st district: Shopping Center Nord**
  This mall has all the main stores selling clothes, shoes, stationery, books, toys, houseware, sporting goods, and pet supplies, and a sandwich shop.
- **22nd district: Donauzentrum**
  This two-story, two-sectioned mall found across from the U-1 Kagran stop houses the same selection of stores as the Shopping Center Nord mall, and includes two grocery stores besides.
- **Vösendorf-Süd, Shopping City Süd**
  This is Europe's largest mall and the parking situation on Saturday can be frightening. It is divided into sections; the largest houses the same stores as a regular mall plus a food court and the Swedish houseware megastore, Ikea. Other sections include a multimedia complex filled with one of the largest movie theaters, small restaurants and cafés, a variety of electronic and houseware stores, and Toys 'R' Us. Interio, a funky houseware store, stands alone across from the complex. Across the highway, but still considered part of this mall, is Media Markt (electronics), Baumaxx (hardware), and Kaindl (houseware and appliances).
- **McArthur Glen Outlet Mall**
  Parndorf (near the border with Hungary) on the A4 Autobahn. Replica of an American outdoor factory outlet

mall built alongside the highway—plenty of brand-name stores with lower prices. Considering the size of the mall, there is only a tiny food court and one café.

Regional Shopping Centres

- **Wiener Neustadt**
  Fischapark Shopping Center
- **St. Pölten**
  Traisenpark
- **Linz**
  Plus City and Hollywood MegaPlexx cinema
- **Graz**
  Shopping City Seiersberg
- **Klagenfurt**
  Südpark in Klagenfurt
- **Salzburg**
  Europark, located on the A1 Motorway
- **Innsbruck**
  DEZ, Austria's first shopping center
- **Vorarlberg**
  Messepark in Dornbirn

All-purpose and Furniture Stores

- **Ikea**
  Website: http://www.ikea.at
- **Interio**
  Website: http://www.interio.at
- **Kika**
  Website: http://www.kika.at
- **Leiner**
  Website: http://www.leiner.at
- **Lutz**
  Website: http://www.lutz.at
- **Möbelix**
  Website: http://www.moebelix.at
- **Möma**
  Website: http://www.moema.at
- **Tschibo/Eduscho**
  Website: http://www.eduscho.at

REAL ESTATE AGENTS AND RELOCATION SERVICES

- **Relocation Service Erika Strohmayer**
  2320 Schwechat, Am Concorde-Park 1/B6
  A-2320 Schwechat
  Tel: (01) 706-2170
  Website: http://www.relocation-services.at
- **Expat Consulting**
  Sonnbergplatz 9/13/1
  A-1190 Vienna
  Tel: (01) 328-8818
  Website: http://www.expat-consulting.com
- **Gasser Real Estate**
  Auhofstrasse 114
  A-1130 Vienna
  Tel: (01) 961-0313
  Website: http://www.vienna-realestate.com
- **Recom Relocation Company (Vienna and Graz)**
  Haizinger Gasse 47/4
  A-1180 Vienna
  Tel: (01) 409-2462
  Website: http://www.well-come-vienna.com
- **Hans Schöll**
  Tigergasse 6
  A-1080 Vienna
  Tel: (01) 402-7561-0 or 408-1505
  Fax: (01) 402-756-144
  Website: http://www.schoell.at
- **ReMax**
  (Numerous offices throughout Austria)
  Naglergasse 29
  A-1010 Vienna
  Tel: (01) 535-5035
  Website: http://www.remax-austria.com
- **R.D. Kalandra**
  Franz-Josefs-Kai 33/6
  A-1010 Vienna
  Tel: (01) 533-3269
  Website: http://www.kalandra.at

USEFUL WEBSITES

- **Austria Café**
  Website: http://www.austria-cafe.com
  Provides numerous links to different websites that deal with any and everything regarding Austria.
- **Virtual Vienna**
  Website: http://www.virtualvienna.net
  Full of great information for those moving to Vienna. Has limited information on other cities.
- **Vienna City Government**
  Website: http://www.wien.gv.at
- **Vienna Expats**
  Website: http://www.vienna-expats.com
  An online forum for expats in Vienna. Any topic will be addressed.
- **About Vienna**
  Website: http://www.aboutvienna.org
- **Kwintessential**
  Website: http://www.kwintessential.co.uk
  In depth country profiles and other cultural guides
- **Studenten-wg.de**
  Website: http://www.studenten-wg.de
  Lots of information for the student in Austria
- **European Rail Guide**
  Website: http://www.europeanrailguide.com
  More than train information, also has city guides.

LODGING WEBSITES

- Website: http://www.kinderhotels.or.at (Children's Hotels)
- Website: http://www.hotels.or.at
- Website: http://www.austria-hotels.com
- Website: http://www.abnet.at/hotel
- Website: http://www.wien.world-stay.com
- Website: http://www.apartment-hotel-wien.at
- Website: http://www.eviennahotels.com
- Website: http://www.familyaustria.at (children-friendly hotels and apartments)
- Website: http://www.schlosshotels.co.at (to stay at a castle)

- Website: http://www.tiscover.com (hotels, campsites, etc., search for Bauernhof to stay on a farm, a very nice and inexpensive way to see Austria)

TOURISM
- **Austrian National Tourist Office**
  Website: http://www.austria.info
- **Tiscover**
  Website: http://www.tiscover.com
  (Loaded with information from lodging to special events to weather reports. Has sections on each of the regions with details on towns and cities.)
- Website: http://www.tourist-net.co.at
- Website: http://www.talkingcities.co.uk
  Vienna guide and city information
- Website: http://www.travelnotes.org
  Very organised travel directory providing country/state information, reviewed web sites, regular travel articles, and online ticketing for car hire, hotel reservations and discounted flights.

Vienna
- **The Vienna Tourist Board**
  Tel: (01) 211-140
  Website: http://www.info.wien.at
- **Vienna Tourist Information Office**
  Albertinaplatz/Maysedergasse 9-19
  A-1010 Vienna
  Tel: (01) 513-4015 or 513-8892

PROVINCES AND REGIONS
- **Burgenland Tourismus**
  Schloss Esterhazy
  A-7000 Eisenstadt
  Tel: (02682) 633-840
  Website: http://www.burgenland.info

Carinthia
- **Kärnten Werbung**

Casinoplatz 1
A-9220 Velden am Wörthersee
Tel: (0463) 3000
Website: http://www.kaernten.at

Lower Austria
- **Fischhof 3/3**
  A-1010 Vienna
  Tel: (01) 5361-06200
  Website: http://www.niederoesterreich.at

Salzburg
- **Salzburger Land Tourismus**
  Wiener Bundesstrasse 23
  Tel: (0662) 6688-0
  Website: http://www.english.salzburgerland.com

Styria
- **Steierische Tourismus GmbH**
  St. Peter Hauptstrasse 243
  A-8042 Graz
  Tel: (0316) 40-030
  Website: http://www.steiermark.at

Tyrol
- **Maria-Theresien Strasse 55**
  A-6010 Innsbruck
  Tel: (0512) 72720
  Website: http://www.tyrol.com

Upper Austria
- **Oberösterrich Tourismus Info**
  Freistädter Strasse 119, A-4041 Linz
  Tel: (0732) 221-022
  Website: http://www.oberoesterreich.at

Vorarlberg
- **Bahnhofstrasse 14**
  A-6901 Bregenz

Tel: (05574) 425-250
Website: http://www.vorarlberg-tourism.at
Website: http://www.vorarlberg.at

Salzkammergut
- **The Salzkammergut**
  Website: http://www.salzkammergut.at

CITIES
Graz
- **Graz Tourist Office**
  Herrengasse 16
  A-8010 Graz
  Tel: (0316) 80-750
  Website: http://www.graz.at
  Website: http://www.graztourism.at

Innsbruck
- **Innsbruck Tourist Office**
  Burggraben 3
  A-6021 Innsbruck
  Tel: (0512) 59-850
  Website: http://www.innsbruck-tourism.at
  Website: http://www.innsbruck.at

Klagenfurt
- **Klagenfurt Tourist Office**
  Rathaus, Neuer Platz 1
  A-9010 Klagenfurt
  Tel: (0463) 537-2223
  Website: http://www.klagenfurt.at

Linz
- **Linz City Tourist Board**
  Old City Hall Building
  Hauptplatz 1
  A-4020 Linz
  Tel: (0732) 7070-1777
  Website: http://www.linz.at

Salzburg
- **Salzburg Tourist Office**
  Auerspergstrasse 6
  A-5020 Salzburg
  Tel: (0662) 889-870
  Website: http://www2.salzburg.info / http://www.salzburg.at

Boat Trips on the Danube
- **Brandner Schiffahrt GmbH**
  Ufer 50
  A-3313 Wallsee
  Tel: (07433) 259-021
  Fax: (07433) 259-025
  Website: http://www.ms-austria.at
- **DDSG Blue Danube Schiffahrt GmbH**
  Schifffahrtszentrum
  Handelskai 265
  A-1020 Vienna
  Tel: (01) 58880
  Website: http://www.ddsg-blue-danube.at

CULTURAL EVENTS
- **Bregenz Festival**
  Platz der Wiener Symphoniker 1
  A-6900 Bregenz
  Tel: (05574) 4076
  Website: http://www.Bregenzerfestspiele.com
- **Brucknerhaus and Brucknerfest Linz**
  Untere Donaulände 7
  A-4010 Linz
  Tel: (0732) 76-120
  Website: http://www.brucknerhaus.at
- **Carinthian Summer Festival**
  Gumpendorfer Strasse 76
  A-1060 Vienna
  Tel: (01) 596-8198
  Website: http://www.carinthischersommer.at
- **Haydn Performances**
  Schloss Esterhazy

A-7000 Eisenstadt
Tel: (02682) 719-3000
Website: http://www.schloss-esterhazy.at

- **Haydn Festival**
  Tel: (02682) 61-866
  Fax: (02682) 61-805
  Website: http://www.haydnfestival.at
- **Innsbruck Altemusik Festival**
  Website: http://www.altemusik.at
- **International Theater (English-language theatre)**
  Porzellangasse 8 and Fundus
  Müllnergasse 6A
  A-1090 Vienna
  Tel: (01) 319-6272
  Website: http://www.internationaltheatre.at
- **Marionette Theater (Vienna)**
  Schloss Schönbrunn
  Hofratstrakt
  A-1130 Vienna
  Tel: (01) 817-3247
  Website: http://www.marionettentheater.at
- **Marionette Theater (Salzburg)**
  Schwarzstrasse 24
  A-5020 Salzburg
  Tel: (0662) 872-4060
  Website: http://www.marionetten.at
- **Mörbisch Festival**
  Joseph Haydngasse 40/1
  A-7000 Eisenstadt
  Tel: (02682) 662-100
  Website: http://www.seefestspiele-moerbisch.at
- **Musikverein**
  Bösendorferstrasse 12
  A-1010 Vienna
  Tel: (01) 505-8190
  Website: http://www.musikverein.at
- **Salzburg Festival**
  Herbert von Karajan Platz 11
  Postfach 140

A-5010 Salzburg
Tel: (0662) 804-5500
Website: http://www.salzburgfestival.com

- **Spanish Riding School**
Michaelerplatz 1
A-1010 Vienna
Website: http://www.srs.at

- **Schubertiade**
Villa Rosenthal
Schweizer Strasse 1
Postfach 100
A-6845 Hohenems
Tel: (05576) 72-091
Website: http://www.schubertiade.at

- **Staatsoper**
Opernring 2
A-1010 Vienna
Tel: (01) 5144-42250
Website: http://www.wiener-staatsoper.at

- **Styriarte**
Sackstrasse 17
A-8010 Graz
Tel: (0316) 812-9410
Website: http://www.styriarte.com

- **Vienna English Theater**
Josefsgasse 12
A-1080 Vienna
Tel: (01) 402-1260-0
Website: http://www.englishtheatre.at

- **Volksoper**
Währinger Strasse 78
A-1090 Vienna
Tel: (01) 5144-43670
Website: http://www.volksoper.at

- **Wiener Festwochen**
Lehárgasse 11
A-1060 Vienna
Tel: (01) 589-22-0
Website: http://www.festwochen.or.at

CINEMAS

See http://www.film.at and go to the OV Cinema link for a full listing of theatres that show movies in their original language.

Vienna

- **Artis**
  Schultergasse 5
  A-1010 Vienna
  Tel: (01) 535-6570
- **Burg Kino**
  Opernring 19
  A-1010 Vienna
  Tel: (01) 587-8406
- **Flotten**
  Mariahilfer Strasse 85-87
  A-1060 Vienna
  Tel: (01) 586-5152
- **Haydn English Language Cinema**
  Mariahilfer Strasse 57
  A-1060 Vienna
  Tel: (01) 587-2262

BOOKSHOPS

- **The British Bookshop**
  Weihburggasse 24-26
  A-1010 Vienna
  Tel: (01) 512-1945
  Website: http://www.britishbookshop.at
  Other branches at:
  - Mariahilfer Strasse 4
    A-1070 Vienna
    Tel: (01) 522-6730
  - Auhof Center Bauteil 3
    Albert Schweitzer Gasse 4A
    A-1140 Vienna
    Tel: (01) 979-198-623
- **Shakespeare & Co.**
  Sterngasse 2
  A-1010 Vienna

Tel: (01) 535-5053
Website:http://www.shakespeare-company.biz

ALTERNATIVE LIFESTYLES

See brochure issued by Vienna Tourism Office.

- **Rosa Lila**
  Linke Wienzeile 102
  A-1060 Vienna
  Tel: (01) 585-4343; (01) 586-8150
  Website: http://www.villa.at
- **Rainbow.at**
  Website: http://www.rainbow.at
- **Homosexual Initiative Vienna (HOSI)**
  Website: http://www.hosiwien.at
- **Homosexual Initiative Linz**
  Website: http://www.hosilinz.at
- **Tyrol**
  Website: http://www.queertirol.com
  Website: http://www.gaytirol.com

RELIGIOUS INSTITUTIONS

- **Christ Church (Anglican/Episcopalian)**
  Jaurèsgasse 17-19
  A-1030 Vienna
  Tel: (01) 714-8900
  Website: http://www.christchurchvienna.org
- **Islamic Center Vienna**
  Am Hubertusdamm 17-19
  A-1210 Vienna
  Tel: (01) 2632-1200
- **Jewish Welcome Service**
  Stephansplatz 10
  A-1010 Vienna
  Tel: (01) 533-2730
  Website: http://www.jewish-welcome.at
- **United Methodist Church**
  Sechshauser Strasse 56/2/6
  A-1150 Vienna

Tel: (01) 893-6989
Email: esumc@chello.at
Service at 11:15 am.

- **Vienna Community Church** (non-denominational)
  Dorotheergasse 16
  A-1010 Vienna
  Tel: (01) 505-5233
  Website: http://www.viennacommunitychurch.com
  Service at 12:00 pm.
- **Votivkirche** (Roman Catholic)
  Rooseveltplatz 8
  A-1090 Vienna
  Tel: (01) 406-1192
  Website: http://www.votivkirche.at
  Mass in English at 11:00 am.
- **Calvary Chapel Vienna** (Evangelical)
  Kollergasse 1
  Am Kolonitzplatz
  A-1030 Vienna
  Tel: (01) 967-8974
  Website: http://www3.calvarychapel.com
  Services at 10:30 am.
- **Church of Jesus Christ of Latter-Day Saints**
  Böcklinstrasse 55
  A-1030 Wien
  Tel: (01) 720-7985
- **International Chapel of Vienna**
  Evangelical and Nondenominational
  Wagramer Strasse 175
  A- 1220 Wien
  Tel: (01) 251-2290
  Website: http://www.intchapel.org
  Service at 10:00 am.
- **Salzburg International Christian Church**
  At Christuskirche
  Schwarzstrasse 25
  Telephone: (0662) 434-314
  Website: http://www.salzburgchurch.org

Bible Fellowship at 10:00 am.
Service at 11:00 am.

FURTHER READING

GENERAL INFORMATION

Living in Vienna: A Practical Guide for the English-Speaking Community. American Women's Association of Vienna, Vienna.

- A must-have for anyone who will be living in Vienna. It provides continuously updated information on every imaginable topic from education to recycling, and lists essential addresses and phone numbers. Please see the AWA website (http://www.awavienna.com) for information on where to purchase the book.

The Xenophobe's Guide to the Austrians. Louis James. London: Oval/Ravette Books, 2000.

- This little book offers amusing commentaries on who the Austrians are and why they do what they do.

HISTORY AND POLITICS

The Austrians: A Thousand Year Odyssey. Gordon Brook-Shepherd. New York: Carroll & Graf Publishers Inc., 2002.

- This comprehensive book offers a good non-academic review of Austria's history. While the title implies detailed information on all eras of Austria's history, the book is biased towards the history of the 20th century.

A Concise History of Austria. Steven Beller. New York: Cambridge University Press, 2007.

- As the name implies, the book provides a general overview of the country's history.

Twilight of the Habsburgs: The Life and Times of Emperor Franz Josef. Alan Warwick Palmer. Berkeley, CA: Atlantic Monthly Press, 1997.

- Franz Josef's personal life is analysed within the context of much larger political issues. The book looks at the political side of a crucial era in Austrian history that has been the subject of much discussion.

Sissi: Elisabeth, Empress of Austria. Brigitte Hamann. Cologne and New York: Taschen, 1997.
- This easy-to-read biography of one of Austria's favourite personalities is neatly written and contains some lovely photographs. It's fun reading for fans of royalty.

The Lonely Empress Elizabeth of Austria. Joan Haslip, Phoenix Press, 2000.
- The book offers a fresh look at the empress who has been studied and written about so often.

A Nervous Splendor: Vienna 1888/1889. Frederic Morton. New York: Penguin, 1980.
- This is an entertaining read if you are interested in what led to the break-up of the empire and the end of the Habsburg dynasty.

Thunder at Twilight: Vienna 1913/1919. Frederic Morton. New York: Da Capo Press, 2001.
- As with his other book, Morton offers an interesting look at Viennese history, this time focusing on the period prior to World War I.

Fin-de-Siècle Vienna: Politics and Culture. Carl E. Schorske. New York: Vintage Books, 1980.
- As the name suggests, this book takes an in-depth look at the close relationship between politics and the arts during this fascinating time in Vienna's history.

Freud: A Life for our Time. Peter Gay. New York: W.W. Norton, 2006.
- This critically-acclaimed book provides insight into Freud's private life and theories.

The Interpretation of Dreams. Sigmund Freud. New York: Avon Books, 1980.
- If you're not clear on what Freud was all about, his most definitive work can be read without prior knowledge of psychoanalysis.

The Austrian Mind: An Intellectual and Social History 1848–1938. William M Johnston. Berkeley: University of California Press, 1983.

- This award-winning book looks at the intellectuals behind the academic, scientific and artistic achievements of this period in Austria's history.

Alma Rosè: Vienna to Auschwitz. Richard Newman with Karen Kirtley. Pompton Plains, NJ: Amadeus Press, 2003.

- An interesting biography tracing Alma Rosè's early life in a well-to-do Viennese Jewish family. As the niece of Gustav Mahler, music was an important part of her life. She helped other Jews to leave Vienna after Austria was annexed by the Nazis, but wound up in Auschwitz where she conducted the only women's orchestra to be formed in a concentration camp.

Simon Wiesenthal: A Life in Search of Justice. Hella Pick. Boston: Northeastern University Press, 1996.

- This book provides the reader with the story of the Nazi-hunter's life.

Guilty Victim: Austria from the Holocaust to Haider. Hella Pick. London and New York: I.B. Tauris, 2000.

- The original German version received much praise. The author focuses on how Austria has been perceived abroad since World War II ended, and provides much interesting information on modern Austria.

Defiant Populist: Jörg Haider and the Politics of Austria. Lothar Hobelt. West Lafayette, IN: Purdue University Press, 2003.

- This book examines the 'Haider phenomenon' in current Austrian politics.

TRAVEL AND TOURISM

Frommer's Austria. Darwin Porter and Danforth Prince. Hoboken, NJ: Frommer's, 2007.

- One of the better travel guides with a lot of practical information for the tourist.

Austria (Eyewitness Travel Guides). Teresa Czerniewicz-Umer, Joanna Egert-Romanowskiej, Janiny Kumanieckiej and Helen Peters. New York: Dorling Kindersley Publishers, Ltd., 2003.
- Beautiful pictures and valuable information for the traveller.

The Rough Guide: Vienna. Rob Humphreys. London: Rough Guides, 2005.
- Probably the best guidebook on Vienna, full of history, anecdotes and valuable practical information.

Rick Steves' Germany and Austria. Rick Steves. New York: Avalon Travel Publishing, 2006.
- This frequently updated travel guide by the popular television show host provides useful and interesting information.

Karen Brown's Austria: Exceptional Places to Stay and Itineraries. Karen Brown. San Mateo: Karen Brown's Guides, CA, 2006.
- This is a guidebook for the romantic who doesn't want to see all of Austria in five days. The author's itineraries take you to out of the way places in addition to the main cities. See also her website at: http://www.karenbrown.com/austria.

Danube, A Sentimental Journey from the Source to the Black Sea. Claudio Magris. The Harvell Press, London, 2001.
- This book cannot and should not be read quickly. The author takes you on a slow journey down the Danube, stopping here and there with a fascinating tale. He explains much of life along the river, not only in Austria.

Walking Austria's Alps Hut to Hut. Jonathan Hurdle. Seattle, WA: Mountaineers Books, 1999.
- This guide contains 11 walking tours. Each hike begins with a good introduction and is supported by detailed information.

Mountain Walking in Austria. Cecil Davies. Milnthorpe, Cumbria: Cicerone Press, 2001.

- This author has grouped Austria's mountains into 25 groups and about 100 different walks.

THE ARTS

Some of the nicest books on the arts may be found in museum gift shops.

Music

Exploring Haydn: Unlocking the Masters Series. David Hurwitz. Pompton Plains, NJ: Amadeus Press, 2005.
- The book is accompanied by a CD to help introduce the reader to the life and works of Haydn.

Mozart: A Cultural Biography. Robert W Gutman. New York: Harcourt Brace, 1999.
- A sensitive look at the life and personality of Austria's most-loved musical composer that also explains in-depth how his work fits in with the music of his time.

Beethoven. His Spiritual Development. J W N Sullivan. New York: Vintage Books, 1960.
- This poignant and intense book on Beethoven's life follows his creative path and describes how his music was affected by his social being, affairs of the heart, deafness, failing health and spirituality.

Beethoven: The Universal Composer (Eminent Lives). Edmund Morris. New York: Harper Collins, 2005.
- A compact biography of this great composer.

Schubert's Vienna. Raymond Erickson (ed.). New Haven: Yale University Press, 1997.
- Various scholars focus on Vienna during the Biedermeier period. They do not just examine developments in music and the other arts, but link them with the political repression of the day.

Johannes Brahms: A Biography. Jan Swafford. New York: Vintage/Random House, 1999.

- Intended for the novice musician, this book offers an introduction to the music and personal life of this wonderful composer.

Bruckner (Master Musicians). Derek Watson. New York: Oxford University Press, 2001.
- A concise book on the life and works of 'God's Musician.'

Second Viennese School. Oliver Neighbour, Paul Griffiths and George Perle. New York: W.W. Norton, 1998.
- If you'd like to know more about Arnold Schoenberg, Anton Weber and Alban Berg, and their revolutionary style of music, this short book offers an explanation as well as biographical accounts of the three men.

Art
Vienna: 1890–1920. Robert Waissenberger. Secaucus: Wellfleet Press, 1988.
- This coffee-table book offers more than just beautiful photographs and reproductions. The politics, arts, architecture, music, and literature of this period are explained in detailed essays complementing the illustrations.

Art in Vienna: 1898–1918, Klimt, Kokoschka, Schiele and their Contemporaries. Peter Vergo. Oxford: Phaidon Press Ltd., 1994.
- This large illustrated book captures the essence of the ideological movement of the Secession toward the end of the 19th century and how paintings, architecture and the applied arts were all affected. Paintings by Klimt, Kokoschka and Schiele are explained in detail, as are the architecture and applied arts of Wagner, Olbrich, Loos and Hoffman.

Gustav Klimt. Gottfried Fliedl. Cologne and New York: Taschen, 2003.
- This large illustrated book on the life and works of Klimt is an easily-read account of the progress and changing

nature of his work from Historicism to Jugendstil (Art Nouveau), his influence with members of the Secession and his fascination in depicting the female nude in his search for a female image of the world.

Egon Schiele: Drawings and Watercolors. Jane Kallir. London: Thames and Hudson, 2003.
- This book consists of beautiful reproductions of his works accompanied by biographical information.

The Applied Arts
Viennese Design and the Wiener Werkstätte. Jane Kallir. New York: George Braziller, 1986.
- With both black and white and colour illustrations, this book showcases the items that came out of the Wiener Werkstätte, including furniture, utensils, glass and clothing. Ample information explains the workshop, its goals, and its products.

Thonet: Classic Furniture in Bent Wood and Tubular Steel. Alexander von Vegesack, with text by Brigitta Pauley and Peter Ellenberg. New York: Rizzoli, 1997.
- This book on the furniture of Vienna's internationally-famous Thonet firm explains the principles and ideas behind their designs. Old and new photos show original pieces both then and now.

Architecture
Otto Wagner: 1841-1918: Forerunner of Modern Architecture. August Sarnitz. Cologne and New York: Taschen, 2005.
- A lovely coffee-table book with beautiful illustrations of his designs.

Otto Wagner (Archipockets). Sol Kliczkowski and Janos Karlmar. Düsseldorf and New York: Te Neues Publishing Co, 2003.
- A pocket-sized guide to the architect's buildings, complete with photographs and detailed information on his designs.

Hundertwasser Architecture: For a More Human Architecture in Harmony with Nature. Friedensreich Hundertwasser, Angelika Muthesius and Angelika Taschen (eds.). Cologne and New York: Taschen, 1997.

- A coffee-table book with beautiful pictures and interesting information on this wonderfully creative artist and architect. This book is a must for any fan of the artist.

Hundertwasser. Pierre Restany. Cologne and New York: Taschen, 2000.

- A paperback book that provides a clear introduction not only to Hundertwasser's architecture, but also to his art.

CUISINE

Austrian Cooking and Baking. Gretel Beer. New York: Dover Publications, 1975.

- A simple book providing very good recipes without fanfare. Dishes range from soups to salads, meats, dumplings, game and desserts.

Cooking the Austrian Way. Helga Hughes. Minneapolis: Lerner Publishing Group, 2003.

- This book, intended for children, is an easy introduction to Austrian cooking.

A Little Book of Viennese Pastry. Jeni Wright. San Francisco: Chronicle Books, 1995.

- A charming little book of recipes and drawings that makes a great gift.

Kaffeehaus: Exquisite Desserts from the Classic Cafes of Vienna, Budapest and Prague. Rick Rodgers. New York: Clarkson Potter (Random House), 2002.

- A beautiful book that makes a wonderful gift. It is full of lovely pictures and authentic recipes that have not been adapted for different markets.

The Wines of Austria. Philipp Blom. London: Faber and Faber, 2006.

- If you're into wines, this book is for you. It gives a history of Austrian wines, discusses the different wine-growing regions, and has several maps to guide you in your search for the perfect wine.

FICTION

The Road into the Open. Arthur Schnitzler. Berkeley: University of California Press, 1992. (First published in 1908.)

- One of the richest portrayals of *fin-de-siècle* Vienna ever written. Following a group of Jewish intellectuals, the author captures the spirit of Vienna as Europe's cultural and intellectual centre, and relates how it came to be threatened by an anti-Semitism that presaged the rise of fascism decades later.

World of Yesterday. Stefan Zweig. Italy: Hesperides Press, 2006. (First published in 1943.)

- In this moving memoir, Zweig describes the horrors of the tumultuous years of the early 20th. The book is a homage to the culture and society that were destroyed during the political upheaval.

Correction. Thomas Bernhard. Chicago: University of Chicago Press, 1979.

- Although the author's style of writing may be dense and difficult to follow at times, this book is worth the effort. One of Austria's best modern authors, Bernhard raises philosophical issues in this story of a suicide.

A Sorrow Beyond Dreams. Peter Handke. New York: New York Review, 2002. (First published in 1974.)

- One of Austria's well-known contemporary playwrights and authors, Handke tells the story of his mother's life and struggles in a post-war Austria which ultimately ended with her suicide.

Darkness Spoken: Collected Poems of Ingeborg Bachmann. Ingeborg Bachmann (translated by Peter Filkins). Chicago: Zephyr Press, 2005.

- A bilingual collection of poems by this respected Austrian poet and novelist.

Tale of the 1002nd Night. Joseph Roth. New York: Picador USA, 1999. (First published in 1939.)
- Written fairy-tale fashion and filled with characters from old Vienna—civil servants, merchants, prostitutes and soldiers. Yet the tale is not a happy one. Taking place in the 1870s, Roth's story is a metaphor for the Austrian Empire's fear of modernity and slow decline during the latter stages of the 19th century.

The Piano Teacher. Elfriede Jelinek. Berkeley: Grove Press, 1989.
- A dark and disturbing story about the relationship between a mother and daughter set in Vienna. Jelinek is a critically acclaimed Austrian writer who won the Nobel Prize for Literature in 2004.

ABOUT THE AUTHORS

Julie Krejci was born in Roswell, New Mexico, USA. She moved several times within the US and Europe during her adolescence and received a Bachelor of Arts in International Relations at Syracuse University and a Master of Arts in Humanities at California State Dominguez Hills. After pursuing a teaching degree, she taught in Spanish in the Los Angeles School District and then went overseas to teach at the American International School in Vienna, Austria. Now married to an Austrian and the mother of two young daughters, she calls Vienna her home. While both authors contributed something to each chapter, Julie is primarily responsible for Chapters 3, 4, 5, 8 and half of Chapters 7 and 9.

ABOUT THE AUTHORS

Susan Roraff was born in Chicago, Illinois, USA. She received a Bachelor of Arts in International Studies and German at Bradley University and spent part of her junior year studying at the University of Vienna. Later, she received her Master of Arts in Latin American Studies from Georgetown University and moved to Chile where she worked at a research organisation. With her Chilean husband, she moved from Chile to Singapore, and then returned to Vienna where her first son was born. She continues to move around the globe with her husband and two young sons, enjoying each new experience. She is also a co-author of *Culture Shock! Chile*. Again, both authors left their mark on the whole book, but Susan is primarily responsible for Chapters 1, 2, 6, 10 and half of Chapters 7 and 9.

INDEX

Titles in the CULTURE**SHOCK!** series:

Argentina	Hawaii	Paris
Australia	Hong Kong	Philippines
Austria	Hungary	Portugal
Bahrain	India	Russia
Barcelona	Indonesia	San Francisco
Beijing	Iran	Saudi Arabia
Belgium	Ireland	Scotland
Bolivia	Israel	Sri Lanka
Borneo	Italy	Shanghai
Brazil	Jakarta	Singapore
Britain	Japan	South Africa
Cambodia	Korea	Spain
Canada	Laos	Sweden
Chicago	London	Switzerland
Chile	Malaysia	Syria
China	Mauritius	Taiwan
Costa Rica	Mexico	Thailand
Cuba	Morocco	Tokyo
Czech Republic	Munich	Turkey
Denmark	Myanmar	Ukraine
Ecuador	Nepal	United Arab
Egypt	Netherlands	Emirates
Finland	New York	USA
France	New Zealand	Vancouver
Germany	Norway	Venezuela
Greece	Pakistan	Vietnam

For more information about any of these titles, please contact any of our Marshall Cavendish offices around the world (listed on page ii) or visit our website at:

www.marshallcavendish.com/genref